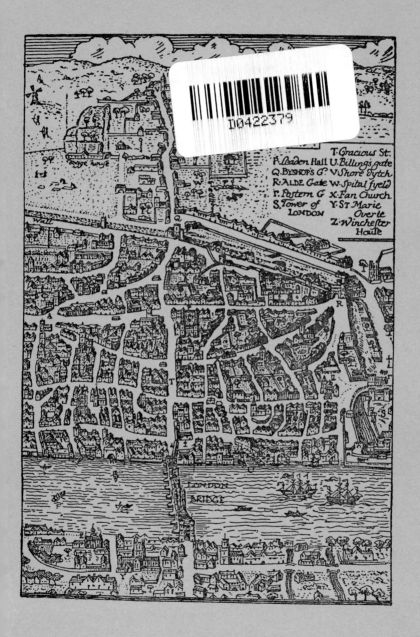

T. Gracious St.
P. Leaden Hall   U. Billings gate
Q. BYSHOPS G?   V. Shore dytch
R. ALDE Gate   W. Spital fyeld
r. Postern G   X. Fan Church
S. Tower of   Y. St Marie
  LONDON   Overie
                   Z. Winchester
                     House

Wall

A

T

LONDON
BRIDGE

A WANDERER IN LONDON

THE TOWER AND THE TOWER BRIDGE

A WANDERER IN LONDON

BY

E. V. LUCAS

WITH SIXTEEN ILLUSTRATIONS BY
NELSON DAWSON

THIRTY-SIX OTHER ILLUSTRATIONS
AND A MAP

TWENTY-FOURTH EDITION

New York
THE MACMILLAN COMPANY
1926

PRINTED IN THE UNITED STATES OF AMERICA BY
THE BERWICK & SMITH CO.

2140

PREFACE TO THE TWENTY-THIRD EDITION

I N this edition, which has long been over-due, but which I could not prepare while the disturbance caused to our galleries by the War was still evident, the new—and, for a long time, definite—re-arrangement of the National Gallery, the Tate Gallery, and the Wallace Collection, is followed. Note is also taken of many changes in London since the last thorough revision some years ago, without, however, trenching upon the preserves of "London Revisited," a companion or supplementary volume, which appeared during the War, describes certain minor galleries and all the statuary and memorial tablets and roams as far afield as Hampton Court.

Fortunately for the world, if less satisfactory to authors who dislike to be out of date, such institutions as the National Gallery and the Tate and the British Museum and the Victoria and Albert, are never complete. Almost every week sees some new picture added, and every day some new exhibit of interest. For instance, even while I was preparing the present edition the Wertheimer portraits by Mr. Sargent, now the property of the nation, were hung in Trafalgar Square.

London's structural changes are also continuous. Devonshire House long since ceased to be ducal; as I write there is rumour of the demolition of the Adelphi and the shifting of Charing Cross Station to the other side of the river; the space between the statue of Lord Holland, seated now among cabbages and beans, and

Holland House at his back, is a school for the intensive culture of golf; Regent Street is to be rebuilt, more Tubes are threatened. Piccadilly Circus at night emulates the great White Way of New York, and an American business firm has provided the island site in the Strand, on the ruins of Holywell Street, with as fine a specimen of steel girder and stone construction as we have, with a magnificent archway on the north which you see before you all the way down Kingsway. When I wrote this book, in 1905, the cinema was in its infancy. There are now hundreds of picture theatres in London, among them two originally planned for Grand Opera. There are also many more theatres proper, but a decline in the popularity of the music hall is noticeable and we have no circus at all.

In 1922 the tree in the midst of Staple Inn—that beautiful spreading plane tree which intended no harm to any one and offered shelter to a thousand sparrows every evening—was cut down.

Among the most beautiful of the recent additions to London's structures I should name the Cenotaph in Whitehall, designed by Sir Edwin Lutyens, and the little Armenian Church, which occurs so surprisingly in all its whiteness and symmetry in the middle of Iverna Court at Kensington. The County Council Hall opposite the Houses of Parliament is impressive and it rises from the river in the good old way; but I am personally doubtful about its red tiles.

Lastly let me say, with extreme satisfaction, that when I wrote this book no such list of Sunday openings as this, which I cut from the "Observer" in February, 1923, could have been printed in any London Sunday paper:—

MUSEUMS AND PICTURE GALLERIES.

National Gallery	2.0	to Dusk.
National Portrait Gallery	2.0	" 4.0 p.m.
British Museum	2.0	" 4.0 p.m.
Wallace Collection	2.0	" 5.0 p.m.

Tate Gallery, Millbank . . . . 2. 0 to 4.0 p.m.
Victoria and Albert Museum . . . . . . 2.30 " 6.0 p.m.
Natural History Museum . . . . 2.30 " 6.0 p.m.
London Museum . . . . 2. 0 " 4.0 p.m.
Science Museum . . . . 2.30 " 6.0 p.m.
Bethnal Green Museum . . . . 2.30 " 6.0 p.m.
Geological Survey and Museum . . . . . 2.30 " Dusk.
Horniman Museum . . . . 2. 0 " 8.0 p.m.
Cuming Museum, Walworth-road . . . . 6. 0 " 9.0 p.m.
Geffrye Museum, Kingsland-road . . . . 2. 0 " 6.0 p.m.

So we do advance a little!

E. V. L.

May, 1923

CONTENTS

LIST OF ILLUSTRATIONS

LIST OF ILLUSTRATIONS xiii

NOTE

The reproduction of the "Holy Family" by Leonardo da Vinci has been made by permission of Mr. F. Hollyer, 9, Pembroke Square, W., from whom carbon prints can be obtained.

A WANDERER IN LONDON

CHAPTER I

NO. 1 LONDON AND PICCADILLY

A Beginning—No. 1 London—Charing Cross in Retirement—A Walk down Piccadilly—Apsley House—The Iron Duke's Statues—An Old Print — Rothschild Terrace — Changes — The March of Utilitarianism—The Plague of New Buildings—London Architecture—The Glory of Disorder—A City of Homes—House-collecting—The Elusive Directory—Kingsley's Dictum—The House Opposite—Desirable Homes—London's Riches—The Smallest Houses in London—A Monument to Pretty Thoughtfulness—The Piccadilly Goat—Old Q—Rogers the Poet.

LONDON, whichever way we turn, is so vast and varied, so rich in what is interesting, that to one who would wander with a plastic mind irresponsibly day after day in its streets and among its treasures, there is not a little difficulty in deciding where to begin, and there is even greater difficulty in knowing where to end. Indeed, to a book on London—to a thousand books on London—there is no end.

But a beginning one can always make, whether it is appropriate or otherwise, and there is some fitness in beginning at Hyde Park Corner, by that square, taciturn, grey house just to the east of it which we call Apsley House, but which I have always been told is really No. 1 London—if any No. 1 London there be. Let us then begin at No. 1 London—just as a Frenchman bent upon discovering the English capital would begin at Charing Cross.

To take a walk down Fleet Street—the cure for ennui
attributed to the most dogmatic of Londoners but
really, I believe, invented for him by another and later
lover of our city, George Augustus Sala—is no longer
an amusing recreation, the bustle is too great; but to
take a walk down Piccadilly on a fine day remains one
of the pleasures of life: another reason for beginning
with No. 1 London. Piccadilly from Hyde Park Corner to Berkeley Street is still eminently a promenade.
But only as far as that. Once Berkeley Street is crossed
and the shops begin, the saunterer is jostled ; while the
Green Park having vanished behind the Ritz Hotel, the
sun and the freshness are lost too. But between those
two points on a smiling day one may enjoy as fair a
walk as in any city in the world.

No. 1 London enjoys its priority only I think in verbal
tradition. To the postman such an address might mean
nothing, although the London postman has a reputation
for tracking any trail, however elusive. The official address of Apsley House is, I fancy, 149 Piccadilly. Be
that as it may, it is No. 1 to us, and a gloomy abode to
boot, still wearing a dark frown of resentment for those
broken windows, although the famous iron shutters have
gone. The London rough rarely mobilises now, and when
he does he breaks no windows; but those were stormier
days. Opposite is the Duke himself, in bronze, on his
charger, looking steadfastly for ever at his old home, where
the Waterloo survivors' dinner used to be held every year,
with numbers lessening and lessening until the victor himself was called away.

An earlier equestrian statue of Wellington once dominated the triumphal arch now at the head of Constitution
Hill (where Captain Adrian Jones, that rare thing, a soldier sculptor, set up his spirited quadriga), but this, I
know not why, was taken down and erected afresh at
Aldershot. A third Wellington trophy is the Achilles
statue, at the back of Apsley House, in the Park, just

across the roadway. This giant figure was cast from cannon taken at Salamanca and Vittoria, Toulouse and Waterloo, and was set up here by the women of England in honour of the great and invincible soldier. There is a coloured print which one may now and then see in the old shops (the last time I saw it was in the parlour of a Duke of Wellington inn at a little village in Wiltshire), of the hero of Waterloo riding beneath the Achilles on his little white horse, with his hand to the salute: one of the pleasantest pictures of the stern old man that I know, with the undulations of Hyde Park rolling away like a Surrey common in the distance. There is also, visible from the tops of omnibus, a bust of the Duke at the side of his house, in the garden.

Our Dukes are no longer made of iron, and Apsley House is desolate, almost sinister. Albeit within its walls are four of Jan Steen's pictures, to say nothing of one of the finest Correggios in England and Velazquez' portrait of himself.

And so we leave No. 1 London frowning behind us, and come instantly to smiling wealth, for the little terrace of mansions between Apsley House and Hamilton Place is a stronghold of that powerful family which moved Heinrich Heine to sarcasm and Hans Christian Andersen to sentiment, and is still one of the greatest forces in European finance.

Never in the recent history of London have so many changes come so rapidly as in the past few years, to which belong not only the rise of the motor and the loss of horse 'buses and cabs, but the elimination of hundreds of landmarks and the sweeping away of whole streets drenched with human association. Such is the ruthless march of utilitarianism and luxury (some of the most conspicuous new buildings being expensive hotels) that one has come to entertain the uneasy feeling that nothing is safe. Certainly nothing is sacred. A garage being required for the motor cars of the Stock Exchange, what,

one asks oneself, is there to prevent the demolition of
the Charterhouse? Since Christ's Hospital could be moved
bodily to Sussex in order that more offices might rise in
Newgate Street, why should not the Brothers be sent to
Bournemouth? The demand for another vast caravanserai
for American visitors on the banks of the Thames may
become acute any day: why should not the Temple site be
utilised? One lives in fear.

I wrote in the first edition of this book that I never
looked at the Adelphi Terrace without a misgiving that
when next I pass it will have vanished; and now it is
to go. Nothing but its comparative distance from the
main stream of commerce can have saved Gray's Inn.
There is an architect round the corner ready with a
florid terra-cotta tombstone for every beautiful, quiet,
old-world building in London. Bedford Row is undoubtedly doomed: Queen Anne's Gate trembles. Clifford's
Inn is going: Holywell Street has gone. He who would
see London before London becomes unrecognisable must
hasten his steps. The modern spirit can forgive everything except age.

Too many London architects dislike large, restful,
unworried spaces and long unbroken lines: hence many
of our new buildings have been for the most part fussy
and ornamental—and not at all, I think, representative
of the national character. Somerset House (save for its
fiddling little cupola) and Carlton House Terrace are
perhaps London architecture at its simplest, the Law
Courts, with all their amazing intricacy and elaboration,
are London's public architecture at its most complex
and unsuitable. St. James's Palace is beautiful, but
Buckingham Palace could hardly be more commonplace.

To Somerset House, the Adelphi, St. James's Palace
and the Tower Bridge, different though they are, the
epithet English can be confidently applied; but Buckingham Palace is French, and it would be difficult to use
the word English of many of the great structures now

A DUTCH LADY
AFTER THE PICTURE BY MICHIEL JANSZ MIEREVELT IN THE WALLACE COLLECTION

rising in London. We seem to have no national school of urban architecture any longer, no steady ideals. The new London that is emerging so rapidly lacks any governing principle. The Ritz Hotel, for example, is Parisian, the Carlton and His Majesty's Theatre are Parisian, and in Russell Square there is a recent hotel that has walked straight from Germany at its most German and grotesque, while the London County Council headquarters has a red roof foreign and medieval.

But if London's completed new buildings are not always satisfactory, their preparations are. There is nothing out of Méryon's etchings or Piranesi's sombre "Carceri" more impressive than our contractors' giant cranes can be—fixed high above the houses on their scaffolding, with sixty vertical yards of chain hanging from their great arms. Against an evening sky, with a little smoke from the engine purpling in the dying sun's rays, and the mist beginning to blur or submerge the surrounding houses, these cranes and scaffoldings have an effect of curious unreality, a hint even of Babylon or Nineveh, a suggestion at any rate of all the majestic building and builders in history. London has no more interesting or picturesque sight than this.

Among the best public buildings of recent days are the National Portrait Gallery, seen as one walks down the Charing Cross Road, and the Institute of Painters in Water Colours in Piccadilly, and the Record Office in Chancery Lane. The South Kensington School of Science is good, so square and solid and grave is it, albeit perhaps a little too foreign with its long and (in London) quite useless but superbly decorative and beautiful loggia; but what can we say of the Imperial Institute and the Natural History Museum and the Victoria and Albert Museum close by, except that they are ambitious and symmetrical—the ideal of the Kindergarten box of bricks carried out to its highest power?

It is as though London had been to a feast of architecture and stolen the scraps. She has everything. She has Queen Anne's Mansions, that hideous barracks, and she has Standen's in Jermyn Street, which is a Florentine palazzo; she has St. John's, Westminster, with its four unsightly bell-towers, and St. Dunstan's-in-the-East with its indescribably graceful spire; she has Charing's Eleanor Cross and the Albert Memorial; she has Westminster Hall and the new Roman Catholic Cathedral; she has Cannon Street Station and the Heralds' College; she has the terra-cotta Prudential Office in Holborn and within a few yards of it the medieval façade of Staple Inn; she has Euston Station and the Ecclesiastical Commissioners' offices at Westminster; she has Park Lane and Bedford Row; she has Chelsea Hospital and Whitehall Court; she has the Gaiety Theatre and Spence's in St. Paul's Church-yard with its plain stone gables; she has the white sever-ity of the Bush Building in the Strand and the Alhambra Theatre with its gilded cupolas; she has Frascati's hot façade in Oxford Street and the little white Armenian Church in Iverne Court; she has the pretentious Wesleyan headquarters and its neighbour, the charming Westmin-ster Town Hall; she has the white Christian Science Church near Sloane Square and the delightful red brick Christian Science Annexe in Palace Gardens Terrace, so Italian and unexpected.

London has learnt nothing from Philadelphia or Paris of the value of regularity, and if she can help it she never will. I suppose that Regent Street and Park Crescent were her last efforts on a large scale to get unity into herself, and then she allowed the Regent Street line to be broken first by the Piccadilly Hotel and later by any one, a draper for choice. But since the glory of London is her disorder, it does not matter. Nothing will change that.

The narrowness and awkwardness of London streets are a perpetual reminder of the Englishman's incapacity or unwillingness to look ahead. In no other city in the world would it have been permitted to build two theatres and the Coliseum in a street so narrow as St. Martin's Lane. Nowhere else is traffic allowed to be so continuously and expensively congested at the whim of private enterprise. In the city itself, in the busy lanes off Cheapside for instance where wagons are sometimes kept eight hours before they can be extricated, this narrowness means the daily loss of thousands of pounds. London's chance to become a civilised city was probably lost for ever at Waterloo. Had Wellington been defeated, carriages might now be running four abreast down Fleet Street. Yet as neither Napoleon nor Baron Haussman ever came our way, we must act accordingly; and the railway companies are still building on their branch lines arches wide enough to carry only a single pair of rails.

But in spite of architectural whimsies, there are in no city of the world so many houses in which one would like to live as in London. In spite of our studious efforts to arrange that every room shall have one or more draughts in it, in spite of our hostility to hot water pipes and our affection for dark and dreary basements, it is generally agreed that the English house can come nearer to the idea of home than that of any other people, and there can be no doubt that the English home is to be found in its perfection in London. Even as I write, the memory of friendly houses, modern and Georgian and of even earlier date, in various parts of England, rises before me: houses over which the spirit of welcome broods, and within which are abundant fires, and lavender-scented sheets, and radiant, almost laughing, cleanliness, and that sense of quiet efficient order that is perhaps not the least charming characteristic of an English country house. Yet it is without treachery to these homes that one commends the comfortable London house as the most attractive habitation in the world; for in spite of so many blemishes which no one feels so much as the mistress of a country house—and the greatest of which is dirt—the

London home is the homeliest of all. Perhaps a touch of grime is not unnecessary. Perhaps houses can be too clean for the truest human dailiness?

While walking about London I have noticed so many houses in which I could live happily; and indeed to look for these is not a bad device to make walking in London inviting, for walking for walking's sake there can be very tedious. One becomes a house-collector: marking down those houses which possibly by some unexpected turn of Fortune's wheel one might take, or which one wants to enter on friendly terms, or which one ought once to have lived in when needs were simpler.

I have sometimes amused myself by jotting down the addresses of the houses I have liked, intending to find out who lived in them; but the "London Directory" seems to be hopelessly beyond the reach of any one not in an office or a public-house.

If ever I were found in these houses it would not be for theft, but to see if their Chippendale was really worthy of them, and how blue their china was, and if they had any good pictures. Perhaps many a burglar has begun purely as an amateur of furniture and decoration. And there are still so many pictures in London houses, in spite of the temptation of American gold. I must not enumerate any of the private collections here, as it might mean vexation to the owners; but I could. I could even give the number of the spacious South Kensington road where Tom Girtin's epoch-making London water colour "The White House at Chelsea" hangs. . . .

I rather think it is Charles Kingsley who says, in one of the grown-up digressions in "Water Babies," that the beauty of the house opposite is of more consequence than that of the house one lives in: because one rarely sees the house one is in, but is always conscious of the other. Kingsley (if it was Kingsley) was good at that kind of hard practical remark; but I fancy that this one means nothing, because the kind of person who would like to live in an ugly house would not care whether the house opposite was beautiful or not. I, who always want too much, would choose above all things to live in a beautiful house with no house opposite; yet since that is hardly likely to be, I would choose to live in a beautiful house with long white blinds that shut out the house opposite (beautiful or ugly) and yet do not exclude what it amuses us in London to call light.

Not that the house opposite would really bother me very much. In fact, the usual charge that is brought against it in this city—that it encourages organ grinders —is to my mind a virtue. London without organ grinders would not be London; and one likes a city to be true to its character, good or bad. Also there is hardly any tune except our National Anthem of which I can honestly say I am tired; and as often as one comes to the conclusion that one can endure even that no longer, it justifies itself and recovers its popularity by bringing some tiresome evening to an end.

In seeking desirable houses I am thinking chiefly of the houses with individual charm: old houses, for the most part, which have been made modern in their accessories by their owners, but which retain externally their ancient gravity or beauty—such as you see in Queen Anne's Gate, or the Master of the Temple's house, or Aubrey House on Campden Hill. I am thinking chiefly of these old comely houses, and of the very few new houses by architects of taste, such as the first Lord Astor's exquisite offices on the Embankment—one of the most satisfying of London's recent edifices, with thought and care and patience and beauty in every inch of it, whether in the stone or the wood or the iron: possessing indeed not a little of the thoroughness and single-mindedness that Ruskin looked for in the cathedrals of France.

But a few desirable houses of the middle or early nineteenth century one has marked approvingly too—

such as Thackeray's house in Kensington Palace Gardens, that discreet and almost private avenue of vast mansions, each large enough and imposing enough to stand in its own park in the country; but here packed close together —not quite in the Park Lane huddle, but very nearly so —and therefore conveying only an impaired impression of their true amplitude. It is of course the houses of a city that give one the most rapid impression of its prosperity or poverty. To walk in the richer residential quarters of London—in Mayfair and Belgravia, South Kensington and Bayswater and Regent's Park, is to receive an overwhelming proof of the gigantic wealth of this people. Take Queen's Gate alone: the houses in it mount to the skies and every one represents—or used to—an income of five figures. I say "used to" because with the Peace a redistribution of wealth set in and chief among those who suffered were the old residents in London mansions, the result being that to walk recently through the more expensive districts was to be confronted by "To Let" and "To be Sold" boards in deplorable profusion or builder's men rapidly reconstructing houses into flats.

Another recent change in London residential quarters is the transformation of districts that might almost be called slums into fashionable quarters by the more artistic of the smart set. They began with the little Georgian and Queen Anne streets between the Abbey and Smile Square and quickly "converted" those, keeping the façade intact but beautifying the interiors. They are still small but very, very *chic*. Next they captured the little streets near Buckingham Gate. I advise the traveller to loiter about both these districts if he is interested in neo-Georgian works. There are some charming doorways and fanlights and green shutters to be seen.

Thackeray's old house in Young Street spreads its bow windows even more alluringly than the new one; but there is a little house next to that, hiding shyly behind evergreens, where I am sure I could be comfortable. This house—it is only a cottage, really—has one of London's few wet, bird-haunted lawns. It is so retiring and whispering that the speculative builder has utterly overlooked it all these years.

Of the exceedingly little houses which one could really inhabit there are several on Campden Hill. There is one in Aubrey Walk which once I could have been very happy in. It could be moved bodily one night anywhere: a wheelbarrow would be enough—a wheelbarrow and a pair of strong arms. It is so small and compact that it might be transferred to the stage of *Peter Pan* as a present for Wendy. I go that way continually just to look at it. And there is the secluded keeper's lodge in Kensington Gardens overlooking the Serpentine. But the most outrageously unreal new miniature house in London is not on the outskirts at all but in the city itself —in Fetter Lane, in fact. I mean the lodge in the garden of the Record Office. South Lodge, near Rutland Gate, has a near relation to it. The quaintest of the old miniature London houses is that residence for the sexton which is built against the wall of St. Bartholomew the Great in Smithfield—a very Elizabethan doll's house; the oddest of the new miniature London houses is a tobacconist's shop in Sherwood Street—like the slice of ham in a sandwich.

But this architectural digression has taken us far from Piccadilly and the crossing at Hamilton Place where we were standing when my pen ran away. At Hamilton Place the clubs begin, one of the first being the Bachelors'; but to me a more interesting matter is the raised platform on the other side of the road, which has been a puzzle to so many persons who have not taken the trouble to read the inscription on it. This runs:—

"On the suggestion of R. A. Slaney, Esq., who for twenty-six years represented Shrewsbury in Parliament, this porter's rest was erected in 1861 by the Vestry of St. George, Hanover Square, for

the benefit of porters and others carrying burdens. As a relic of
a past period in London's history it is hoped that the people
will aid in its preservation."

When I first came to London, Piccadilly still had its
goat. I remember meeting it on the pavement one day
in 1892, opposite Hamilton Terrace, and wondering how
it got there and why the people, usually so curious about
the unusual, were taking so little notice of such a phenom-
enon, as it seemed to me. It must have been soon after
then that it died and, with true London carelessness, was
not replaced.

Were it not for the traffic, omnibuses, carriages and
cabs all day and until long after midnight, and in the
small hours traction engines rumbling into Covent
Garden with wagon loads of cabbages and vegetables from
the Thames valley—Piccadilly opposite the Green Park
would be the perfect place for a house. But it is too
noisy. Once, however, it was chiefly residences, such as
Nos. 138 and 139, which stand upon the site of the abode
of the disreputable "Old Q" who posed to three generations as the model debauchee, and by dint of receiving
9,340 visits of two hours each from his doctor during the
last seven years of his life, and a bath of milk every morning, contrived to keep alive and in fairly good condition
until he was eighty-six. It was in the half of Old Q's
house which afterwards was called No. 139, and was pulled
down in 1839 and rebuilt, that Byron was living in 1816
when his wife left him for ever. Lord Palmerston for
some years occupied what is now the Naval and Military
(or "In and Out") Club; and Miss Mellon the actress,
who married Mr. Coutts the banker, lived at No. 1 Strat-
ton Street, which was for so long the residence of the
Baroness Burdett-Coutts. In the good old knife-board
days one had the history of these houses from communi-
cative and perhaps imaginative 'bus drivers. Their suc-
cessors, the chauffeurs, cannot tell any one anything,
partly because they are men at the wheel, and partly

THE LADY WITH A FAN
AFTER THE PICTURE BY VELAZQUEZ IN THE WALLACE COLLECTION

because they are not within speaking distance of any of their fares, and partly because they are engineers and moderns, and therefore not interested in the interesting, and have cultivated in perfection the unseeing eye. The iron law of utilitarianism which called them into being is the foe of so many of the little amenities of life.

And so we come to Berkeley Street, and the strolling part of the walk is over. Anyone who is run over at this corner—and that is no difficult matter—will have the satisfaction of knowing that he shares his fate with the author of "The Pleasures of Memory." Being only a little past eighty at the time, Rogers survived the shock many years.

This reminds me that the infrequency with which Londoners are run over is one of the most amazing things in this city. To ride in a taxi in any busy street, is, after a short time, to be convinced that the vehicle has some such power of attraction over human beings as a magnet has over needles. Men rise up from nowhere apparently with no other purpose than to court death, and yet all seem to view the advancing danger with something of the same air of astonishment as they would be entitled to assume were they to meet a railway train in Kensington Gardens. It seems to be a perpetual surprise to the Londoner that vehicles are making any use of his roadways.

CHAPTER II

ROMANCE AND THE WALLACE PICTURES

Dull Streets—London and London—The Rebuilder again—Old Paris—The Heart of the Matter—A Haunt of Men—External Romance—Dickens and Stevenson—The True Wandering Knight —The Beautiful Serpentine—London Fogs—Whistler—The Look-out down the River—Park Lane—Dorchester House—Tyburn— Famous Malefactors—The Fortunate John Smith—The Wallace Collection—Rembrandt and Velazquez—Andrea del Sarto—Our Dutch Masters—Guardi and Bonington—Miniatures and Sèvres.

THE more I wander about London the less wander-able in, for a stranger, does it seem to be. Those who live in it and necessarily must pass through one street in order to get to another are not troubled by squalor and monotony; but what can the traveller make of it who comes to London bent upon seeing inter-esting things? What can he make of the wealthy deserts of Bayswater? of the grimy Vauxhall Bridge Road? of the respectable aridity of the Cromwell Road, which goes on for ever? of the dull monotony of Gower Street? What can he make of the hundreds of square miles of the East End? And what, most of all, of the interminable dis-tricts of small houses which his train will bisect on almost every line by which he can re-enter London after one of his excursions to the country? Nothing. He will not try twice.

And yet these poorer districts are London in the fullest sense of the word, although for the most part when we say London we mean the Strand and Piccadilly. But the Strand and Piccadilly might go and it would not really matter: few persons would suffer extremely; whereas were Poplar or Bermondsey, Kentish Town or Homerton, to fall in ruins or be burnt, thousands and thousands of Londoners would have lost all and be utterly destitute.

It perhaps comes to this, that there is no one London at all. London is a country containing many towns, of which a little central area of theatres and music halls, restaurants and shops, historic buildings and hotels, is the capital; and it is this capital that strangers come to see. For the most part it is this capital with which the present pages are concerned. London for our purposes dwindles down to a very small area where most of her visitors spend all their time—the Embankment, Trafalgar Square, and Piccadilly, Regent Street and the British Museum, the Strand and Ludgate Hill, the Bank and the Tower. That is London to the ordinary inquisitive traveller. Almost everything that English provincials, Americans and other foreigners come to London to see, is there.

The more I know of London, the more I am impressed by the timid orbits of Londoners. Indeed, so fixed are most of us in our grooves that you might say that the only Londoners who habitually leave the beaten track are the drivers of taxis and messenger boys.

Ask your London friends what they have been doing to-day, and you will quickly discover how circumscribed are their movements in this vast, fascinating and endlessly new and varied city. Most will say that they went to the office in the morning, out to lunch at the regular place, back in the evening, always by the same routes. Even those who are not in business, and therefore should be free to explore, did as little. They walked to this shop or that, to this club or that, on somewhere to lunch, then some more shopping or clubbing, and so home again, chiefly by accustomed routes. Ask either set of people to name anything new that they saw during the day—any

London thing that they hadn't seen before—and most of them will be unable to do so.

I suppose there are to be found a few Londoners who treat this city as a naturalist treats the country-side, and are always investigating, scrutinising, hoping for treasure-trove. I hope so. Such a one I used to be, before I had too much to do, and such a one I still am in a less adventurous way. Only the other day, for instance, did I (at great personal peril) ascertain precisely the situation of the angular stone which marks the exact position of Tyburn Gallows, sixty-nine feet north of the tablet on the railings by the Marble Arch. Motor 'buses and taxis did their best to put an end to my inquisitive career, but persistence prevailed. And only recently did I fully realise the beauty and unexpectedness of that isolated Georgian mansion in Rochester Row, which is now, I believe, the Grenadier Guards' hospital. I am one of the few enterprising strangers, unconnected with West-minster School, who watch cricket in Vincent Square and who know that all through September the most exciting unadvertised matches can be seen free at Lord's.

The odd thing is that though London has its villages, the villagers are Londoners, too. Life among streets moulds urban characters; just as life among hedges and fields moulds rural characters. Not yet, for instance, does the rustic have to look each way before he can cross the road, but the Londoners must ever do it; and such vigil-ance leaves its mark. The result is that the provincial villager, when he comes to town, is instantly to be detected. He has a score of non-metropolitan characteristics, apart altogether from his clothes and boots, while the London villager, even though he never leaves Church Street, Ken-sington, or Upper Street, Islington, or Artillery Row, or Berwick Street, or the Mile End Road, or the Boro' High Street, is still of the centre.

These streets, which I have named almost at random, are at some distance from each other, and their differences

PICCADDILY LOOKING EAST

are therefore not remarkable: but one of the strangest things about London is the differences that you can find between streets that actually adjoin. Walk, for example, up Bond Street, and turn to the left into Oxford Street, on the south side, and notice how completely the people have changed. On the north side of Oxford Street, where the great drapery houses are, you find a few women who are to be seen also in Bond Street; on the south side, none. Or turn out of Oxford Street into Tottenham Court Road on the west side and notice how the people have changed. Walk out of the cosmopolitan Strand into Fleet Street and notice how women vanish. You find a few in St. Paul's Churchyard, again drawn together by the lure of clothes; but in Cheapside the realm of men is again entered, and there are no more women until White-chapel. At evening all this city region empties. Where has everyone gone? Each to his own village.

A tidal wave of utilitarianism has lately rolled over the city and done irreparable mischief, and London no longer offers much harvest for the gleaner of odds and ends of old architecture, quaint gateways, unexpected gables. Such treasures as she still retains in the teeth of the rebuilder are well known: such as Staple Inn and the York Water Gate, a house or two in Chelsea (mostly doomed), the city churches, a corner or two near Smith-field, Butcher's Row, Aldgate, and so forth. She has nothing, for example, comparable with the Faubourg St. Antoine in Paris, where one may be rewarded every minute by some beautiful relic of the past. London, one would say, should be first among cities where symbols of the past are held sacred, but in reality is the last.

Hence I am only too conscious as we walk up Park Lane (having returned to No. 1 London to begin again), that we shall be wandering in streets that present little or no attraction to the stranger from the shires or the pil-grim from over seas. For beyond some mildly interest-ing architecture Mayfair streets can offer nothing to anyone that is not interested in their past inhabitants. Better to have stuck to Piccadilly or Oxford Street, with their busy pavements: much better, perhaps, and at the same time to have accepted the fact that London is before all things a city of living men and women.

That is what the traveller must come to see—London's men and women, her millions of men and women. If he would eat, drink and be merry, he must go elsewhere; if he would move in beautiful and spacious thoroughfares, he must go elsewhere; if he would see crumbling architecture or stately palaces, he must go elsewhere; but if he has any interest in the human hive, this is the place. He can study it here day and night for a year, and there will still be vast tracts unknown to him.

For a great city of great age and a history of extraordinary picturesqueness and importance, London is nearly destitute of the external properties of romance. But although, except here and there—and those in the more placid and law-abiding quarters, such as the Inns of Court —the dark gateway and the medieval gable are no more, I suppose that no city has so appealed to the imagination of the romantic novelist. The very contrast between the dull prosaic exterior of a London street and the passions that may be at work within is part of the allurement.

It was undoubtedly Dickens who first introduced Englishmen to London as a capital of mystery and fun, tragedy and eccentricity: it was Dickens who discovered London's melodramatic wealth. But Dickens did not invent anything. It was Stevenson in his "New Arabian Nights" who may be said to have invented the romantic possibilities of new streets. Dickens needed an odd corner before he set an odd figure in it; the Wilderness, for instance, came before Quilp, the Barbican before Sim Tappertit; but Stevenson, by simply transferring the Baghdad formula to London, in an instant transformed, say, Campden Hill and Hampstead, even Bedford Park and

Sydenham Hill, into regions of daring and delightful possibilities. After reading the "New Arabian Nights" the tamest residence holds potentialities; and not a tobacconist but may be a prince in disguise, not a cabman but may bear a roving commission to inveigle you to an adventure.

In ordinary life to-day, even in London among her millions, adventures are, I must admit, singularly few, and such as occur mostly follow rather familiar lines; but since the "New Arabian Nights" there has always been hope, and that is not a little in this world.

Even without Stevenson I should, I trust, have realised something of the London cab driver's romantic quality. He is the true Wandering Knight of this city. He does not in the old way exactly hang the reins over his horse's neck—or, rather, to be modern, he does not permit his steering wheel to turn itself—but he is as vacant of personal impulse as if he did. His promptings come all from without. There he sits, careless, motionless (save for quick eyes), apathetic. He may sit thus for an hour, for two, for three, unnoticed; he may be hailed the next moment. He may be wanted to drive only to a near station —or to a distant suburb. One minute he has no purpose in his brain: the next he is informed by one and one only—to get to St. Pancras or Notting Hill, the theatre or the bank, the Houses of Parliament or Scotland Yard, in the shortest space of time. And this romantic is the servant of every one who has a shilling—bishop or coiner, actress or M.P.

I want to say one other word about romantic London before we really enter Park Lane. Beneath one of her mists or light fogs London can become the most mysterious and beautiful city in the world. I know of nothing more bewitchingly lovely than the Serpentine on a still misty evening—when it is an unruffled lake of dim pearl-grey liquid, such stuff as sleep is made of. St. James's Park at dusk on a winter's afternoon, seen from the suspension bridge, with all the lights of the Government offices reflected in its water, and the turrets and gables of Whitehall Court against the sky, has less mystery but more romance. It might be the lake before an enchanted castle. And while speaking of evening effects I must not forget the steam which escapes in fairy clouds from the huge chimney off Davies Street, just behind the Bond Street Tube Station. On the evening of a clear day this vapour can be the most exquisite violet and purple, transfiguring Oxford Street.

To artists the fog is London's best friend. Not the black fog, but the other. For there are two distinct London fogs—the fog that chokes and blinds, and the fog that shrouds. The fog that enters into every corner of the house and coats all the metal work with a dark slime, and sets us coughing and rubbing our eyes—for that there is nothing to say. It brings with it too much dirt, too much unhealthiness, for any kind of welcome to be possible. "Hell is a city much like London," I quoted to myself in one of the worst of such fogs, as I groped by the railings of the Park in the Bayswater Road. The traffic, which I could not see, was rumbling past, and every now and then a man, close by but invisible, would call out a word of warning, or some one would ask in startled tones where he was. The hellishness of it consisted in being of life and yet not in it—a stranger in a muffled land. It is bad enough for ordinary wayfarers in such a fog as that; but one has only to imagine what it is to be in charge of a vehicle, to see how much worse one's lot might be.

But the other fog—the fog that veils but does not obliterate, the fog that softens but does not soil, the fog whose beautifying properties Whistler may be said to have discovered—that can be a delight and a joy. Seen through this gentle mist London becomes a city of romance. All that is ugly and hard in her architecture, all that is dingy and repellent in her colour, disappears.

"Poor buildings," wrote Whistler, who watched their transformation so often from his Chelsea home, "lose themselves in the dim sky, and the tall chimneys become *campanili,* and the warehouses are palaces in the night, and the whole city hangs in the heavens."

I have said that it was Dickens who discovered the London of eccentricity, London as the abode of the odd and the quaint, and Stevenson who discovered London as a home of romance. It was Whistler who discovered London as a city of fugitive, mysterious beauty. For decades the London fog had been a theme for vituperation and sarcasm: it needed this sensitive American-Parisian to show us that what to the commonplace man was a foe and a matter for rage, to the artist was a friend. Every one knows about it now.

Fogs have never been quite the same to me since I was shown a huge chimney on the south side of the Thames, and was told that it belonged to the furnaces that supply London offices with electric light; and that whenever the weather seems to suggest a fog, a man is sent to the top of this chimney to look down the river and give notice of the first signs of the enemy rolling up. Then, as his news is communicated, the furnaces are re-stoked, and extra pressure is obtained that the coming darkness may be fought and the work of counting-houses not interrupted. All sentinels, all men on the look-out belong to romance; and from his great height this man peering over the river shipping and the myriad roofs for a thickening of the horizon has touched even a black London fog with romance for me. I think of his straining eyes, his call of warning, those roaring fires. . . .

Park Lane is interesting in that every house in it has personal character; while a few are beautiful and more than one might have been built to stand among trees in its own deer park: a remark that applies to Dorchester House, to Londonderry House, and to Grosvenor House, all of which quietly take their place in this street almost as submissively as the component parts of a suburban terrace. Such natural meetings of architectural incompatibles form one of London's most curious characteristics. There are, I believe, in Park Lane no two houses alike; but now and then one comes upon one more unlike the others than one would have thought possible—as for example that richly carved stone façade at the end of Tilney Street, a gem in its way, but very, very unexpected here.

In Dorchester House, by the way, are many of the pictures collected by that very catholic lover of art, Mr. Holford, and these are shown to visitors. Among them is the famous long view of Dort by Albert Cuyp, and a magnificent Rembrandt. The famous room decorated by the English Michelangelo, Alfred Stevens, the designs for which are at the Tate Gallery, is here. Stevens did not live to finish it, but enough was done to prove the astonishing variety and power of his genius.

Before it was Park Lane and wealthy this pleasant thoroughfare—half-town and half-country, catching all the sun that London can offer in summer and winter— was known as Tyburn Lane, Tyburn Tree, where highwaymen and other malefactors danced upon air, being at the north end of it, near the Marble Arch, now so foolishly isolated—a gateway leading to nowhere. The last hanging at Tyburn was in 1783, after which the scene was moved to the front of Newgate (now also no more). We have the grace to do such deeds in secret to-day; but nothing in our social history is more astonishing than the deliberateness with which such grace came upon us.

Tyburn was the end of a few brave fellows, and many others. Perkin Warbeck, who claimed the throne, died here, and Fenton, who killed Buckingham; Jack Sheppard very properly had a crowd numbering 200,000, but Jonathan Wild, who picked the parson's pocket on the way to the gallows, had more; Mrs. Brownrigg's hanging was very popular, but among the masses through whom

SUSANNA VAN COLLEN AND HER DAUGHTER
AFTER THE PICTURE BY REMBRANDT IN THE WALLACE COLLECTION

Sixteen-stringed Jack wended his way, with a bouquet from a lady friend in his hand, were probably more sympathisers than censors. The notorious Dr. Dodd, in 1777, drew an immense concourse.

These curious Londoners (Hogarth has drawn them) once at any rate had more (or less) than they were expecting, when, in 1705, John Smith, a burglar, was reprieved after he had been hanging for full fifteen minutes, and being immediately cut down, came to himself "to the great admiration of the spectators" (although baulked of their legitimate entertainment), and was quickly removed by his friends, enraptured or otherwise, to begin a second, if not a new, life.

But I must not speak of curious Londoners as though they were extinct. The twentieth century knows them too, and it is still the romance or lure of crime that chiefly brings them together. Executions are no longer public, but thousands of persons still stand outside the prison doors on the fatal morning—that is, if the murderer is sufficiently sinister or picturesque; while the funeral of a popular character, such as Dan Leno or that very accomplished and faithful Londoner, George R. Sims, can attract an immense following. Hogarths come and go but human nature does not change.

And here, having come to Oxford Street before I intended, let us forget malefactors and the gallows in walking through the Wallace Collection at Hertford House, which is close by, and gain at the same time some idea of London's wealth of great painting: turning aside just for a moment to look at the very charming raised garden in the Italian manner which has been ingeniously built over a subterranean electric light station in Duke Street. This is quite one of the happiest of recent architectural fancies in London, with its two domed gateways, its stone terraces and its cypresses. One might almost be on Isola Bella.

Opinions would necessarily differ as to what is the

greatest picture on the walls of Hertford House, but I suppose that from the same half-dozen or so most of the good critics would select that one. It is not in me to support my choice with professional reasons, but I should be inclined to name Rembrandt's "Parable of the Unmerciful Servant." Near it, in the large gallery, come the same painter's portraits of Jan Pellicorne and his wife, and Velazquez' "Portrait of a Spanish Lady," sometimes called "La Femme à l'Eventail," of which I, for one, never tire, whether I think of it as a piece of marvellous painting or the record of a sad and fascinating personality. And here may also be seen Frans Hals' "Laughing Cavalier."

There are also such masterpieces as Andrea del Sarto's "Virgin and Child with St. John the Baptist and two Angels," notable for the beauty and the maternal sweetness and kindliness of it, and the quiet ease of the brush; wonderful examples of Dutch art; of British art, in particular Reynolds; some superb Rubens'; much of the best work of the French fête champêtre school, including twenty-four Bouchers, and certainly not least, a record number both in oil and water-colours of that young master, Richard Parkes Bonington, who in his brief life of twenty-seven years brought both these branches of painting to perfection. The Wallace Collection has eleven of his oils and twenty-five water colours.

The Wallace Collection is one of the most remarkable assemblages of works of art—pictures, furniture, porcelain, armour—that can ever have been brought together by one man; for although two or three others contributed to it, notably the late Sir Richard Wallace, the bulk of the collection was formed by the fourth Marquess of Hertford (1800-1870). Whatever else his predecessors, the first three Marquesses, and his heir, Sir Richard Wallace, may have bought, it was the fourth Marquess, one of whose homes was in this house, who acquired the thirty-six

Boningtons, twenty-four Bouchers, twenty-one Greuzes, fourteen Canalettos, thirteen Murillos, twelve Rubens', twelve Rembrandts, nine Guardis, nine Watteaus, eight Reynolds', and eight Fragonards. These figures attest to his catholicity. "I only," he wrote to a friend, "like pleasing pictures."

Sir Richard Wallace, his natural son and heir, completed the collection and added all the armour. To him we owe the Corot and the Rousseau, but he also was no revolutionary in artistic taste. Sir Richard's widow, Lady Wallace, left this priceless treasure-house to the nation.

The Wallace Collection not only illustrates what can be done by two wealthy virtuosi; it also supplements very usefully the National Gallery. The French schools, for example, both of the eighteenth and nineteenth centuries, are very poorly represented in Trafalgar Square; here they are very strong.

We will now pass through the rooms in order and glance around.

From the main entrance Room No. I is to the right, notable for two Nattiers. In the middle is a case of French royal souvenirs.

In Room II, very splendid and ornate, lectures are given.

In Room III we find majolica ware, church ornaments, medals and renaissance bronzes. Two large scenes of Venice by Canaletto are here.

In Room IV are swords and shields and the porcelain of Sèvres.

Rooms V, VI and VII are devoted to European armour, including two complete sets for a cavalryman, one French of the fifteenth century, and one German, of the sixteenth.

In Room VIII are bronzes, furniture and some French pictures by Le Moine, Rigaud and Philippe de Champaigne.

In the Founders Room will be found "Perdita" Robinson by Sir Joshua and Mrs. Siddons by Lawrence.

In Room IX will be found "Perdita" again, this time by Romney: very alluring. Here also is a brilliant George IV when Prince of Wales, by Hoppner, and an exquisite head of Mary Stuart which, if it is not by Clouet, could hardly be more like his work.

In Rooms X and XI are French pictures, including a number by Oudry.

As you go upstairs note the very characteristic and charming busts by Houdon, particularly that on the left, Madam Victoire, daughter of Louis XV. Turning to the left, at the top, we enter Room XII where the Venetians hang. The Guardis are among the best that exist. S. Maria della Salute was never painted more seductively than in No. 503.

Room XIII is Dutch and it has some exquisite things, all small: two serene groups of shipping, marvellously composed, by William van de Velde; a masterly Netscher, No. 237, as inevitable as a Vermeer although without his magic; a church interior by Emanuel de Witte; two tiny Rembrandt heads; a Cuyp and a Paul Potter.

Room XIV is also Dutch and here we find two Jan Steens; an avenue by Cuyp; two Terburgs, one of them —No. 236—a miracle of soft and delicate painting; a very interesting work by that rare painter Boursse, No. 166, of whom the National Gallery has nothing; a typical Van der Heyden; a typical Maes; and two or three Metsus.

We now pass from Holland to France. As I have said, the Wallace Collection is peculiarly rich in French pictures, eighteenth century and later. We come to the nineteenth century in Room XV where the oil works of Bonington, who had great influence in France—there are Delacroix's hanging near which confess their paternity— are also to be found. Nothing in the room is more beautiful than Nos. 273 and 375 by this artist, who is very poorly represented in the National Gallery. Here also are two of the scholarly works of Prud'hon, notable for the drawing beneath the paint. Rousseau's famous "Glade in the Forest of Fontaineblеau" is here and Corot's "Macbeth and the Witches." There is also a fine Jules Dupré, No. 299. The rest of the pictures are mainly Decamps' and Meissoniers.

We now enter the large room where the masterpieces hang, and on the right come at once upon Rembrandt's magnificent portrait of "Susanna van Collen, wife of Jean Pellicorne, and her Daughter" (reproduced in this book), at the other end of the wall being the pendant "Jean Pellicorne with his Son Gaspar." Between is a lovely Cuyp, "The Ferry-boat on the River," and a Hobbema in which every leaf may be counted. On the next wall we come at once to a sweet Dutch lady (reproduced in this book), by Mierevelt. I note the chief works as they now occur: a superb copy of Velazquez by his son-in-law Mazo, Reynolds' portrait of Mrs. Carnac; a lively portrait by Philippe de Champaigne; Rembrandt's "Unmerciful Servant" one of his greatest works; Hals' "Laughing Cavalier" who is not really laughing but facing the world with an insolent confidence (see the photograph opposite page 28); Velazquez' "Lady with a Fan," that incomparable work (see opposite page 12); another Hobbema; Gainsborough's full-length of a lady whom we have already seen depicted by two other masters, Reynolds and Romney—Mrs. "Perdita" Robinson, with a collie; Reynolds' portrait of Miss Bowles, also with a dog; Rembrandt's beautiful portrait of his son Titus; Van Dyck's grave and distinguished "Wife of Philippe le Roy"; a characteristic Pieter de Hooch (No. 27); Rubens' great landscape, "The Rainbow"; another and better Pieter de Hooch, beautifully lighted; Sir Joshua's "Mrs. Nesbitt with a Dove," and lastly an enchanting Cuyp.

The next wall is notable for its two Murillos and a romantic scene by Claude.

After some dashing sketches by Rubens we come, on

the last wall, to Velazquez again: "Don Balthasar Carlos in Infancy." Then to a glorious Rubens, clear as crystal, "The Holy Family with Elizabeth and John the Baptist"; Gainsborough's charming portrait of little Miss Haverfield; Reynolds' very popular "Mrs. Richard Hoare with her Infant Son," and, better still, the bewitching "Nelly O'Brien." Lastly another Velazquez, sombre and noble: the same little Don, but now older and on a pony; and another vivid Rubens: "Christ's Charge to S. Peter."

In the next room, XXVII, the favourite picture is probably that of the little Italian boy reading, which used to be hidden away downstairs. This is part of a fresco on plaster, by Vincenzo Foppa, and it was originally painted on the wall of the palace in the Via de' Bossi at Milan. Sir Richard Wallace bought it, together with the Beccafumi (No. 525), on the opposite wall, in 1872. Other remarkable pictures in the room are the two Luinis, so gentle and soothing; the very beautiful Andrea del Sarto, one of his finest works; a Murillo; a Ruisdael; the curious great allegory by Pourbus; and one of Bronzino's several austere portraits of Eleanor of Toledo.

In the next room, XVIII, we find the French masters of the eighteenth century, the *Fête Galanté* school. Here is Fragonard, with the delicious "Schoolmistress" (No. 404), and the adorable little boy as Pierrot. Here is Lépicié, a predecessor of Meissonier in minuteness but more homely in his sympathies. Here is Madame Vigée le Brun. Here is the accomplished Nattier. Here are Greuze, Watteau and Pater.

In the next room, XIX, we find some of them again, but the dominating figure here is Bouchen.

In Room XX Greuze reigns, but an Englishman is permitted to enter in the person of George Morland with a pretty domestic scene, "A Visit to the Boarding School," hung here no doubt to show how like him was his French contemporary, so seldom seen in London, Louis Leopold

THE "LAUGHING" CAVALIER

AFTER THE PICTURE BY FRANS HALS IN THE WALLACE COLLECTION

Boilly. Morland was born in 1763 and was dead by 1804, worn out by dissipation. Boilly, two years his senior, lived on till 1845. His two pictures illustrating "The Sorrows of Love" have great charm. On the wall dividing Rooms XX and XXI are a number of Bonington's water colours, proving that he was equally a master of interiors with dramatic scenes in progress and of landscape. And what a colourist! Morland's life was short, but Bonington's, with no contributory recklessness on his part, was tragically shorter: only twenty-seven years. I have marked in particular among these water colours, Nos. 656, 700, 701, 704, 727, 733. In Room XXI we find two excellent portraits by De Vos, a formal little Claude with an enchanted ship in it, more Greuze, and a Pater, No. 397, artificial but very pleasing. And here, as in every other room, are specimens of furniture, all French and all remarkable. The many clocks, too, should be studied. More furniture is in the last and circular room, more tapestry, more Greuze, and a sumptuous service of Augsburg silver gilt plate.

Upstairs are other pictures not of the highest rank. A visitor not finding an old favourite should inquire of the attendant and it will, if possible, be shown to him. The catalogue is one of the best—if not quite the best— that I know.

CHAPTER III

MAYFAIR AND THE GEORGIANS

The Stately Homes of London—Shepherd Market and the Past—
Gay's "Trivia"—Memorial Tablets—Mayfair—Keith's Chapel—
Marriage on Easy Terms—Curzon Street—Shelley and the Lark—
Literary Associations—Berkeley Square—The Beaux—Dover Street
—John Murray's—Grosvenor Square—South Audley Street and
Chesterfield House.

OF the vast tracts of wealthy residential streets in
Bayswater and Belgravia and South Kensington
there is nothing to say, because they are not
interesting. They are too new to have a history (I find
myself instinctively refusing to loiter in any streets built
since Georgian days), and for the most part too regular
to compel attention as architecture. But Mayfair is
distinct: Mayfair's bricks and stones are eloquent.

Mayfair, whose oldest houses date from the early years
of the eighteenth century, strictly speaking, covers only
a very small area; but we have come to consider its
boundaries Piccadilly on the south, on the north Oxford
Street, on the east Bond Street, and on the west Park
Lane. Since most of the people who live there have one
or more other houses, in England or Scotland, Mayfair
out of the season is a very desolate land; but that is
all to the good from the point of view of the wanderer.
Indeed in August it is like a city of the dead. It is still
one of the most difficult districts to learn, and so many
are its *culs-de-sac*—often a mews, where horses once
stamped but where now motor horns hoot—and so

capricious are its streets, that one may lose one's way
in Mayfair very easily.

In Shepherd Market, just here, which is one of the
least modernised parts of London, it is still possible to
feel in the eighteenth century. It lies just to the south
of Curzon Street, in the democratic way in which in
London poor neighbourhoods jostle wealthy ones, and it
is a narrow street or two filled with bustling little shops
and busy shopkeepers. Many of the houses have hardly
been touched since they were built, nor have the manners
of the place altered to any serious degree. Gentlemen's
gentlemen, such as one meets about here, remain very
much the same: the coachmen and butlers and footmen
who to-day emerge from the ancient Sun Inn, wiping
their mouths, are not, save for costume, very different
from those that emerged wiping their mouths from the
same inn in the days of Walpole and Charles James Fox.
Edward Shepherd, the architect who built Shepherd
Market, lived in what is now Crewe House, the very
attractive and countrified low white house in its own
grounds with a little lodge, opposite the Duke of Marlborough's square white palace.

A thought that is continually coming to mind as one
walks about older London and meditates on its past is
how modern that past is—how recently civilisation as
we understand it came upon the town. Superficially
much is changed, but materially nothing. Half an hour
spent on the old "Spectator" or "Tatler," or with
Walpole's "Letters" or Boswell's "Johnson," shows you
that. The London of Gay's "Trivia," that pleasant
guide to the art of walking in the streets of this city, is
at heart our own London—with trifling modifications.
The Bully has gone, the Nicker (the gentleman who broke
windows with halfpence) has gone, the fop is no longer
offensive with scent, wigs have become approximately a
matter of secrecy, and the conditions of life are less
simple; but Londoners are the same, and always will

be, I suppose, and the precincts of St. James still have
their milkmaids.   It is too late in the day to quote from
the poem, but my little edition has an index, and I quote
a little from that, partly because it is interesting in itself,
and partly because it transforms the reader into his own
poet.   Here are some entries:—

> Alley, the pleasure of walking in one
> Bookseller skilled in the weather
> Barber, by whom to be shunned
> Butchers, to be avoided
> Cane, the convenience of one
> Coat, how to chuse one for the winter
> Countryman, perplexed to find the way
> Coachman, his whip dangerous
> Crowd parted by a coach
> Cellar, the misfortunes of falling into one
> Dustman, to whom offensive
> Fop, the ill consequence of passing too near one
> Father, the happiness of a child who knows his own
> Ladies dress neither by reason nor instinct
> Milkman of the city unlike a rural one
> Overton the print seller
> Oyster, the courage of him that first ate one
> Prentices not to be relied on
> Periwigs, how stolen off the head
> Playhouse, a caution when you lead a lady out of it
> Shoes, what most proper for walkers
> Stockings, how to prevent their being spattered
> Schoolboys mischievous in frosty weather.
> Umbrella, its use
> Wig, what to be worn in a mist
> Way, of whom to be inquired
> Wall, when to keep it

From these heads one ought—given a knack of rhyme—
to be able to make a "Trivia" for oneself; and they
show that the London life of Gay's day—"Trivia" was
published in 1712—was very much what it is now.

From No. 1 London the best way to Shepherd Market
is by Hamilton Place and Hertford Street, or it may be
gained from Piccadilly by the narrow White Horse Street.
Hertford Street is a street of grave houses where many

THE SHRIMP GIRL

AFTER THE PICTURE BY HOGARTH IN THE NATIONAL GALLERY

interesting men and women have lived, only one of whom, however—Dr. Jenner, the vaccinator, at No. 14 —has a tablet. The erection of tablets in historic London—a duty shared by the County Council and the Society of Arts—is very capricious, a result partly due to the reluctance of owners or occupiers, to have their walls thus distinguished for gapers. Mayfair, so rich in residents of eminence, has very few tablets. Upon Hertford Street's roll of fame is also Capability Brown, who invented the shrubbery, or at any rate made it his ambition to make shrubberies grow where none had grown before, and was employed on this task, and on the laying out of gardens, by gentlemen all over England. Sheridan lived at No. 10 during four of his more prosperous years, in the house where General Burgoyne (who was also a playwright) died. Bulwer Lytton was at No. 36 in the eighteen-thirties.

Mayfair proper, which takes its name from the fair which was held there every May until the middle of the eighteenth century, on ground covered now by a part of Curzon Street and Hertford Street, has changed its character as completely as any London district. In those days it was notorious. Not only was the fair something of a scandal, but the Rev. Alexander Keith, in a little chapel of his own, with a church porch, close to Curzon Chapel, was in the habit of joining in matrimony more convenient than holy as many as six thousand couples a year, on the easiest terms then procurable south of Gretna Green. Among those that took advantage of the simplicities and incuriousness of Keith's Chapel was James, fourth Duke of Hamilton, in his curtain-ring marriage with the younger of the beautiful Miss Gunnings. Curtain-ring and Keith notwithstanding, this lady became the mother of two Dukes of Hamilton, and, in her second marriage, of two Dukes of Argyle. Keith meanwhile died in the Fleet prison. Not only is his chapel no more, but Curzon Chapel, its authorised neighbour and scandalised rival, is no more, for a few years ago the Duke of Marlborough, wishing to build a new town house, used its site. In exchange for the old conventicle there is now close by, on the other side of the street, one of the most striking of London's new temples—the Church of Christ Scientist.

Curzon Street might be called the most interesting street in Mayfair. Although it has these two new buildings and newly-fronted houses, it retains much of its old character, and it is still at each end a *cul-de-sac* for carriages, which is always a preservative condition. Now and then one comes to a house which must be as it was from the first—No. 35, for example—which has the old windows with white frames almost flush with the façade (a certain aid to picturesqueness, as Bedford Row eminently shows), and the old tiled roof. Like so many houses in this neighbourhood, No. 21 retains its extinguishers for the torches of the link boys. To give a list of Curzon Street's famous inhabitants would not be easy; but it was at No. 19 that Lord Beaconsfield died, and at No. 8 died the Miss Berrys, of whom Walpole has so much that is delightful to say.

Curzon Street's tributaries have also preserved much of their early character: Half Moon Street, Clarges Street, the north part of which has the quaintest little lodgings, Bolton Street, and so forth. In Half Moon Street, named, like many other London streets and omnibus destinations, after a public house, lived for a while such very different contemporaries as Hazlitt, Shelley and Madame d'Arblay. "There was," says Hogg in his life of his friend, "a little projecting window in Half Moon Street in which Shelley might be seen from the street all day long, book in hand, with lively gestures and bright eyes; so that Mrs. N. said he wanted only a pan of clear water and a fresh turf to look like some young lady's lark hanging outside for air and song."

Clarges Street, which is next Half Moon Street on the

east, has its roll of fame too. Dr. Johnson's blue-stock-inged friend Mrs. Elizabeth Carter died at a great age at No. 21, and Nelson's Lady Hamilton occupied No. 11, from 1804 to 1806. Edmund Kean lived at No. 12 for eight years, and Macaulay lodged at No. 3 on his return from India. No. 32, in Mr. Kinnaird the banker's days, was one of Byron's haunts. Bolton Street, near by, which not so very long ago was the most westerly street in London, was the home of Pope's friend Martha Blount, who inspired some of his most exquisite compliments; and it was there that Madame d'Arblay moved in 1818 and was visited by Sir Walter Scott and Samuel Rogers.

At its east end Curzon Street narrows to a passage between the gardens of Devonshire House and Lansdowne House, which takes the foot passenger into Berkeley Street. Once, however, a horseman made the journey too: a highwayman, who after a successful coup in Picca-dilly, evaded his pursuers by dashing down the steps and along this passage—a feat which led to the vertical iron bars now to be seen at either end.

Berkeley Square is smaller than Grosvenor Square but it has more character. Many of the wealthy inhabitants of Grosvenor Square are willing to take houses as they find them; but in Berkeley Square they make them pecu-liarly their own. At No. 11 Horace Walpole lived for eighteen years (with alternations at Strawberry Hill), and here he died in 1797. At No. 65 Clive committed suicide. "Auld Robin Gray" was written at No. 21.

To the task of tracing the past of this fashionable quarter there would of course be no end, and indeed one could not have a much more interesting occupation, but this is not that kind of book, and I have perhaps said enough to send readers independently to Wheatley and Cunningham,[1] who have been so useful to me and to

[1] "London Past and Present: Its Histories, Associations and Traditions," by H. B. Wheatley, based upon Peter Cunningham's "Handbook of London." Three volumes. Murray.

whom old London is more familiar than new London.
For any one bent on this pleasant enterprise of re-peopling
Mayfair, Berkeley Square is a very good starting point.
Charles Street, Bruton Street, and Mount Street all lead
from it, of which Charles Street perhaps retains most of
its ancient peace and opulent gravity. One of its newer
houses, with three dormer windows, has some of the best
wrought-iron in London. At No. 42 lived, in 1792, Beau
Brummell; while another Charles Street dandy—but
only half a one, since he smirched his escutcheon by
writing books and legislating—was the first Lord Lytton.
Here also Mr. Burke flirted with Fanny Burney, before
Mrs. Burke's face too. Later, Beau Brummell moved to
4 Chesterfield Street, where he had for neighbour George
Selwyn, who made the best jokes of his day and dearly
loved a hanging. In Bruton Street—at No. 24—lived in
1809 another George who was also a wit, but of deeper
quality, George Canning.

Through Bruton Street we gain Bond Street, London's
Rue de la Paix, which only a golden key can unlock; but
into Bond Street we will not now stray, but return to
Berkeley Square and climb Hay Hill,—where the Prince
of Wales, afterwards George IV, with a party, was once
waylaid by footpads; but to little profit, for they could
muster only half a crown between them—and so come
to Dover Street, where once lived statesmen and now
are modistes. Among its old inhabitants were John
Evelyn, who died in the ninth house on the east side
from Piccadilly, and Harley, Earl of Oxford, in whose
house, the second from Piccadilly on the west side, Pope
and Swift and Arbuthnot used to meet in what Arbuthnot called Martin's office—Martin being Scriblerus, master
of the "Art of Sinking in Poetry." In another Dover
Street house lived Sir Joshua Reynolds' sister, whose guests
often included Johnson and his satellite.

Albemarle Street, which also is no longer residential
and has been given up to business, also has great tradi-

LADY READING A LETTER
AFTER THE PICTURE BY TERBURG IN THE WALLACE COLLECTION

tions. Lord Bute lived here, and here Zoffany painted the portrait of John Wilkes; Charles James Fox lived here for a little while, and Robert Adam and James Adam, who with their brothers built the Adelphi, both died here. Louis XVIII, when in exile in 1814, stayed at Grillion's Hotel, now no more. But the most famous house is John Murray's, at No. 50, where the "Quarterly Review," so savage and tartarly, was founded, and whence so much that is best in literature emerged, whose walls are a portrait gallery of English men of letters. Byron's is of course the greatest name in this house, but Borrow's belongs to it also. Scott and Byron first met beneath this roof.

It was at the Mount Coffee House in Mount Street, which takes one from Berkeley Square to Grosvenor Square, that Shelley's first wife, Harriet Westbrook, about whom there has been too much chatter, lived, her father being the landlord; but Mount Street bears few if any traces of that time, for the rebuilder has been very busy there. And so leaving on the left Farm Street, where Mayfair's Catholics worship, we turn into Grosvenor Square. Grosvenor Square is more than two hundred years old and has had many famous residents. It was in an ante-room of the Earl of Chesterfield's house here that Johnson cooled his heels and warmed his temper. Mr. Thrale died in Grosvenor Square, and so did John Wilkes, at No. 30. At No. 22 lived Sir William and Lady Hamilton, with "Vathek" Beckford, and thither went Nelson after the battle of the Nile. When gas came in as the new illuminant, Grosvenor Square was sceptical and contemptuous, and it clung to oil and candles for some years longer than its neighbours.

The two Grosvenor Streets, Upper and Lower, have rich associations too. Mrs. Oldfield died at No. 60 Upper Grosvenor Street in 1730; at No. 13 Scott and Coleridge had a memorable meeting in 1809. The two Brook Streets, and indeed all the Grosvenor Square tributaries, are also worth studying by the light of Wheatley and Cunningham; while South Audley Street, although it is now principally shops, is rich in sites that have historic interest. At 77, for instance, lived Alderman Wood, the champion of Caroline of Brunswick, who was his guest there on her return from Italy in 1820. Many notable persons were buried in Grosvenor Chapel, among them Lady Mary Wortley Montagu and John Wilkes. This is one of the prettiest churches in London and just round the corner, on the south side, is one of the snuggest of London's little houses.

At the corner of South Street is a fine example of Georgian solidity, No. 71. Next but one to it, No. 73 South Audley Street, we notice a severe and very attractive portico, and a little later the superb modern façade of Bute House. The house within its own walls and gates at the south-east corner of South Audley Street is Chesterfield House, built in the middle of the eighteenth century for the famous fourth Earl of Chesterfield, who wrote the "Letters," and who by his want of generosity (but that was in Grosvenor Square) stimulated Dr. Johnson to a better letter than any of his own. It is now the London home of Princess Mary. And at this point we enter Curzon Street again.

INTERIOR OF A DUTCH HOUSE

AFTER THE PICTURE BY PETER DE HOOCH IN THE NATIONAL GALLERY

ST. JAMES'S AND PICCADILLY EAST

FOR one still interested in the very core of aristocratic life it is a pleasant walk from Mayfair to that other Park Lane, Queen's Walk, lined also with its palaces looking westward over grass and trees —these, however, being the grass and trees of Green Park. Some of London's most distinguished houses are here—among them Hamilton House and Stafford House, where the London Museum is lodged. Arlington Street, where the upper Queen's Walk houses have their doors, has long been dedicated to high politics. Every brick in it has some political association, from Sir Robert Walpole to the late Lord Salisbury. Horace Walpole lived long at No. 5, and was born opposite. At No. 4 lived Charles James Fox; and it was at lodgings in Arlington Street in 1801 that Lady Nelson parted for ever from her husband, being "sick of hearing of 'Dear Lady Hamilton.'"

St. James's Place also has political associations, but is

more tinged with literature than Arlington Street. Addi
son lived here, and here lived Pope's fair Lepel. Fox,
who seems to have lodged or lived everywhere, was here
in 1783. "Perdita" Robinson was at No. 13; Mrs. Delany
died here; and Byron was lodging at No. 8 when "English
Bards and Scotch Reviewers" burst on the town. But the
king of St. James's Place was Samuel Rogers, who lived
at No. 22 from 1803 until 1855, when he died, aged ninety-
five, and in that time entertained every one who was
already distinguished, and distinguished the others by
entertaining them.

St. James's Place is the quietest part of aristocratic
London. Even in mid afternoon in the season it is possible
to see no sign of life in any of its odd ramifications. Every
house is staid; every house, one feels, has had its history
and perhaps is making history now; wealth and birth
and breeding and taste are as evident here as they can
be absent elsewhere. One doubts if any Cockney child,
even the most audacious, venturing up the narrowest of
narrow passages from the Green Park into this Debret-
tian backwater, ever dared to do more than peep at
its blue-blooded gravity and precipitately withdraw. I
would go to St. James's Place for a rest cure: it is a
sanctuary to which the motor bus will never penetrate.

Arlington Street and St. James's Place have kept their
residential character; but St. James's Street and Pall
Mall have lost theirs. They are now the principal male
streets of London. Women are the exception there, and
there are no London streets so given up to women as
these to men. The buildings are clubs and a few men's
shops, most famous of which in the past was Hoby's,
the bootmaker. Hoby claimed to have won Vittoria, and
indeed all Wellington's battles, by virtue of the boots he
had made for him in St. James's Street and the prayers
he had offered for him in Islington, where he was a Metho-
dist preacher. I suppose there are still characters among

PORTRAIT OF A TAILOR

AFTER THE PICTURE BY MORONI IN THE NATIONAL GALLERY

London tradesmen; but one does not hear much about them. Interest in character seems to have died out, the popular ambition to-day being for every man to be as much like every other man as he can. Hoby was splendid. When Ensign Horace Churchill of the Guards burst into his shop in a fury, vowing never to employ him again, the bootmaker quietly called to one of his assistants, "John, put up the shutters. It's all over with us. Ensign Churchill has withdrawn his custom." Hoby kept all the Iron Duke's orders for boots; I wonder where they are now. I know personally of only one great man's letter to his bootmaker, and that is on the walls of a shop near Charing Cross, and in it Thomas Carlyle says that there at last, after many years, have his feet found comfort.

Before St. James's Street was given up to clubs—White's with its famous bow window, Boodle's, Brooks's, the Thatched House, to mention the old rather than the new—it had its famous inhabitants, among them Edmund Waller, Gillray the caricaturist, who committed suicide by throwing himself from a window at No. 29, Campbell the poet, and James Maclean the gentleman highwayman. At No. 3, Messrs. Berry's wine office, is a pair of giant scales on which every one of importance in club life for the past century and more has been weighed, and a record kept, filling volumes.

St. James's Street has the great scenic merit of terminating in the gateway of St. James's Palace, a beautiful, grave, Tudor structure of brick. The palace, now the home of the Prince of Wales and of various court officials, was the royal abode from the reign of William II, in whose day Whitehall was burnt, to George IV. Queen Mary died there. Charles I was imprisoned there before his execution and walked to Whitehall on the fatal morning from this place—to bow his comely head down as upon a bed. General Monk lived in the palace for a while, and Verrio, the Italian mural painter, who covered fair white ceilings with sprawling goddesses and cupids, had his home here in the reign of James II. In 1814 Blücher lodged in Ambassador's Court, and, settled in his window with his pipe, bowed to the admiring crowds—an agreeable picture to think upon. Ambassador's Court is still one of the quietest spots in London, and indeed the palace is a very pleasant place in which to retire from the streets, for those who prefer the repose of masonry to the repose of nature, such as St. James's Park offers. Levées are still held at St. James's; but the old practice of hearing the Laureates declaim their state poems has been abandoned without any particular wrench. Every morning at eleven the lover of military music may enjoy the Guards' band.

And so we come to the Park, of whose beauty I have already said something, and to the splendours of the Mall, which is London's Champs Elysées, and to the monotonous opulence of Carlton House Terrace. The new gateway at Whitehall, and the Victoria Statue opposite Buckingham Palace, are part of the memorial to the great queen; the Edward Memorial is at the foot of Regent Street, opposite the Athenæum Club.

Pall Mall is not only more sombre in mien but has more seriousness than St. James's Street. The War Office is here, and here are the Carlton and the Athenæum. Marlborough House is here too. But it was not always thus, for at the house which is now No. 79, but has been rebuilt and rebuilt, once lived Mistress Eleanor Gwynn, over whose garden wall she leaned to exchange badinage with Charles II. The impostor Psalmanazar lodged in Pall Mall, and so did Gibbon, greatest of ironists. Gainsborough painted there, and Cosway, and there was the house of John Julius Angerstein, whose collection of Old Masters formed the nucleus of our National Gallery.

Captain Thomas Morris's pleasant song about the charms of the sweet shady side of Pall Mall over all the allurements of the country has never found any echo in

PORTRAIT OF A YOUNG SCULPTOR
AFTER THE PAINTING BY ANDREA DEL SARTO IN THE NATIONAL GALLERY

me. I find Pall Mall equally forbidding in wet weather or fine. There is something chilling about these huge, sombre, material monasteries called clubs, solemn temples of the best masculine form, compounded of gentlemen and waiters, dignity and servility. They oppress me. Pall Mall has no sweet shade; its shade is gloomy.

Turning up between the Army and Navy and the Junior Carlton clubs one comes to St. James's Square, once another abode of the rich and powerful, and now a square of clubs and a few private houses with the statue of William III in their midst famous for his horse's voluptuous tail. In 1695, when it was already built round, the square was a venue for duellists, and in 1773 a mounted highwayman could still carry on his profession there. At Norfolk House, No. 31, George III was born. The iron posts at No. 2 were cannon captured off Finisterre by Admiral Boscawen. At No. 15 lived Thurlow. At the north corner of King Street was Lord Castlereagh's, and here his body was brought after his suicide in 1822. It was round this square that Johnson and Savage, being out of money, walked and walked for hours one night, "in high spirits and brimful of patriotism," inveighing against the ministry and vowing to stand by their country. Later Johnson used often to quote the stanza about the Duchess of Leeds—

> She shall have all that's fine and fair,
> And the best of silk and satin shall wear,
> And live in a coach to take the air,
> And have a house in St. James's Square,—

saying that it "comprised nearly all the advantages that wealth can give." But King Street's chief interest for me is centred in Christie's rooms, for here one may see during the season so many beautiful pictures—better often than our National Gallery examples—and even if one may not buy one can attend the private views or even the sales themselves, provided that one has no awkward nervous affection which might be mistaken by the auctioneer for the frenzied nods of the millionaire collector. In course of time nearly every privately owned picture finds its way to Christie's, and I advise all visitors to London in the season to get into the habit of dropping into the rooms on the chance of finding a masterpiece. Christie's is not the only picture sale room hereabouts, but the best. The others should be visited too, and every other shop in King Street, Bury Street and Carfax Street is a little gallery too, even if, for the principal picture dealers, Bond Street must be sought.

All the streets in this neighbourhood have their pasts: Bury Street, where Swift had lodgings when he was in London, and Steele, after his marriage, and Moore and Crabbe; Duke Street, where, at No. 67, Burke had rooms; and Jermyn Street, home of bachelors whose clubs are their father and their mother, where in its palmy residential days lived great men and women, even Marlborough himself and Sir Isaac Newton. Gray lodged here regularly, over Roberts the hosier's or Frisby the oilman's; and in 1832, in a house where the Hammam Turkish Bath now is, Sir Walter Scott lay very near his end.

To the end of all, in the case of many illustrious persons, we come at St. James's Church, between this street and Piccadilly, one of Wren's red brick buildings and a very beautiful one too, with a font and other work by Grinling Gibbons and a Jacobean organ. Here lie cheerful Master Cotton, who helped with the "Compleat Angler," and Van de Velde the painter of sea-fights, and the ingenious but reprehensible Tom d'Urfey, and Dr. Arbuthnot, friend of Pope and Swift and Gay and wit. Mrs. Delany is also here, and Dodsley the bookseller, and the dissolute Old Q, and Gillray; and here was baptised the great Earl of Chatham. And so we come to Piccadilly again—the business part of it—with its crowded pavements, its tea rooms and picture galleries and restaurants.

St. James's Church is Piccadilly's most beautiful old

ALFRED WERTHEIMER
FROM THE PAINTING BY JOHN S. SARGENT IN THE NATIONAL GALLERY

building; the Institute of Water Colour Painters its most impressive new one; Burlington House is its principal lion, and the Albany its quietest tributary. Many famous men made their home in this mundane cloister, where all it well-ordered, still and discreet—like a valet in list slippers. Monk Lewis had his cell at No. 1a, to be followed there many years later, by Sir Squire Bancroft; Canning was at 5a; Byron at 2a, in rooms that afterwards passed to Lytton; Macaulay was at 1e for fifteen years—in the eighteen-forties and fifties. Mr. Gladstone also was a brother of the Albany for a while. Only by the expedient of pretending to have a friend here (whose name one must first ascertain) can a stranger get past the janitor into the Albany.

Of Burlington House, since it changes its exhibitions twice a year, there is little to say in a book of this character. As a preliminary step for the full enjoyment of the Bond Street tea shops there is nothing like the summer Academy, where thousands of pictures wet from the easel are assembled; but the winter exhibitions of Old Masters are among the first intellectual pleasures that London offers, and are a recurring reminder of the fine taste and generosity of the English collector, and the country's wealth of great art.

Few people find their way to the permanent Diploma Gallery at the top of Burlington House, where hang the pictures with which in a way every Royal Academician pays his footing, together with a few greater works. But to climb the stairs is important, for the Diploma Gallery contains what might be called without extravagance the most beautiful drawing in London—a Holy Family by Leonardo da Vinci, reproduced opposite page 48. The picture being in monochrome, the reproduction does it less injustice than usual, preserving much of its benign sweetness, and the lovely maternity of it. A bas-relief of Michelangelo and a figure of Temperance by Giorgione are other treasures of this gallery. Reynolds' sitter's

chair and easel and three or four fine portraits are also
here; Maclise's vast charcoal cartoon of the meeting of
Wellington and Blücher: sixty-six designs for Homer by
Flaxman; Watts' Death of Cain; and a number of
impressionistic oil sketches by Constable, some of them
the most vivid presentments of English weather that exist.
The rest is strictly diploma work and not too interesting.
The sculpture room, full of diploma casts, yellow with
paint or London grime, is, I think, the most depressing
chamber I ever hurried from; but a few of the pictures
stand out—Reynolds' portrait of Sir William Chambers,
and Raeburn's "Boy and Rabbit," and Sargent's "Venetian Interior," for example. But it is Leonardo and
Michelangelo and Constable that make the ascent necessary.

A few years ago it was to Piccadilly that every fortunate
child was taken, to hear the Christy Minstrels; but this
form of entertainment having been killed in England,
within doors at any rate, that famous troupe is no
more. The St. James's Hall has been razed to the ground,
and a vast and imposing hotel has risen on its site;
yet in the latter nineteenth century the names of Moore
and Burgess were as well known and as inextricably
associated with London's fun as any have ever been.
But burnt cork has gone the way of sawdust and London
now has neither Ethiopian entertainers nor a circus.
And the Music Hall is not what it was, en-
croached upon by revue and threatened by the
omnipresent cinema.

Gone too is the Egyptian Hall, that other Piccadilly
Mecca of happy childhood, where incredible illusions held
the audience a-gape twice daily. Maskelyne still remains,
but there is no Cook any more, and the new Home of
Mystery is elsewhere. Change! Change! But the
Burlington Arcade remains, through which, half stifled
by heat and patchouli, one may if one likes regain the
quietude of Georgian London: for one comes that way

ST. JAMES'S STREET AND ST. JAMES'S PALACE

to Cork Street and Old Burlington Street and Boyle
Street and Savile Row, which have been left pretty much
as they were. In Old Burlington Street lived General
Wolfe as a youth; and here lived and died the poet
Akenside. Pope's friend Arbuthnot lived in Cork Street.
Savile Row being the headquarters of tailoring is now
almost exclusively a masculine street, save for the little
messenger girls who run between the cutters and the
sewing rooms; but once it was a street of family mansions, many of which are not much altered except in
occupants since they were built in the seventeen-thirties.
Poor Sheridan, who once lived at No. 14, died at No. 17
in great distress—just before assistance came to him from
the Regent, who had been postponing it for weeks and
weeks, a failure of duty which led to Moore's most scathing poem. George Tierney, who fought a duel with Pitt,
lived at No. 11, which previously was tenanted by Joseph
Hill, to whom Cowper wrote rhyming epistles. Grote's
house is marked by a tablet.

One of Piccadilly's claims to notice I must not overlook
its windows. Though not so wholly given up to shops
as Regent Street or Bond Street, where everything can be
bought, Piccadilly contains certain shops of world-wide
fame, whose windows I for one never tire of studying.
One of these is that condiment house on the south side
where, according to Sydney Smith, the gourmets of
England will make their last stand when their country
is under invasion. It is still as wonderful as in the days
of the witty Canon: the ends of the earth still combine
to fill it with exotic delicacies. Close by is, I suppose, the
best known taxidermist and naturalist's in the world,
where you may see rhinoceroses' heads and hartebeests'
horns, bear hat-stands and coiled boa-constrictors, ostriches
and kingfishers (both harmless creatures more beautiful
in life than death) all ready for English halls. "A tiger-
skin rug," said another wit, "is the Ro. Ward of accuracy."

Bond Street, which Socrates would find more than

filled with articles that he could do without, is more complete as a shopping centre. You may buy there anything from a muff-warmer to a tiara, from caravan-borne tea to an Albert Cuyp; for jewellers and old and new picture dealers have especially made it their own. In the matter of jewels London is still faithful to its old specialising habit—the best jewellers being still in Bond Street and close by, and its diamond merchants still congregating almost exclusively in Hatton Garden; but a decentralising tendency has steadily come upon the town. Not so very long ago, for example, Wardour Street stood for old furniture, and Holywell Street for old books. But to-day Holywell Street does not exist, and old book and old furniture shops have sprung up all over London, while Wardour Street is now dedicated to the movie industry. Long Acre, once wholly in the hands of carriage-makers, is now a centre for motor cars, which may, however, be bought elsewhere too. Publishers, once faithful to Paternoster Row, have (following John Murray) now spread to the west. Departmental London, so far as retail trade is concerned, is practically no more.

The saddest change in the shops of London is in the chemists: the greatest, in the tobacconists. There must now be a tobacconist to every ten men of the population, or something near it, and the new ones are in every way unworthy of the old: they know no repose, as a tobacconist should; they serve you with incredible despatch and turn to the next customer. To loiter in one of their shops is beyond consideration; and no Prince Florizel could be a tobacconist to-day, unless he was prepared for bankruptcy. Of course there are still a few old-fashioned firms on secure foundations where a certain leisure may be observed; but it is superficial leisure. I feel convinced that below stairs there is a seething activity. And even in these shops one cannot really waste time, although to enable one to do that with grace and a sense of virtue is of course the principal duty of the leaf. It

HOLY FAMILY

AFTER THE DRAWING BY LEONARDO DA VINCI IN THE DIPLOMA GALLERY,
BURLINGTON HOUSE

will prove our decadence, our want of right feeling, of reverence, when you try in vain in all London to find tobacconists with enough piety to retain the wooden Highlander who once was as necessary and important to the dealer in Returns and Rappee as is the figure of Buddha to a joss house or a striped pole to a barber. I know at this moment of only two such shops.

Sadder still is the decay of the chemist. There are here and there the real old chemist's windows, with a row of coloured jars such as poor Rosamond lost an excursion for; but how rare these are! One is in West Halkin Street—all honour to it! Our new business habits, imported chiefly from America, have in no respect done so much injury—æsthetically—as in substituting the new store-druggist's crowded window for the old chromatic display. In the modern stress of competition there is no room to spare for pure decoration; and so the purple jars have gone. And within all is changed too. An element of bustle has come into the chemist's life. Of old he was quiet and sympathetic and whispering: now his attitude is one best described by the words "Next, please." I wonder that the sealing wax remains. In some of the new chemists the difficulty is to find bottles at all. Only by struggling past novels and photograph frames can this be done.

Another commercial sign of the times in London is the increase of newsagents (in addition to the kerb-stone salesmen), and with them the rise of the demon distributor. No recent London street type is more noticeable than he: a large-boned centaur, half-hooligan, half-bicycle, who, bent double beneath his knapsack of news, dashes on his wheel between the legs of horses, under wagons and through policemen, in the feverish enterprise of spreading the tidings of winner and starting price. But he is fast disappearing in favour of the motor-driven vehicle. Every day more motor cars are projected upon the London streets: every day blocks assume larger dimensions and I see no chance of any improvement until roads are widened (at prohibitive cost) or viaducts such as that at Holborn over Farringdon Street come in.

And here is a London conundrum:—

What is this?——

It is a common object of the London streets. In fact, London would not be London without it.

It is most visible and active in August and December.

You hardly ever see it in the country.

You never see it at night.

It was once so tiny as to be helpless. It is now helpful or nothing.

Although once so tiny it would never be bigger than it is now.

It is outside size.

It would be terrible doubled.

Although never larger than a hot-water bottle it can stop a motor bus.

It ought to be whiter than snow, but as the day wears on it isn't.

It is never so white as on occasions of State—such as Lord Mayor's Day, Royal weddings, Arrivals of Foreign Rulers.

Few sights are more welcome to timid persons.

None are more unwelcome to the impatient. Indeed it can reduce the impatient to frenzy.

It is at its best in the open air.

He would be both a bold and foolish man who dared to resist it.

No one shakes it till the evening.

Unlike the barometer, its rise is more irritating than its fall.

It is an impressive sight even to taxi drivers.

It causes us to lose trains and be late for meals and appointments.

THE NATIVITY

AFTER THE PICTURE BY PIERO DELLA FRANCESCA IN THE NATIONAL GALLERY

It has probably saved more lives than were lost in the War.

None the less it is the constant cause of rage and profanity.

It is, very possibly, futile in the home.

There is no appeal against it.

The Parisians could do with a few like it.

When not working it is the most ordinary affair.

It has certain superficial resemblances to yours.

The answer is the hand of a policeman on point duty.

Bond Street's past has been almost wholly buried beneath modern commerce, but it is interesting to recollect that it was at No. 41, which was then a silk-bag shop on March 18, 1768, that the creator of Uncle Toby and Corporal Trim died. It was at No. 141 New Bond Street that in 1797 Lord Nelson lay for three months after the battle of Cape St. Vincent, where his arm was shot.

From Bond Street one is quickly in Regent Street, once more among the shops and in the present day; but Regent Street is not interesting except as part of a great but futile scheme to plan out a stately and symmetrical London in honour of an unworthy prince. Of this, Portland Place, Park Crescent and Regent's Park are the other portions. The project was noble, as the width of Portland Place testifies, but it was not in character with London, and it failed. No second attempt to provide London with a Parisian thoroughfare—with anything approaching French width and luxury—occurred until the Mall was taken in hand and the space in front of Buckingham Palace was made symmetrical. Every day the regularity of Regent Street, as planned by Nash, is impaired. In no London thoroughfare have the rebuilders been so lively since the War.

Regent Street in its turn leads to Oxford Street, where the great drapery shops—I should say, emporiums—are: paradises of mannequins and super-mannequins. More attractive to me is the little, almost Venetian, knot of flower-sellers who have made the island in Oxford Circus their own, in summer adding to its southern air by large red umbrellas. Of such women one should buy one's flowers.

CHAPTER V

TRAFALGAR SQUARE AND GREAT ENGLISHMEN

London's finest site—Nelson—The French salutes—Trafalgar Day — The Steeple-jack — St. Martin's-in-the-Fields — The Gymnast — "Screevers" — Bands — The Cenotaph — London's Statues — The National Portrait Gallery.

OF Trafalgar Square London has every right to be proud. Here at any rate, one feels, is a genuinely national attempt at a grandoise effect. The National Gallery façade is satisfactory in its British plainness and seriousness; St. Martin's Church, with its whiteness emerging from its grime, is pure London; the houses on the east and west sides of the square are commendably rectangular and sturdy; the lions (although occupied only in guarding policemen's waterproofs) are imposing and very British: while the Nelson Column is as tall and as commanding as any people, however artistic or passionately patriotic, could have made it. It is right. I am not sure but it touches sublimity. Apart, I mean, altogether from the crowning figure and all that he stands for in personal valour, melancholy and charm, and all that he symbolises: conquest itself—more than conquest, deliverance. Indeed, with the idea of Nelson added, there is no question at all of sublimity; it is absolute. I like the story of the French sailors who visited London in 1905 rising to salute it as they were driving past on their way to the West End. Would they have saluted Wellington's statue at Hyde Park Corner, I wonder? May be; but certainly not with the involuntary spontaneity that marked the Trafalgar Square demonstration. (Fortunately, exhaustive as was our hospitality, they were not taken to the grave of Sir Hudson Lowe at St. Mark's in North Audley Street.)

Every now and then the Nelson Column is festooned in honour of Trafalgar Day, and for a while its impressiveness is lost. Wreaths at the foot were better. Patriotism and hero-worship, however, do not resent broken lines; and the ropes of evergreens that twine about the pillar draw thousands of people to Trafalgar Square every day. I remember the first time I saw the preparations in progress. Turning into the square from Spring Gardens, I was aware of a crowd of upturned faces watching a little black spot travelling up the pillar. It reached the top, disappeared and appeared again, waving something. It was a Steeplejack, an intrepid gentleman from the north of England, if I recollect aright, who had the contract for the decorations, and with whom, on his descent, it was the privilege of several newspaper men to have interviews.

I was tempted after reading one of these to seek him myself, and either induce him to take me to the top with him, or hand him a commission to describe the extent of Nelson's view from that altitude, which, under the title "What Nelson Sees," would, I thought, make a seasonable and novel Trafalgar Day article. But I dared neither to converse with the living hero nor climb to the dead one, and that article is still unwritten. On a clear day Nelson must have a fine prospect to the south—not quite to his ancient element, of course, but away to the Surrey hills, and east and west along the winding river.

St. Martin's Church—the real name of which is St. Martin's-in-the-Fields (how far from fields to-day!) stands upon its hill as proudly almost as St. Paul's, and has not a little of St. Paul's grave dignity. From its steps many Londoners get their impression of State pageants: I was standing there on the only occasion that I have ever seen a Shah. Among those who lie beneath this church is Nell Gwynn, and Francis Bacon was christened there.

St. Martin's spire was once used for a strictly secular purpose, when, in 1727, Violanti, an Italian acrobat, fastened one end of a rope three hundred yards long to its summit, and the other to a support in the Royal Mews beyond St. Martin's Lane, and descended upon it head foremost with his arms and legs outstretched, among the crowd being "the young princesses with several of the nobility." The pavement to the north and south used to be the canvas of two very superior "screevers"—as the men are called who make pastel drawings on paving-stones. London has fewer "screevers" than it used, and latterly I have noticed among such of these artists as remain a growing tendency to bring oil paintings (which may or may not be their own work) and lean them against the wall, supplying themselves only the minimum of scroll work beneath. To such go no pennies of mine—unless of course the day is dripping wet. On a dry pavement the "screever" must show us his pictures in the making: they must, like hot rolls, be new every day. We will have no scamping in this art.

If "screevers" are fewer, bands are far more numerous. The German band, naturally, is no more; but in its place have sprung up scores and scores of performers of home-growth, often ex-service men, who rattle their collecting boxes with a determination that the discordant Teuton never dared. Returning for a moment to the "scree-ver," I have observed that he rarely now depicts cutlets and sections of salmon, but relies rather upon landscape and portraits of celebrities.

Trafalgar Square, with Nelson and the surrounding figures of stone, notable among them the beautifully easy presentment of Gordon, brings us to the general considera-tion of London statues, of which there are many here and there, although, since we are not naturally a statue-erect-ing or statue-valuing people, as the French are, for the most part they escape notice. Among the French, indeed, wherever you go, a livelier love of country and a more personal pride in it are to be found.

The old gibe against that nation that it has no word for home, and no true sense of home, might be met by the reminder that France itself is the home of the French in a way that England can never be called the home of the English. An Englishman's home is the world; a Frenchman's France; and he is never wearied in beautifying that home, and praising it, and keeping it homely. Such pride has he in it that there is hardly a place in the whole country without its group of statuary in honour of some brave or wise *enfant* of the State, which is decorated at regular intervals and whose presence is never forgotten. It is impossible to do anything for France and escape recognition and tribute. With the English, patriotism is taken for granted; but the French nourish it, tend it like a favourite flower, enjoy every fresh blossom.

The War certainly made a change in this matter of respect and memory in England and few, if any, of the Memorials that have been piously set up all over the country are neglected. In London the beautiful Cenotaph in Whitehall has fresh flowers laid at its foot every day, and so has many another—the Cross of Sacrifice in Sloane Square in particular springs to mind.

But for statues as statues we still do not much care. It is true that on certain anniversaries we also decorate some of our statues—Beaconsfield's, Gordon's, Nelson's; but we do so, I fear, less as a people than as a party. Charles the First's statue facing Whitehall has its wreaths once a year, but they come from a small body of "Legitimists"; the Gladstone statue in the Strand will no doubt be decorated too for a few years, but it will not be a national duty, and none of those who take primroses to Parliament Square on April 19 will be represented.

In "London Revisited" I endeavoured to make a complete list of London public statues, but the list extends continually. Among the latest, not including War

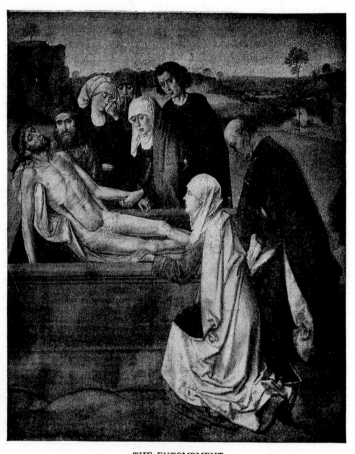

THE ENTOMBMENT
AFTER THE PICTURE BY DIRK BOUTS IN THE NATIONAL GALLERY

Memorials, is that of Edward VII, just by the York
Column, displacing Sir William Napier who is now to be
found opposite Queen's Gate in Kensington Gardens—the
gate that is made memorable by the exquisite figures of
deer on each side. Opposite Sir John Franklin's memorial,
also in Waterloo Place, is now a statue of Captain Scott,
the more recent and equally ill-fated Arctic explorer,
the work of his widow. On the little lawn under the
National Gallery is a life-size figure of George Washington, very modest. Near by at the foot of the Charing Cross
Road is the Cavell Memorial, with a charming maternal
figure at the apex. Opposite the entrance of Dean's Yard
is a replica of St. Gaudens' famous figure of Abraham
Lincoln, with the great, lonely but impressive chair behind
him. In Portland Place is a statue of Field Marshal Sir
George Stuart White, and Clive has been moved from
his old position to the St. James's Park end of King
Charles's Street.

Among older and more memorable of London's statues,
I recall as I write Queen Anne in front of St. Paul's and
again at her beautiful gate by St. James's Park; George I
on the top of the spire in Bloomsbury; George II in
Golden Square; George III in a little scratch wig on a
prancing horse at the east end of Pall Mall; George IV,
riding without stirrups, and visibly uncomfortable, in
Trafalgar Square; James II (looking too much like Mr.
Forbes-Robertson the actor) behind the Admiralty; Queen
Elizabeth on the wall of St. Dunstan's-in-the-West; Mary
Queen of Scots for some reason or other on a new façade
in Fleet Street; Queen Victoria, by Blackfriars Bridge,
standing, and in Kensington Gardens, seated; Cromwell
in the shelter of Westminster Hall, very nigh the replaced
bauble; Richard Cœur-de-Lion, splendidly warlike, on
his horse, by the House of Lords; the Duke of York of
discreditable memory on his column in Waterloo Place,
doing all he can by his sheer existence to depreciate the
value of the national tribute to Nelson close by; Welling-

ton at Hyde Park Corner and again before the Royal
Exchange; Havelock in Trafalgar Square; Captain
Coram by his Foundling Hospital; Gladstone in the
Strand; Dr. Johnson, pitifully meagre, close by; Shake-
speare in the middle of Leicester Square, within hail of
the Empire and the Alhambra, and again, with Chaucer
and Milton, in Hamilton Place, and still again, in connection with the editors of his first folio, Heminges and
Condell, at their parish church of St. Mary the Virgin,
Aldermanbury; Milton outside St. Giles's, Cripplegate;
Lord Strathnairn at Knightsbridge; Boadicea, in her cha-
riot, on Westminster Bridge; Darwin, Huxley, Owen and
Banks in the Natural History Museum; William Pitt, a
gigantic figure, in Hanover Square; Charles James Fox
in Bloomsbury Square and at Holland House; Carlyle
in Chelsea; Sir Hugh Myddelton in Islington Green;
Canning (who has a sparrow's nest under his arm every
spring) in Parliament Square; Cobden in Camden Town:
Sir Robert Peel (in profile very like Lamb) in Cheapside;
Lord Herbert of Lea and Florence Nightingale in Waterloo
Place; Cardinal Newman by the Brompton Oratory;
John Wesley opposite Bunhill Fields; Robert Stephenson
at Euston; Byron, seated, in Hamilton Gardens and in
relief in St. James's Street and again in Holles Street;
Robert Burns, Robert Raikes and Sir Arthur Sullivan
in the Embankment Gardens; Sir Wilfrid Lawson
there too, looking thirstily at the Thames; W. S.
Gilbert on a medallion opposite; the Duke of Cambridge in Whitehall; Sir Henry Irving in the Charing
Cross Road; and Prince Albert, often unrecognized
in Holborn Circus, and again, all gold, in Kensington Gardens, seated beneath a canopy not without
ornamentation. This, though far from complete, may
be called a good list; and I doubt if there are many
Londoners who could have supplied from memory half of it.

Indoor collections of statues and busts are to be seen
in the Abbey, in St. Paul's, in the National Portrait

Gallery and the Tate Gallery, in the Houses of Parliament and the British Museum; while the long façade of the Institute of Royal Painters in Water Colours in Piccadilly has a fine row of the masters in that medium—De Wint and David Cox, Girtin and Turner, for example. On the roof of Burlington House, again, are many artists.

The practice of setting groups of allegorical statuary on the façades of houses has grown. Perhaps the most striking recent addition is the pediment of Africa House in Kingsway, which represents a big-game hunter's apotheosis. Australia House in the Strand has also some giant figures intended, I suppose, to exert an Antipodean lure. Other giants will be found on the new London County Council palace.

Statuary on buildings seems to be watched with a very jealous eye. Many readers of this book may remember the controversy caused by Mr. Epstein's series of statues on the façade of the "British Medical Association" building in the Strand, the objection being to certain realistic details. There was no bending to that storm, but when, a few years later, some feminine "rondeurs" over the door of the United Kingdom Assurance Office in the Strand were publicly criticised, a prompt reduction of their opulence was effected. Opposite this office, on the other side of the Gladstone monument, is another Assurance building, the General, which has on its façade some of the most charming stone figures in London—cherubs in helmets: for all I know members of the angelic fire brigade.

To the National Gallery in Trafalgar Square we shall return later; but after my digression on statutes and the English pride or want of pride in their great men, this is the time to enter the National Portrait Gallery, hard by, where pictures of most of the nation's principal sons since the days when painters first got to work among us (less than a poor four hundred years ago, so modern is our culture,) may be studied. In masterpieces the gallery is not rich—nor need it be, for the interest is rather in the sitter than in the artist—yet it has many very fine portraits (quite a number of Reynolds', for example), a few superlatively fine, and not many wholly bad. Taken as a whole it is a very worthy collection, and one of which England has every reason to be proud. A composite photograph of each group of men here would make an interesting study, and it might have significance to a Lavater—unless, of course, the painters have lied.

The numbering of the rooms begins on the top floor, and, as for a while at any rate, chronological order is respected, it is well to make a start there.

The earliest English portrait is in Room I, that of Richard II. We then jump to Tudor times and the school of Holbein. Here is Henry VIII and here is his valiant daughter Elizabeth, painted twice, brocaded and pale.

In Room II we find Tudor worthies such as Shakespeare, Ben Jonson, Michael Drayton.

Room III is Stuart. Charles I is here, painted by Van Dyck; his daughter, Elizabeth Queen of Bohemia ("Ye meaner beauties of the night") is here too, and there is a group of the Villiers family by Honthorst.

Room IV is a small recess given to Cavaliers.

Room V has a large painting of a Peace Conference in 1604, very different from Sir William Orpen's treatment of a more recent gathering. Van Dyck's picture of Charles I's children hangs here.

In the next room, VI, we come to Cromwell, by Robert Walker, and Milton.

In Room VII Charles the Second is found; and a number of Sir Peter Lelys are here, notably Mistress Eleanor Gwynn.

The most notable picture in Room VIII is the dead Monmouth by Sir Godfrey Kneller.

In Room IX the same painter has a portrait of the author of "The Beggar's Opera." In the middle is an astonishingly life-like coloured modelled head of Colley Cibber. There is also the head, but not coloured, of Hogarth.

THE MADONNA OF THE MEADOW

AFTER THE PICTURE BY MARCO BASAITI IN THE NATIONAL GALLERY

In Room X we find Richard Wilson, famous for his golden landscapes, as a painter of princes; Peg Woffington in bed, and a realistic portrait of Whitefield converting a listener.

Charles James Fox, modelled by Nollekens, and painted as a robust country squire by Hickel, is one of the dominating figures in Room XI. Warren Hastings by Lawrence and Burke by Reynolds are also here, and there is a fine head of Garrick in clay.

Room XII is given to eighteenth-century artists and men of letters, Reynolds as a young man, by himself, being one of the masterpieces. Dr. Johnson and Goldsmith, both by Sir Joshua, hang here, and George Coleman by Gainsborough. A little portrait of Gibbon by Henry Walton makes him very podgy.

We now leave the top floor, passing a series of electrotypes of Westminster Abbey statues and, also on the top landing, a very fine portrait of Henrietta Maria by Honthorst, and explore the floor beneath, where the reference section is situated, being Rooms XIV to XXII. This is an immense assemblage of persons of note in every walk of life, beginning with Tudors and Stuarts in Room XIV, miscellaneous eighteenth century in Rooms XV to XVIIA, and then artists and musicians, authors and statesmen, of the eighteenth century, in Rooms XVIII and XIX. In Rooms XX-XXII are the nineteenth-century men of eminence. All these are valuable as portraits; but the best painting of the heroes of the same period is reserved for three rooms below. First, however, we go through a series of royal paintings coming right to our own time on landings XXIII and XXIV, Sir John Lavery's group of the reigning Royal Family being one of the most modern.

To most visitors of the National Portrait Gallery the three rooms XXV-XXVII are the best, and particularly XXV, where Mr. Sargent's Henry James, Octavia Hill and Coventry Patmore are to be found, and Millais' Thomas

Carlyle, and G. F. Watts' Matthew Arnold, Browning, Tennyson and Swinburne, and Richmond's R. L. Stevenson. A bust of Thackeray as a boy is very interesting.

In Room XXVI are the great scientific men of the Victorian Age, and in Room XXVII actors, artists and musicians, Bastien-Lepage's little vivid painting of Henry Irving being the masterpiece.

On the ground floor are the Victorian soldiers, sailors and statesmen, the Duke of Wellington occurring more than once. One of the finest pictures is Sir John Moore by Lawrence. Millais' Disraeli and Ouless's John Bright remain in the memory.

CHAPTER VI

THE NATIONAL GALLERY : ITALIAN MASTERS

THE National Gallery was founded in 1824, its origin being the purchase of thirty-eight pictures from the collection of the late John Julius Angerstein, of Lloyd's, for £57,000 by Lord Liverpool's Government. They would now be worth many times that sum.

The numbers on the frames should always be noted because they indicate at what period the pictures were acquired, and this helps to reveal the extraordinary growth of the Gallery in the last few years. One of the latest numbers that I find at the time of this revision is No. 3714 on the little Fabritius in Room XII. That was hung in 1923, ninety-nine years after the Gallery was begun; which suggests that the rate of addition to its treasures has been about thirty-eight pictures a year. But a neighbouring picture that happens to have its date of acquisition as well as number, Velazquez' portrait of Admiral Pulido Pareja, in Room XVII, shows us that there has been no such steady increase. That picture was acquired in 1890 and is numbered 1315. As the Gallery began in 1824, it means that whereas fifty-six years were spent in amassing the first thirteen hundred pictures, the following thirty-three years have seen the addition of two thousand six hundred more. Another date in the same room helps again. Velazquez' "Venus and Cupid" was acquired in 1906 and is No. 2057 ;

so that in the seventeen years since then over sixteen hundred pictures have been added. This is a great achievement.

Not all of the pictures are, however, here ; for the Tate Gallery, a branch of the National Gallery, shares the numbering and hangs as many, if not more, pictures on its walls, as we shall see when the times comes to visit Milbank.

It would be difficult to give our National Gallery too much praise. Its present post-war arrangement seems to me almost beyond criticism. Every time I look in—and I am there certainly once a week—I am more and more impressed by the excellence of the collection, in gross and in detail.

The numbering of the rooms is rather capricious, but I think it better, for the most part, to follow it here.

At the head of the entrance stairs we find the earliest painting of all—portraits from Egyptian mummy cases. Here also is one of Cimabue's big black-mantled Madonnas that were carried in procession through the streets. The blue robe came later. This painting is one of the earliest of modern times. Cimabue is assumed to have been born in 1240 and to have died in 1301.

Room I now lodges the Italian primitives, and beginning at the right wall and walking round you can follow the evolution of painting from the purely ecclesiastical symbols of the fourteenth century—chiefly of the Sienese school—to Uccello's great battle piece, painted some time in or after 1432. Everyone in this room was feeling his way, among the chief and most influential of these pioneers being Masaccio (1401-1428), and Andrea del Castagno (1410 ?-1457) whose " Crucifixion," No. 1138, has a strange mastery for so early a day. But for these two painters Italian art might have developed very differently. In this room also you will find the sweet and gentle fancies of Gentile da Fabriano and Fra Angelico, who painted saints as though they were saints themselves. The last picture of all, the **Bernardino Fungai**, No. 1331, is an adorable work.

In Room II we find far more accomplishment. Much had yet to be done in compassing light and shade, but drawing is now established. This room is chiefly Botticelli's and his associates and followers. To the lay mind there is little enough to choose between Botticelli and the School of Botticelli: both produced works of exquisite beauty. Here also you will find Lippo Lippi, Botticelli's master and the hero of Browning's monologue ; Lorenzo di Credi, who, though not of the same rank, made very pleasing things ; and two pictures which the authorities give to the school of that fine artist and influence, Andrea Verrocchio (Andrew of the True Eye) in whose studio Leonardo da Vinci learned his craft. Both are very beautiful. Note in No. 781, " The Angel Raphael and Tobias," with what triumphant airy lightness the angel is moving ; in the other, No. 296, " Madonna and Child with Angels" foreshadowings of the Leonardo type of girl's face are visible.

We must cross the big room No. I again to reach Room III, where Piero della Francesca rules. A very gentle sway is his. One of my favourite pictures has always been his " Nativity," No. 908. Time has been not too kind to the painter's colours, but in another way it has befriended him, both in this work and in the " Baptism of Christ," near it, for the faint tones that age has brought about are very soothing and unlike anything else in the gallery. These two pictures are getting on for five hundred years old. Note the drawing of the man divesting himself, in No. 665. Piero's pupil, Luca Signorelli, who, in his turn, influenced Michelangelo, is also in Room III. Note in No. 1133, " The Nativity," the careful painting of the wild flowers. Piero's wild flowers and birds you will have noticed too. That very engaging painter, Pintoricchio, whose Piccolomini frescoes lure so many people to Siena, displays great versatility in this

room for he has an exquisite little " Madonna and Child,"
703, and the curious and very interesting fresco (transferred to canvas), representing the return of Ulysses—
No. 911. Finally there is the serene and mellow triptych
by Perugino, No. 288, famous for the figures of the angels
Raphael and Michael.

In the next room, IV, we find Perugino again, in the
large pale fresco No. 1441, " The Adoration of the
Shepherds," painted for the church of Fontignano in
1522 and removed from there in 1843. It belongs to
the Victoria and Albert Museum, but has been lent to
the National Gallery for a long while and is better here.
Other pictures to note here are the Matteo di Giovanni
" Assumption of the Virgin," No. 1155, a most satisfactory altar piece for a church frequented by simple
souls ; and another of the many representations of the
mystical marriage of S. Catherine and the Infant Christ,
by Lorenzo da San Severino II. The child slips what is
very like a real ring, so thick is the appliqué gold, on the
third finger of the saint's right hand ; but she was not,
of course, then a saint. The artist has made her more
comely than she was and altogether it is a very pretty
fancy. The curious, and in part reassembled, Pesellino
hanging close by, " The Trinity," with two angels brought
from different sources, and a panel lent by the King, to
assist in the completion, is an example of patient and
pious research.

Although the numbering of the rooms is not consecutive
I think it would be well, at this point, before going to
Room V to enter the Dome and visit the three other
rooms that radiate from it, for all have a similar character,
being given up to large church pieces, nor are they
strictly chronological.

The earliest works are those of Orcagna in Room VIII,
at the end of which is the famous Raphael known as
" The Ansidei Madonna," painted in 1505-6 for a church
in Perugia. Raphael is here at his most grave and

MOUSEHOLD HEATH

AFTER THE PICTURE BY OLD CROME IN THE NATIONAL GALLERY

mellow. On the left wall we find Orcagna, who lived as long ago as the first half of the fourteenth century and was not only painter but goldsmith, sculptor, architect and worker in mosaic—as all students of Florence know. On the opposite wall are the altar pieces of that very interesting and amusing, if not great, painter, Carlo Crivelli of the Venetian School, who in addition to his skill as a draughtsman and his ingenuity in welding real stones and lumps of gold into his paint, had very pretty thoughts and fancies and the admirable habit of signing his works in full. To the conjecturing expert this may be deplorable, but to the simple-minded it is a virtue. Crivelli was fond of giving his celestials very human accessories—such as fruit and flowers and creatures of earth and air. In No. 724 there is, for example, a swallow; in No. 668 there are ducks. Look at the predella of No. 724, in which poor S. Sebastian is being pierced by arrows at the closest range. You will find S. George and the Dragon here too.

In the Dome we come, on the right, to a rich and glowing altar piece by Francia ; then, past the next entrance, to a very interesting Luca Signorelli, with an attractive town on the water's edge in the distance ; then to a Perugino so bland as to be insipid ; and then a sweet assemblage of benign personages by Cima. The room opposite No. IV is No. XI, where that great master of portraits, Moretto of Brescia, whom we shall find in the large Venetian room, may be seen as an ecclesiastical painter. The two angels that guard the door are very charming. Here also are altar pieces by other Italian painters of great distinction and power, but not quite of the highest rank, such as Foppa and Garofalo and Parmigiano, while Paul Veronese, who refused to be humble or even to sanction humble things, has a vast canvas representing the "Adoration of the Kings" in a stable of palatial dimensions.

The fourth room leading from the Dome is XVI, where

you will find the very antithesis of Veronese's splendours in No. 1849 by "Pacchiarotto who worked in distemper" : a "Nativity" in as modest a shed as could be depicted. Here also is the great Botticini "Assumption," where the Virgin rises from a tomb now filled with lilies in a meadow not very far from Florence, whose dome and spires are seen in the distance. On either side kneel the donors : Signor Palmieri and his wife. In the heavens is the celestial host. Two pretty altar pieces by Bertucci, No. 282, and Girolamo, No. 748, should be looked for : each has little musicians making melody. And I like the rich colours of the Ortolano, No. 669.

We now go back to Room No. I to gain No. V, where the school of Lombardy is to be found, chief of it being Leonardo da Vinci, whose "Virgin of the Rocks" hangs here. By this—the beginning of the sixteenth century—the art of painting had reached perfection. Everything was known. There has been other painting since Leonardo, but none better. Several of Leonardo's followers are here : Luini, Boltraffio, Cesare da Sesto, Ambrogio da Predis. Here also is a scholarly, self-conscious work by Bramantino : "The Adoration of the Kings," No. 3073. Some pleasant Borgognones will be found too, agreeable in design and colour but weak in drawing. Boccaccino's "Procession to Calvary," No. 806, is interesting.

In Room VI we leave Lombardy and enter Venetia. The first picture on the right is a work of dazzling distinction and delight, "SS. Antony and George," No. 776, painted before 1450, by Pisano, or Pisanello, who is chiefly famous for his medals. Next it is another picture by the same hand, but not so brilliant, "The Vision of S. Eustace." We now come to that severe and most thoughtful of painters, Andrea Mantegna, who usually preferred strength to sweetness, but in No. 274, "Madonna and Child with Saints," has both. This is a very beautiful picture. An even more beautiful—touched with a deeper emotion and painted with a rare simplicity—is the "Crucifixion" by Antonello da Messina, No. 1166, which I have always thought one of the most notable pictures in the whole Gallery. Antonello, who was born in 1430 and died in 1479, painted this in 1477. In his work he combined Italian and Flemish methods, and it is probable that he sojourned in Flanders.

We come now to the two Bellinis, in whose work the Gallery is rich. Giovanni is the more remarkable and the five pictures confidently given to him are all treasures. The portrait of Doge Leonardo Loredano, No. 189, is probably the most popular, but there is some amazing work in No. 1233, " The Blood of the Redeemer," which is full of light. It is interesting to remember that Titian and Giorgione were probably pupils of the Bellinis. Another pupil was Basaiti, the painter of the charming " Madonna of the Meadow," No. 599, which brings so much fresh air into this room. Cima, the painter of No. 300, also came under the Bellini influence, and so did Catena, whose gentle placid scene of "A Warrior adoring the Infant Christ," No. 234, is on the opposite wall. Catena was influenced also by Giorgione and two pictures which might be by him, and one which is, hang close by. Who else could have painted Nos. 1160 and 1173 it would be difficult to say, but there is a conspiracy to deprive Giorgione of everything but his School. For some years No. 269 was taken from him, but I am glad to see that the old ascription has been replaced. This figure has enough resemblance to the figure of San Liberale in the famous altar piece at Castel Franco (Giorgione's birthplace) to be called a study for it. Samuel Rogers, the banker-poet, owned the picture and bequeathed it to the nation. His ghost should be pleased to read Giorgione's name, without dilution, again beneath it. It would not surprise me if it were found that Giorgione (who, after all, must have painted something) had a hand in No. 270, which bears Titian's name.

Three other artists to scrutinise in this room are

Piombo, who began by being Venetian and rich in
colour, and then passed under the severe influence of Michelangelo, and Carpaccio, who is represented here by a
scene in the S. Ursula series, smaller than any of those
in the Accademia in Venice and not of the same quality.
Lastly, Carlo Crivelli, whose altar pieces we saw in Room
VIII. In this room is his "Annunciation," No. 739,
where the golden shaft of light, bearing the message of
the Holy Ghost to the poor little Virgin, reaches her
through a loophole left by the builder for the purpose!
The picture is full of detail, all worth study, and not the
least attractive accessory is the little inquisitive child on
a balcony at the left.

Immediately on the right of the entrance to Room VII,
is a curious and fascinating battle scene, more important
as decoration than as a picture, by an unknown Ferrarese
artist, No. 1062. Next is the first of a number of fine
portraits by Moretto of Brescia, and then we come to
the first of the portraits by his pupil Moroni, who some
think surpassed him. Each seems to me superb ; Moroni
has nothing better than Moretto's Italian nobleman,
while Moretto has nothing better than Moroni's lawyer
and tailor. Moroni perhaps was gentler.

And now Titian, of whose paintings the National
Gallery possesses seven that are unquestioned, including
that supreme achievement "Bacchus and Ariadne,"
No. 35, which burns like a jewel. It was one of the
earliest pictures bought for the Gallery, the date being
1826, or three hundred and six years after it was painted,
and it has now passed its fourth centenary and is still
gloriously glowing with life. Titian both as a religious
painter and as a portrait painter is also found on this
wall, and here is No. 270 which Giorgione might possibly
have painted. The two men were of the same age and
both studied under the Bellinis, but whereas Giorgione
died of a fever at the age of thirty-three, Titian lived to be
ninety and nine and was painting almost to the last minute.

No. 1 in the collection—Sebastian del Piombo's "Raising of Lazarus"—divides the wall in two. Here was once a doorway, which the picture has closed. On the other side, with its back to this, is "The Ansidei Madonna" by Raphael, under whose influence Piombo passed when he left Venice for Rome. Later, Michelangelo tinctured his style and it has been suggested that the great master may have touched this work, which was painted for Giulio de' Medici in competition with Raphael's "Transfiguration." Hanging next it is a "Holy Family," No. 1450, with a fine freedom of design, also by Piombo.

We come now to the more recent Venetians: the daring and splendid Tiepolo, last of the Old Masters; Guardi with his sparkling water and palaces; Canaletto, with his accurate architecture; and Longhi, the Venetian Hogarth. The best Canaletto is perhaps No. 127, presented to the Gallery by one of its earliest and best friends, himself an amateur artist, Sir George Beaumont.

And now we find a run of the sumptuous Paul Veronese, including two allegorical subjects, drawn as only a giant could draw; his golden S. Helena, the "Vision of the Cross," perhaps the most spiritual of all his works; and the great "Family of Darius before Alexander," a glorification of the Pisani family of Venice.

Lastly—for I have already said something of the Morettos and Moronis—there is that magnificent piece of drawing and colour and invention, Tintoretto's "Origin of the Milky Way." I once startled and embarrassed a dinner table of artists and art critics by asking which was the best picture in the National Gallery. On my modifying this terrible question to the more human form, "Which picture would you choose if you might have but one?" and limiting the choice to the Italian masters, the most distinguished critic present (the late Mrs. Meynell) named at once Tintoretto's "Origin of the Milky Way." One could understand the selection, so splendid in vigour and colouring and large audacity is this wonderful work;

but it would never be my choice to live with. Another, an artist, also without hesitation chose Titian's "Bacchus and Ariadne"; and I can understand that too. Before leaving this room I recommend the reader to come to an independent decision with regard to these two pictures, which face each other.

My own impression and belief is that "The Origin of the Milky Way" was painted for a ceiling, but the official catalogue (which, by the way, is a very interesting book) does not support this view.[1]

The room that leads from the long Venetian Gallery where we now are is No. IX and is given to Dutch pictures. But before we enter it there is another Italian room which, though out of the numerical sequence, should be seen now, so that the Italian survey may be complete: Room XXIX. We come at once to another Botticelli, the Mars and Venus, with its masterly draughtsmanship, and here is Correggio, that voluptuous colourist, who although his pictures often have religious titles, was a Pagan at heart and never so happy as in his masterpiece here, the "Mercury instructing Cupid." Then comes the wistful and aristocratic portrait of a "Young Sculptor," by Andrea del Sarto, one of the best known pictures ever painted, and then the giant hand of Michelangelo is found, in the "Entombment," which, were it finished, might be the greatest picture in the world. Another unfinished work by Michelangelo is on the next wall. Even in their broken state they are among the most beautiful things in the Gallery, as well as the firmest.

After the dashing allegory of Bronzino, with such power in its drawing, we come to Raphael again, but here he is represented only by small pictures. The Child in No. 744 is surely one of the triumphs of pigment. His vivacity is complete. The whole picture is as near perfection as one can ask. Note the pyramidal scheme of composition. Whether or not Raphael painted No. 2069, "The Madonna

[1] The 1921 edition does not refer at all to this view.

of the Tower," we shall never know, but its golden mistiness is very pleasing. Raphael's little gay romantic scene No. 213, with the drawing from which it was traced hanging beneath it, is delicious; and we get an idea of the variety and catholicity of his mind from its presence here, among the Church pieces. Next is another very typical example of Andrea's tender sorrowful manner. The other pictures of special note are the very beautiful Filippino Lippi, No. 293, one of the gems of the Gallery, the amusing Gozzoli with its goldfinches, and Piero di Cosimo's romantic and tragic "Death of Procris" set in a fairyland scene.

The room leading from XXIX is XXVII, and here are gathered examples of the seventeenth-century Italians, the painters of the decline, such as Guercino, and Carlo Maratti and Baroccio and Carlo Dolci and Guido Reni and the Carracci. After the great men, these will not do; but they had brilliancy and power. It is better to begin with these pictures rather than to end with them.

In the basement are a number of Italian paintings of a lower quality than those that we have been seeing. If any old friend is missing, it should be looked for there.

CHAPTER VII

THE NATIONAL GALLERY : DUTCH, FLEMISH AND SPANISH SCHOOLS

WE come now to the Dutch pictures, which are
distributed without any chronology—for the
great Dutchmen were practically contemporaries, without predecessors and without followers—in the
rooms, IX, X and XII.

The Tuscans, Umbrians, Ferrarese, Parmese, Lombar-
dians, Sienese—these found in the Scriptures their principal sources of inspiration; these painted the Holy Child,
the Virgin Mary and the blessed company of saints, with
a persistence which I for one cannot too much admire and
rejoice in. Looking to Rome and Romish patrons for their
livelihood, they had little choice, more particularly in the
earlier days when simplicity was in their very blood; nor
would they have wished a wider field. We may say, at
any rate of the Tuscans and Umbrians and Sienese, that
their colours were mixed and their panels made smooth
for the glory of Our Lady. But in the Dutch rooms we
are among painters whose art was the servant of the State
rather than the Church. Farewell to mild Madonnas and
chubby Christs: farewell to Holy Families and the company of the aureoled. Art has descended to earth:
become a citizen, almost a housewife. Heaven is unim-
portant: what is important is Holland and the Dutch.
Let there be Dutch pictures! A religious subject may
creep in now and then, but (unless Rembrandt holds
the brush or the burin) it will not be a religious picture.
Worldliness has set in thoroughly. We have travelled

74

PORTRAIT OF TWO GENTLEMEN
AFTER SIR JOSHUA REYNOLDS' PICTURE IN THE NATIONAL GALLERY

very far from Fra Angelico and Francesca's "Nativity."

I hope I shall not be misunderstood about Dutch art, for which I have the greatest admiration. All I mean is that there is no preparation for a loving appreciation of it so unsuitable as the contemplation of the old Italian masters. No emotional student of the Umbrians and the Venetians, no one whose eyes have just been filled with their colour and glory, is in a fit state to understand the dexterity and homeliness of Gerard Dou and Terburg, De Hooch and Jan Steen, the austere distinction of Van Dyck, the magic of Vermeer, or even the stupendous power of Rembrandt. A different attitude is expected by Italian masters and the northern masters: the Italians ask for wonder, delight; the Dutch for curiosity, almost inquisitiveness. It is the difference between rapture and interest. Always, however, excepting Rembrandt: he stands alone, towering.

Perhaps one should not combine the north and the south in one visit at all, but confine each visit to a single group.

Weak as the National Gallery is, here and there, no one can deny the thoroughness and superlative excellence of its Netherland rooms. The English have always appreciated Dutch art. To have nineteen Rembrandts is alone no small matter; but there are also five Hals', and five De Hoochs, and nine Jan Steens, and three Terburgs, and fifteen Cuyps, and six Van der Heydens, and two Vermeers, and twenty-one Jacob Ruisdaels, and nine Hobbemas, including the best of all. I doubt too if Van Dyck ever surpassed the distinction and power of our "Cornelius van der Geest."

The best pictures of the Dutch school are in Rooms X and XII. But there is much that is interesting in Room IX, which we now enter. One of the first pictures is a typical Van Huysum flower piece with a yellow hollyhock in the midst. Then an equally typical Nicolas Maes, with a subject very popular with Dutch figure painters, "The Idle Servant." Near it is a charming Van Goyen, one of the many placid river scenes with shipping which we are to see as we pass through these rooms, all painted with such serene beauty that there is hardly any choice. Less typical is "The Forge," No. 2591, a modern-looking work attributed to Metsu but little like him. A rich misty Cuyp, No. 2546, hangs near and also a study of trees by a rare master, Vroom, No. 3475, with a distant view which Rousseau might have painted. No. 3047 is our first De Hooch, but better are in store in Room XII. We find another example of the placid school, by Jan van de Cappelle, in No. 2588, and then a fine example of a roystering group such as Codde, Duyster, Coques and Dirk Hals are famous for: No. 2575 which used to be called a Palamedes but is now given to Velsa. The light in it is very striking. Another "placidian," the exquisite Willem van de Velde, now confronts us with No. 980, but there are even better examples of his genius on the next wall. The large picture attributed to De Hooch, No. 2552, ought to be, I think, in the basement. Beyond it is an interesting portrait by Raguinea; a good still-life by one of the several men who, in the generous Dutch way, practised this form of painting with equal distinction, Jan Jansz van de Velde (among the others are Heda and Claesz) ; and then a golden landscape by Jan Both. We come now to the first Hobbema, very like a Jacob Ruisdael. Another hangs near it, No. 2571; but better still are in Room XII. Two fine Hondecoeters are here, another beautiful Cuyp and Saenredam's light and lustrous church interior, No. 2531. Our first Jan Steen is here, but far better are to come. Here, however, is a masterpiece beyond improvement in Gerard Dou's "Poulterer's Shop" which is inexhaustible in its detail and charm. Its pendant, by his derivative, Willem van Mieris, is only a shade less marvellous in minuteness, but far less charming. Gerard Dou's gift for painting large portraits exceedingly small may

TRAFALGAR SQUARE

also be studied here in No. 1415. A pretty De Hooch should be noted—No. 794.

The next room, X, is full of wonderful work testifying to the astonishing and sudden and brief efflorescence of Dutch painting in the seventeenth century when, in a period of some fifty years, there seems to have been a painter of genius ready to supply every possible need. One of the first of the great pictures is a Van Goyen, No. 151; and near it is another Jan van de Cappelle, No. 2587, the last word in restful beauty. Here also are works by other gentle craftsmen, such as Cuyp, and Van de Velde and Karel du Jardin. We come to something sterner in No. 221, our first Rembrandt, the portrait of the artist himself, bottle-nosed and mature. A good Teniers the Younger is No. 862, and then comes another Rembrandt, the delicious "Diana Bathing." The National Gallery, I may say again, has no fewer than nineteen works by this supreme master. And now we come to the very pick of the Jan Steens, "The Skittle Players," where all the coarseness and carelessness of the great painter are purged away and nothing but delicacy and gaiety and the most scrupulous craftsmanship remain. It seems almost impossible that the convivial Jan should have brought himself to paint the foliage with such patience; but I suppose he did. A very good example of the minute work of Dou's pupil, Godfried Schalcken, is to be found in No. 199, and then one of Rembrandt's Rabbis. Next, our first Van der Heyden, the best of all painters of brick walls, and near it an even more attractive topographical work by Berck-Heyde of Haarlem, No. 1420; but Van der Heyden excels him in light and gaiety a little farther on, in No. 992. Another fine Rembrandt, "Portrait of an Old Man," and a very attractive Paul Potter, and then we come to Rembrandt's portrait of himself when young, a glorious work. A landscape by Salomon van Ruisdael hangs over the Van der Heyden, paving the way for one of his nephew Jacob's masterpieces, the lovely "Shore at Scheveningen." The Rembrandt close by, No. 45, was one of the pictures which gave the Gallery its start, in 1824.

Another Berck-Heyde with some perfect painting in it is No. 1451, and another Jacob van Ruisdael, No. 990, helps to show what a various master he was. We now come to Frans Hals, but that giant has nothing here that is so fine as his "Laughing Cavalier" at the Wallace Collection. The great Cuyp with the man in red on horseback, another of the Angerstein pictures, hangs close by, and in the middle of the wall is the new Honthorst, in which Christ is being catechised by a judge: not a masterpiece but very effective. The Dutch family group by Sweerts makes a very efficient contrast, its lighting being so cool and clear. Another sweet Jan Both, also a very early picture in the collection; another Rembrandt, "A Man with a Cap"; and another vast golden Cuyp, a view of his own Dort, and we have seen the best pictures in the room.

Coming to Room XII we find still more examples of many of the painters we have already been admiring and some new ones, such as Vermeer of Delft and Terburg, and Carel Fabritius. Beginning with the right wall we find Terburg's crowded scene, but painted with amazing skill: "The Peace of Münster," No. 896, which wants some "reading from left to right" directions under it. Another Terburg (or Terborch) near it is more in his own "pocket Velazquez" manner, No. 1399: "Portrait of a Gentleman," a distinguished arrangement of blacks and reds. Between them is Jan Steen's "Music Master," No. 856, one of the most delicate of his pictures. After a Metsu or so we come to the Vermeer which Mr. Salting bequeathed: No. 2568, a charming work, but not the equal in brilliancy of the one near it, No. 1383, "Lady Standing at the Virginals" where this painter's almost miraculous deftness in applying colour and creating air can be studied. Over the first Vermeer is a little view of Delft after the explosion

THE PAINTER'S DAUGHTERS
FROM THE PAINTING BY THOMAS GAINSBOROUGH IN THE NATIONAL GALLERY

in 1654—the explosion being that in which Vermeer's master, Carel Fabritius, lost his life. We come to a delicious little Delft scene by this rare painter just by the door. Other pictures on this wall are a little Gerard Dou portrait, No. 968, and a figure by his pupil Mieris, almost equal to the master, No. 2589; another Terburg, another Metsu, and Nicholas Maes' very pretty "Cradle," No. 153, wherein it is easy to see that Rembrandt was this painter's instructor.

Beyond the door is another fine Maes, No. 159, "The Cook Maid" and near it a work by the same hand on a much larger scale, "Card Players," No. 1247, a fine animated, sombre group to which Rembrandt's name used to be affixed. Ochtervelt's exquisitely painted and drawn "Lady at her Toilette," No. 2553, next catches the eye, and then a Van Goyen winter scene, and then Rembrandt's portrait of, possibly, Françoise van Wasserhoven. In No. 836 by Koninck all Holland seems to be spread out, and then we find another of that country's many superb portrait painters in Bartholomew van der Helst, who is represented by the figure of a Dutch lady in wonderful lace, No. 1937. After another Ochtervelt, No. 2143, this time of a lady in rose-coloured satin, painted with great distinction, we have Rembrandt's little "Philosopher," No. 3214, a recent acquisition, before us. This is unlike any other Rembrandt in the Gallery and has for me a peculiar fascination. There are other Rembrandts on this wall, including the "Old Lady," No. 1675, the "Burgomaster," No. 1674, and the "Woman Bathing," No. 54, that astonishing work of genius, but No. 72, the noble landscape with Tobias and the Angel which for so long was given to him and which also hangs here, is now attributed to Adriaen Brouwer, who is more generally known for his tavern scenes. Other notable pictures on this wall are a Hobbema, almost too dazzlingly clear, No. 832; a very skilful portrait group by Thomas de Keyser, No. 212; a charming Mierevelt,

No. 2292, where we find lace again painted to perfection; and above it another golden mellow Cuyp, No. 1289.

On the left wall are some very fine things, including the De Hoochs and Hobbema's famous "Avenue at Middelharnis." But first a church interior by Emanuel de Witte, a masterpiece of architectural drawing as well as of human accessories. Then the best of the De Hoochs here—and I think of all De Hoochs—No. 834, the "Interior of a Dutch House," where you will find some discreet convivialists set in a room with a skill rarely approached and almost never surpassed. The very light of day floods it. If you will look very carefully at the woman by the fireplace you will see that the painter once had another figure here, probably a man whose pipe she was lighting, but he changed his mind and expunged it. The man at the table on the right also, I think, once had a glass in his hand. Over this picture is a beautiful little placid sea piece, No. 1462, by Hendrik Dubbels, who seems to have been one of several marine artists of that wonderful day equally accomplished. W. van de Velde in No. 2574 close by, certainly is not better. Then, between two dashing heads by Frans Hals, comes the favourite Middelharnis Avenue, which is perhaps as well known as any landscape in the world. The secret of its charm I have never quite ascertained; but no one can deny it. Another De Hooch, No. 835, very delightful, but not the equal of the one with the *pentimenti* in it, and then we come to our last Rembrandt, No. 237, a smiling Dutch brunette, who seems actually to live, and to the very interesting fish market scene by the same hand that painted the church scene, De Witte, No. 3682, a very recent addition and a picture of great originality and daring. A companion piece is in the Boymans Museum at Rotterdam.

These are all the Dutch paintings of the first class,

LADY AND CHILD
AFTER THE PICTURE BY ROMNEY IN THE NATIONAL GALLERY

but in the basement a large number of others may be seen, by application, together with works of other schools which fail to attain to the required level upstairs.

From Holland we pass to Flanders. In Room XIV (there is no Room XIII) we find Rubens, of whose astonishing output the National Gallery owns thirty-five examples, some of which, however, are only studies but are none the worse for that. And here is also Van Dyck, who is represented by ten works. Both Rubens and Van Dyck were among the painters who figured in the Angerstein Collection, and the first picture that we find as we enter this room and turn to the right is the Angerstein Van Dyck portrait of Cornelius van der Geest, which is one of the finest portraits in the world. Rubens' hot and huddled "Rape of the Sabines" comes next, one of the Sabines being astonishingly like the old ladies who sit just in front of us at the theatre. Then another superb Van Dyck head—that of an Italian sitter when he was working in Genoa, and opposite is the sitter's wife, the Marchesa Cattaneo, auburn-haired and mischievous. Rubens' voluptuous "Triumph of Silenus" is between them. Then another Rubens, "The Brazen Serpent," and then the cool tones and easy treatment of Susanne Fourment (not Helen Fourment, as is so often stated) the painter's sister-in-law. The picture is also known as the "Chapeau de Paille." The other Rubens, of special note are the two landscapes, especially the large one, No. 66, with such a vast mileage of Belgium in it and the painter's own country home, the Château de Steen, in the left foreground. Observe how this splendid abundant genius handles partridges: to him, who saw everything big, they are as huge as capons. The other chief pictures are the brilliant "Holy Family," by Jordaens, which probably was never intended to be a Holy Family at all; and the remaining Van Dyck portraits, in particular the full-length of the two Lenox youths, No. 3605, and the "Lady and Child," No. 3011.

Of early Flemish works the National Gallery has beautiful examples. Directly one enters the room where Rogier van der Weyden and Van Eyck are to be seen, one notes that the cheerful piety of Francesca and Fra Angelico, and the sheer love of innocent beauty of Botticelli and Filippino Lippi, are absent. A note of sadness instead, a northern earnestness, and also something of a realistic interest in humanity. The full materialism of later Netherlandish art is not yet; there is still much left of the rapt religious spirit; but these early Flemish painters have an eye on this world too. It is in their minds that living men and women deserve painting as much as the hierarchy of heaven. We find realism at its most extreme in No. 944, the "Two Usurers" of Marinus van Reymerswael, and in certain of the religious pictures too, notably Gerard David's "Christ being nailed to the Cross," Peter Brueghel's "Adoration of the Magi" and the triptych by the "Master from Delft." Joachim Patinir introduces us to domestic landscape in Nos. 1084 and 1082, both purporting to depict incidents in the life of the Virgin but more interesting for their backgrounds of fairy-tale scenery, busy with romantic Chaucerian happenings. Even more remarkable as innovation is No. 1298, from the same hand, one of the most exquisite pieces of colour in the whole collection—a river scene frankly, and nothing else, painted four hundred years ago. This Patinir, whose work is not often to be seen, was a friend of Dürer, who painted his portrait and no doubt encouraged him.

Room XV has almost too much that is good. One is bewildered by such a high standard of exquisite finish and the eye tires of the prevalence of red. But it is ungrateful to write like this, for early Flemish art is always interesting and one must avoid fatigue by taking the pictures slowly, one by one. The masterpiece of the room— and possibly of the whole National Gallery—at any rate there is nothing painted more marvellously—is the portrait of "Jan Arnolfini and his Wife," by Jan van Eyck. This picture is both a triumph of miniature painting and of big painting. You derive two kinds of satisfaction from it: in the gross and in detail. The husband and wife soon become as real as people that we meet. Perfect though this picture is, it was painted before most of the artists on whose feats the popularity of the National Gallery largely depends were born. Jan van Eyck painted this picture in 1434 and died in 1441; Michelangelo, Titian, Raphael, Andrea del Sarto, Correggio, Perugino, Rembrandt, Velazquez, Rubens—not one of these was yet living.

When minuteness of detail in painting is mentioned it is customary to cite the work of Gerard Dou and his school—notably the two Mierises—examples of whose amazing delicacy we saw in the Dutch rooms. But nothing done by Dou is more remarkable than the details in this Van Eyck. If you take a magnifying glass—a very instructive and amusing companion in every picture gallery—you will see that around the mirror are ten scenes from the life of Christ. You will also see how the hairs of the fur are painted, and the lines on the lady's hand: legibly enough for a palmist to predict her fate. It has been remarked that the mirror, in gathering up reflections of the contents of the room, takes note only of the single orange on the window sill, and not of those on the lid of the chest. My guess is that Van Eyck added the oranges on the lid of the chest as an afterthought, the picture wanting warming at that point, and then, for once being the least little bit absent-minded, forgot to add them in the mirror.

This priceless picture came to England as one of the spoils of war. It had once belonged to Margaret of Austria and later to Mary of Hungary. After that it went to Spain, and a French General removed it from Madrid as loot in 1789. In course of time it found its way to Brussels, and in 1815 was again looted, this time by an

English General, who sold it to the National Gallery in 1842. England is fortunate to have had the last word.

After the Arnolfini my favourite picture in this room is No. 664, which when I wrote this book was attributed to Rogier van der Weyden, but is now given to Dirk Bouts. Among so much that is red and hot, this picture has a gentle coolness. It seems to have been painted with sincerity: there is real grief on these faces.

Near the big Van Eyck are some other marvellous minute works by himself and by Petrus Cristus; and then we come to another very interesting early master, Robert Campin (1375-1444). No. 2608 has a very unusual and attractive colour scheme. In No. 2609, even if you do not admire the type of Madonna, you cannot but rejoice in the little town seen through the window. The two portraits by the same painter are very fine, especially the woman in the white head-dress.

In Gerard David the Gallery is also rich, and there is another delicious town in No. 1079 by him, with the simple mild Kings presenting their gifts. Near it is a picture of Christ being nailed to the Cross ascribed to Gerard David, No. 3067, a most curious, repulsive, but very interesting work which is in treatment and in thought the completest antithesis to the "Adoration." The Adoration of the Magi was a favourite subject with the Flemish painters, and we find an intricate and masterly treatment of it by Mabuse in No. 2790, where so much of an artist's craft may be seen, and again in No. 3556 by Peter Brueghel, but this treatment seems to be satirical. It is the least religious religious painting I ever saw.

Close by is the beautiful soft Quinten Massys which has recently been given to the Gallery—No. 3664: the "Virgin and Child with SS. Catherine and Barbara." It is odd to think that when this gentle and distinguished picture came into the auction room not long since, no art director wanted it! One of the most popular pictures in this room is Mabuse's pretty plump brocaded "Jacqueline de Bourgogne," No. 2211.

Room XVII has the chief works of the Spanish School: few but choice. Whether or not Velazquez painted the "Venus and Cupid" will probably never be known; but here it is, always with a little knot of people before it. This was the picture which suffered so badly during the suffragette disturbances, so that Venus's back had practically to be re-painted. Velazquez's son-in-law, Del Mazo, is supposed by some experts to be the artist; and one claims to have found his signature. Undoubted works both by Velazquez and Del Mazo hang near by, chief of the Velazquez' being the Philip IV, the portrait of the Admiral Pulido Pareja, and the "Christ at the Column." There is also the "Christ in the House of Martha and Mary," the still-life in which is painted with superb gravity.

Murillo is also in Room XVII, with a Holy Family and the little "S. John and the Lamb" a favourite with mothers; and here is El Greco for those that can find pleasure in his work, of whom I rarely am one. The portrait of that ripe and commanding Spanish beauty, Dona Isabel Cobos de Porcel, by Goya, is almost too living. Another aspect of Goya's variety is to be found in its pendant, the portrait of Dr. Péral, so calm and cool. The sombre solidity of Zurbaran's genius is responsible for the full-length gipsy lady: No. 1930.

The little room—XVIII—leading out of this one has a few more Spanish works, chief among them the famous landscape with figures by Velazquez, No. 197: Philip IV hunting the wild boar under conditions that look almost too unsportsmanlike. Here also is Del Mazo with a portrait of Marianne of Austria. But the picture to which I turn first and last is the recent acquisition called "S. Paul," No. 3590, by an unknown artist. This is a very fascinating work, and not the less so for its suggestion of Whistler's famous portrait of his mother, now in Paris.

On the landing is a large Canaletto and two more of Paul Veronese's Allegories, in which the figures are posed in such a way as to give the artist the greatest difficulty and pleasure in mastering it.

CHAPTER VIII

BRITISH, FRENCH AND GERMAN PICTURES

WE are now to wander through the galleries to the left of the entrance stairs. On the landing we find a delightful oil sketch by Gainsborough —"Mrs. Graham as a Housemaid." Here also is a sunlit landscape by Frederick Walker, and opposite it is Holman Hunt's "Triumph of the Innocents," a picture which, to me, is without any appeal whatever.

The first room, XIX, a very small one given to early German work, leads out of Room XX. Its masterpiece is Holbein's portrait of Christina of Denmark, daughter of Christian II of Denmark, who was born in 1523 and in 1534 married the Duke of Milan. The Duke died in the following year and Holbein painted this most attractive of widows in 1538, when she was still only twenty. The same master's "Ambassadors" is also here, with the curious distorted representation of a skull in the foreground, to see which properly one must get one's eye on a level with it at a point to the side. The Ambassadors are, on the left, Jean de Dinteville, Lord of Polisy, and on the right George de Selve, Bishop of Lavaur. Chief of the other pictures in this room are those by Lucas Cranach (note the amusing "Charity," No. 2925, and that demure quaint little lady, No. 291), and by the Master of Liesborn who is always interesting, and the very fine portrait by Dürer of his father, painted in 1497.

In Room XX we find a very mixed assemblage of French works. The gallery cannot be called rich in French art, although it has some fine Claudes, the best of which we shall see later, in the little Turner room; but in Room XX are two beauties—Nos. 1319 and 61. Here also are several works by Nicholas Poussin, but they have gone very dark.

There is also a series of early portraits of the Clouet School, with a very interesting Mary Queen of Scots; a portrait, in triplicate, of Richelieu by Philippe de Champaigne, and again, full length, by the same artist; and finally some early church works of which No. 1302, "S. Bertin borne to Heaven," by Simon Marmion, is very quaint.

In Room XXI we find modern and recent French art, with a few Dutch pictures added, the gift of Mr. J. C. J. Drucker. Among them are works by Matthew and Jacob Maris. An early Corot and a Daubigny are also on this wall and a powerful oil sketch of the "Deposition." Manet's "Firing Party," and a "Soldier Examining the lock of his Rifle" are here too—the soldier being as typically French as any portrait you ever saw, with all the sadness and fatalism and intentness of the French face in perfection. A late Corot hangs next and it is interesting to compare this, in his studio manner, with the early one near the door, when he painted out of doors. We come now to good examples of Ingres, Millet, Chardin and Fragonard, but for Fragonard, as for Lancret and Boucher and Watteau, who are represented here by ones and twos, the Wallace Collection is the place. Chardin, however, did not appeal to Lord Hertford. The National Gallery has two examples of his delicate material art, and the Greuzes here are not inferior to those in Manchester Square. A recent acquisition is a pretty little blue Peronneau pastel, a child with a kitten. For the rest, there is a dashing Mignard, a very typical Georges Michel, some Puvis sketches full of a movement that he often lost in his large frescoes, a very good Boudin, and a glorious flower piece by Fantin Latour.

ADMIRAL PULIDO PAREJA

AFTER THE PICTURE BY VALAZQUEZ IN THE NATIONAL GALLERY

Room XXII is dominated by Constable, and you find him in every mood. We begin with "Weymouth Bay," a very modern work, full of rushing clouds and movement. At the other extreme is No. 1815, which is a storm not of weather but of paint. In Nos. 1246, 1819 and 1822, you see what a lot the Barbizon men learned from this Englishman, who was exhibiting at the Paris Salon, together with Bonington, in 1824. There are two Boningtons here, as against the great number in the Wallace Collection, but one of them, No. 2664, is a masterpiece. Here also is Old Crome, with the golden "Windmill"; and Turner with two enchanted Venetian scenes, and a yacht race at Cowes in which you can hear the hissing of the foam; and W. P. Frith with his "Derby Day," a picture I never tire of not looking at; and William Dyce with his fascinating "Pegwell Bay," a triumph of minute painting and big effect; and Millais with portraits of Mrs. Jopling-Rowe, very simply painted, and Mr. Gladstone, meek and mild; and Alfred Stevens with his portrait of Mrs. Collmann, one of the masterpieces of English portraiture; and John Sargent, with the commanding "Lord Ribblesdale." And then we come to the last wall, where Millais' "Ophelia" hangs, and Rossetti's "Ecce Ancilla Domini," and Whistler's lovely "Nocturne— Blue and Silver, Cremorne Lights," and his "Symphony in White, No. 2: The Little White Girl." Lastly look at the breezy day by David Cox, and see in No. 2649 how tame and trim Constable, who began so bravely in this room with "Weymouth Bay" and its bluster, could now and then become.

In Room XXIV we come at once upon a sublime Old Crome, No. 2645, "Moonrise on the Marshes of the Yare," in which the moon grows brighter as you watch it. The composition is absolute. Next it is still another kind of Constable, showing how ready he was to adapt his method to the scene: the quiet "Malvern Hall," in which the hush of an English evening is perfectly captured

and the rooks caw almost audibly. Above it hangs a very
complete contrast in manner, "The Salt Box, Hampstead
Heath." A second Old Crome, "The Poringland Oak,"
has another beauty of evening sky. The boys were put
in by Crome's friend, Michael William Sharpe. And now
another Constable, this time one of his smashing impressionistic works: No. 2651, one of many studies for the
artist's great pictures of Salisbury Cathedral. The painting is amazingly dexterous, the brush being called upon to
do impossible things, even to depicting the Bishop on
his lawn.

After a Barker of Bath landscape we find Turner's
vast and restless "Calais Pier," where thoughts of the
horrors of the old Channel crossings are so vivid as to
spoil one's pleasure. Next it, is the best Lawrence in the
Gallery—the sparkling Mrs. Siddons, No. 785, with eyes
lifelike, so far superior to the full-length hanging opposite. And now we come to the same painter's portrait
of John Julius Angerstein, whose pictures formed, in
1824, the nucleus of this marvellous collection. Angerstein's thirty-eight pictures had to be bought; but those
collected by George Salting, over one hundred and thirty
in number, which became the nation's property in 1910,
were a free bequest. The Old Crome moonlight scene
and the Constable "Malvern Hall," and "Salisbury
Cathedral" in this room were among them. And not only
did George Salting leave pictures to the National
Gallery, but miniatures to the British Museum and
a collection of porcelain and other treasures worth hundreds of thousands of pounds to South Kensington. His
praises cannot be sufficiently sounded.

A rather careless but masterly Raeburn; another
great Turner marine; and then a family group brought
to life with a thousand delicate touches by the accomplished Zoffany: No. 3678. Note the painting of the
silks and the little Vermeerish points of light. Turner's
great impressionistic riot, "Rain, Steam and Speed,"

THE CITY FROM WATERLOO BRIDGE

next confronts us and reminds us of how wide a span
his career covered, for it was painted as recently as 1844;
and then his golden placid "Ulysses," perhaps as fine a
piece of colour as any painter ever produced, studies for
which will be found at the Tate. And on the other side
of a soft and pleasing Hoppner is the wizard again, this
time with the famous "Temeraire," one of the most beautiful pictures in the world. "The Fighting Temeraire
towed to her last Berth" is the full title, and the painter's
brush is as emotional as his pen. After such a work
James Ward's landscape in the manner of Rubens falls
flat, and we are glad of the interposition of Raeburn's
full-length of "Miss Mary Hepburn" before we come to
another of the masterpieces of the Gallery, the first of
four of the greatest landscapes in the world. This is
"Mousehold Heath" by Old Crome: that mellow spreading prospect, with wild flowers at our feet and the golden
sky over all. Strange are the vicissitudes that masterpieces can suffer. This picture, now one of the most
treasured possessions of the Gallery, was once torn in
two and used as a sunblind! Next is that extraordinary
piece of realism, Turner's "Frosty Morning," which
almost causes one to stamp one's feet for cold as one looks
at it. Turner, as we shall see again at the Tate, was a
jealous man, only too conscious of the success of other
artists, and there is plenty of proof that he often tres-
passed into rivals' fields just to show how various and
accomplished he could be. But for Crome's fame we might
never have had this picture. Next, and after a splendid
Raeburn, is Constable's famous "Hay Wain." There
are examples of Constable's genius that one may think
finer, but this is a great picture. Next it, however, is a
greater—Turner's, "Crossing the Brook." I don't say
that jealousy of Constable led to this lovely work, but it
would not surprise me. Look at the country in the middle
distance. No painter, not even Koninck, has ever suggested more square miles,

Room XXV is the most popular in the whole Gallery because it contains the pick of the British portraits; and portraits are, ultimately, the favourite form of art with British people. The dominating figures are Reynolds, Gainsborough, Romney and Hogarth; but Van Dyck's full length of Charles I on horseback is the largest canvas.

Beginning at the right we come at once to some little glowing Wilsons, of which No. 1064 is the most beautiful. Nothing indeed in the Gallery is more beautiful. An example of the clean-cut method of Francis Cotes is here, and also a work by a painter rarely met with, Henry Walton, a pupil of Zoffany, who has been called the English Chardin, but is a long way behind the French master. We now come to Gainsborough and Reynolds, the one with a happy little woodland scene and the other with a dashing sketch of a portrait group. And then Gainsborough's famous Mrs. Siddons in the blue dress and the black hat. Mrs. Siddons was then, in 1784, twenty-nine. In the portrait which we saw by Lawrence, in the last room, where she is so unlike Gainsborough's representation of her, she was—in the small one—forty-two and in the full-length forty-nine. We now come to our first Hogarth—No. 1663—and have the opportunity of seeing what a colourist he could be and what a master of broad brushwork. A few steps farther on we shall find "The Shrimp Girl," that astonishing feat of dexterity, almost magic, which increases our regret that he should have given so much time to the dramatic series: that the satirist and moralist should have so triumphed over the painter. Between the Hogarths is a fine dignified Reynolds full-length, Captain Robert Orme. And now comes one of the gems of the collection, Gainsborough's delicious cool painting of his two little girls, both so young, fresh and flowerlike. Another golden Wilson and another Hogarth, where the painting of the woman's bodice—such a pretty arrangement of

MADONNA AND LAUGHING CHILD

FROM THE CLAY STATUETTE BY ANTONIO ROSSELLINO (OR DESIDERIO DA SETTIG-
NANO) IN THE VICTORIA AND ALBERT MUSEUM

mauve and green and white ruffles!—is again marvellous.

On the other side of the door is Hogarth's curious "Calais Gate" where so much is happening, even to a procession of priests in the distance, touched in with delicate precision. The Romney next it is one of the favourite pictures in the Gallery, a "mother's picture," a remark that applies also to two of the Reynolds' on the same wall—the "Heads of Angels," and "The Age of Innocence"—and possibly also to the group of Lady Cockburn and her children, one of the pictures by our great British master which has kept its original glowing hues. His rival is here too, with the famous "Dr. Schomberg." At the end of the wall is another Hogarth—a group of heads—and next it the sketch for a mural work by Sir James Thornhill, with whose daughter Hogarth eloped.

We now pass a number of early English portraits, including a curiously realistic unknown picture of Mrs. Joshua Horton, a sinister old lady, and come to the other long wall, where another beautiful work by Sir Joshua is waiting for us—the "Two Gentlemen," so mellow and distinguished. A rather hard group by Romney, then a classical landscape by Wilson, and then a comic group by Gainsborough, the Baillie family, where Mr. Baillie, the proud father, is at least eight feet high, but is atoned for by the prettiest of little girls at the left, and we have reached the great Gainsborough: "Wood Scene, Cornard, Suffolk," where his mastery of landscape is absolute. Reynolds' "Three Graces" has never much delighted me, but the dignity and repose of his Countess of Albemarle are never without their appeal. This is one of the pictures in which the colour is fading away. The same artist's "Holy Family" retains its richness, but it is not a work that carries any conviction, and Joseph is made older than by almost any other painter. In fact the disparity in age between Joseph and the Madonna is grotesque, and Reynolds ought to have known better. The large "Stable Interior" by Morland, so comfortable and woolly, completes this wall.

At the end we find a vivacious Downman, a quaint Devis, and some not very pleasing Highmores. The gems are the portrait of Constable's wife, painted with great tenderness by her husband, and a tiny masterpiece by Gainsborough—Miss Singleton—where every touch is joy.

In Room XXVI are, at the time of writing, the Sargents: that brilliant series of portraits of members of the family of Asher Wertheimer, the art dealer. Among them have been hung a number of specimens of the work of the great English masters of portraiture, Reynolds, Gainsborough, Opie, Lawrence; but to my mind our modern master does not in the least suffer by comparison. For such assurance and certitude of brushwork you have to go back to Frans Hals to find a parallel. I look upon the portraits of Mrs. Wertheimer and of Alfred Wertheimer in his laboratory as two of the great pictures of the world. The others have all astonishing passages, but these two seem to me to be on a higher plane.

Among the other pictures in this room are a very good example of the genius of George Stubbs, proving him to have been a great painter not only of horses but of England, and one of Gainsborough's most charming landscapes. There is also a very pleasant Downman, No. 3544.

Room XXVIII and last is given to Turner and Claude— the two Turners which were specifically left to the Gallery to be hung next the two Claudes that the artist believed himself to have surpassed. With that opinion I agree. And I go further. I believe that there is no more beautiful picture in the world than "The Sun Rising through Vapour," No. 479. Other of Turner's oils are here too, all remarkable; but of them and of the many water colours in the cases I say nothing, as they are periodically changed. Enough that the greatest genius in English painting may be studied here in great comfort.

For the bulk of his work, which he bequeathed to the nation, you must go to the Tate.

CHAPTER IX

THE STRAND AND COVENT GARDEN

The Strand—A Cosmopolitan Street—Waterloo Bridge and white stone—The Adelphi—The Brothers Adam—Adelphi Terrace and Buckingham Street—Samuel Pepys, a great Londoner—The old Palaces—The Covent Garden stalwarts—A modern bruiser—New thoroughfares—Will's Coffee House—Charles and Mary Lamb—The Lyceum—Benedick and Beatrice—Dr. Primrose and Olivia—Essex Street—The picturesque omnibus—A Piccadilly scene—St. Mary's Le Strand—The Maypole—St. Clement Danes—The Law Courts.

I COULD not, I think, explain why, but I have more distaste for the Strand than for any street in London. I would avoid it as carefully, from pure unreasoning prejudice, as Count D'Orsay and Dick Swiveller avoided certain other districts on financial grounds. This, I fear, proves me to be only half a Londoner—if that; for the Strand to many people *is* London, all else being extraneous. They endure their daily tasks elsewhere only because such endurance provides them with the means to be in the Strand at night.

The most Bohemian of London streets, if the Strand could cross to Paris it would instantly burgeon into a boulevard. Its prevailing type is of the stage: the blue chin of Thespis is very apparent there, and the ample waistcoat of the manager is prominent too. Except at night, on the way to the Gaiety, the fashionable youth avoid the Strand; and indeed the best-dressed men and women are not seen on its pavements, howsoever they may use its carriage way. But with these exceptions, all London may be studied there; and other nations too, for the great hotels and Charing Cross station tend to cosmo-politanise it. Probably at no hour of the day or night are more than half the Strand's population true Londoners.

If the Strand is too much for you, as it may easily be, the escape is very simple. You may be on the banks of the Thames in two minutes from any part of it, or on the beautiful Adelphi Terrace, or among the flowers and greenery of Covent Garden, or amid the peace of the Savoy chapel or the quietude of Essex Street. Standing at the Surrey end of Waterloo Bridge on a sunny afternoon you get one of the best views of London that is to be had and learn something of the possibilities of the city's white stone. Somerset House from this point is superb, St. Paul's as beautiful and fragile as any of Guardi's Venetian domes. Above the green of the trees and the Temple lawns and the dull red of the new Embankment buildings, broken here and there by a stone block, you see Wren's spires pricking the sky, St. Bride's always the most noticeable; and then, far back, gleaming with its whiteness and the gold of its figure of Justice, is the mas-sive Central Criminal Court, to add an extra touch of light. Culminating statues gilded or otherwise are begin-ning to be quite a feature of London buildings. The New Gaiety Theatre has one; Telephone House in Temple Avenue has a graceful Mercury; over the Savoy portico stands a noble Crusader; over Romano's doorway dance a group of bronze Cupids. Less ambitious but not less pleasing is the gold galleon forming a weather-vane on what used to be the Astor Estate office, which is as fine in its way as the Flying Dragon on Bow Church in Cheapside. I suppose that every one of London's bridges could claim to have wonderful views; indeed, each might claim the best. From the Tower Bridge you see the Tower and the shipping; from London Bridge you see the Tower Bridge; from the Charing Cross foot-bridge, when there is no traffic to distract, the prospect is very similar to that from Waterloo Bridge with the advantage that that fine structure is included, and on a misty morning London is enchanted and the new Bush Building is seen rising above Somerset House like a medieval Castle Keep.

The Adelphi, which dates from 1768, consists of the Terrace, standing high overlooking the river, and its neighbouring streets, John Street, Robert Street, James Street, William Street and Adam Street, together with the arches beneath. It was the work of the Scotch architects Robert, John, James and William Adam, who in its generic title and in those four streets celebrate for ever their relationship and their names. The Terrace must be seen from the Embankment or the river if its proportions are to be rightly esteemed; and one must go within one of the houses to appreciate the beauty of the Adam ceilings and fireplaces, which are the perfect setting for the furniture of Heppelwhite and Sheraton. English taste in decoration and design has certainly never since reached the height of delicacy and restraint it then knew

No house in the Terrace has been replaced or very seriously tampered with, and all have some interesting association, chief among them being No. 4, where in 1779 the gaiety of nations was eclipsed by the death of Garrick The other Adelphi streets have historic memories too Disraeli always believed that he was born at No. 2 James Street, in a library, although the facts seem to be against him; at No. 18 John Street is the Society of Arts, and at No. 2 Robert Street lived Thomas Hood, who sang the "Song of the Shirt."

More ancient is the district between the Adelphi and the Charing Cross District Railway station. Here we go back a hundred years before the Adelphi was built, to associations with the great name of Buckingham—Buckingham Street, Duke Street, and Villiers Street being its chief quarters. Of these Buckingham Street retains most signs of age. Samuel Pepys lived there for many years in the south-west corner house overlooking the river, whi

he probably came to think his own; Peter the Great
lodged at the opposite corner; Jean Jacques Rousseau
and David Hume were together in Buckingham Street in
1765, before they entered upon their great and unphilo-
sophic quarrel; Etty painted at No. 14 and Clarkson
Stanfield's studio was below him.

Pepys' companion diarist John Evelyn resided for a
while in Villiers Street, which is now given up to cheap
eating-houses and meretricious shops, and on Sunday
evenings is packed with rough boys and girls. Steele
lived here after the death of his wife. The street is much
changed since then, for Charing Cross station robbed it
of its western side.

I am inclined to think that when all is said Pepys is the
greatest of the Londoners—a fuller, more intensely alive,
Londoner than either Johnson or Lamb. Perhaps he
wins his pre-eminence rather by his littleness, for to be a
Londoner in the highest one must be rather trivial or at
least be interested in trivialities. Johnson was too serious,
Lamb too imaginative, to compete with this busy Secre-
tary. Neither was such an epicure of life, neither found
the world fresh every morning as he did. It is as the
epicure of life that he is so alluring. His self-revelations
are valuable in some degree, and his picture of the times
makes him perhaps the finest understudy a historian
ever had; but Pepys' greatness lies in his appreciation of
good things. He lived minute by minute, as wise men
do, and he extracted whatever honey was possible. Who
else has so fused business and pleasure? Who else has
kept his mind so open, so alert? Whenever Pepys found
an odd quarter of an hour he sang or strummed it away
with a glad heart; whenever he walked abroad his eyes
were vigilant for pretty women. No man was more
amusable. He drank "incomparable good claret" as it
should be drunk, and loved it; he laughed at Betterton,
he ogled Nelly Gwynn, he intrigued with men of affairs,
he fondled his books, he ate his dinner, all with gusto

and his utmost energy. Trivial he certainly was, but his enjoyment is his justification. Samuel Pepys was a superb artist in living. He was a man of insatiable inquisitiveness: there was always something he considered "pretty to see"; and it was this gift of curiosity that made him the best of Londoners. He had also the true Londoner's faculty of bearing with equanimity the trials of others, for all through the Great Plague and the Great Fire he played his lute with cheerfulness.

Turning into the pleasant Embankment Gardens at the foot, one comes at once upon the York Water Gate, which was built by the Duke of Buckingham on the shore of the river to admit boats to his private staithe, those being the days when the Thames was a highway of fashion. To-day it is given up to commerce. But he did not complete his design of rebuilding the old Palace; the gate is all that now remains; and the site of York House is covered by Buckingham Street and its companion—just as the site of Durham House, where Raleigh lived, is beneath the Adelphi, and that of Arundel House beneath Arundel Street and its neighbourhood, and that of old Somerset House beneath the present building of the same name.

Only two relics of the old Strand palaces remain: the York Water Gate and the Savoy chapel, one of London's perfect buildings, dating from 1505 and offering in its quietude the completest contrast to the bustle of the surrounding neighbourhood. The outside walls alone represent the original structure, and they, I fancy, only in parts. Among those who lie beneath its stones are Mrs. Anne Killigrew, whom Dryden mourned, and George Wither the poet, who sang divinely in prison of the consolations of the muse.

The memorial to that stalwart journalist W. T. Stead which has been set up on the river side of the Embankment opposite the foot of Essex Street, should be looked for, because it has on it two of those charming littl

bronze figures for which Sir George Frampton, the
sculptor who designed it, is justly famous. St. George's
spear is periodically renewed and as regularly stolen. A
little farther on towards the city is the War Memorial
to the submarine heroes. On the Adelphi side will be
found the group of statuary which Belgium gave to
England in token of her help and sympathy in the War.
I am not very fond of it, but there is something in its
austerity that commands respect. A close examination
of Cleopatra's needle and the attendant sphinxes will
reveal the wounds inflicted by a German bomb which
fell near here one memorable night. The scarred place
at the foot of the Nelson Column, on the pedestal of one
of the lions on the Cockspur Street side, was due, however,
only indirectly to War, for it was the result of a bonfire
lighted there by some over-enthusiastic revellers on
Armistice Night. The War Memorial to the Air Force
is on the Embankment opposite the County Council
Hall.

[Covent Garden being for the most part a wholesale
market, it has none of the interest of the Paris Halles,
where the old women preside over stalls of fruit and vegetables arranged with exquisite neatness, and make up
pennyworths and two pennyworths with so thoughtful an
eye to the preservation of economy. We have nothing
like that in London. In London if you want two pennyworth of mixed salad you must buy six pennyworth and
throw away the balance, economy being one of the virtues
of which we are ashamed; nor do we encourage open-air
stalls except for the poor. Hence where it is retail
Covent Garden deals only in cut flowers and rare fruits.]

There is something in the constitution of the London
porter, whether he unloads ships or wagons, carries on his
head vegetables, fish, or the products of farthest Ind,
which arrests progress, keeps him apart and out of the
movement. You notice this at the Docks, which are of
course remote from the centre, but you notice it also at

Covent Garden, within sound of the very modern Strand.
Covent Garden remains independent and aloof. New
buildings may arise, petrol instead of horses may drag in
the wagons from the country, but the work of unloading
and distributing vegetables and flowers remains the same,
and the porters have an immemorial air and attitude
unresponsive to the times; while the old women who sit
in rows in the summer shelling peas have sat thus since
peas first had pods. Not only does the Covent Garden
porter lead his own life insensitive to change, but his
looks are ancient too: his face belongs to the past. It
is not the ordinary quick London face: it has its scornful
expression, of course, because London stamps a weary
contempt on all her outdoor sons; but it is heavier, for
example, than the Drury Lane face, close by. Perhaps
the soil is responsible for this: perhaps Covent Garden
depending wholly on the soil, and these men on Covent
Garden, they have gained something of the rural stolidity
and patience.] ꜱᴛᴏᴘ

One could not have a better view of the Covent Garden
porters collectively than fell to my lot one day recently,
when I found some scores of them waiting outside the boxing club which used to be Evans's Rooms in Thackeray's
day, and before that was Lord's Hotel, looking expectantly
at its doors. I waited too, and presently there emerged
alone a fumbling stumbling figure, a youth of twenty-four
or so, neatly dressed and brushed, but with his cheeks
and eyes a mass of pink puff. The daylight smote him
almost as painfully as his late adversary must have done
the night before, for this is now the National Sporting
Club, where the big boxing contests are held, and he had
come for his prize money. He stood there a moment
on the steps, while Covent Garden, which dearly loves
a fight with or without the gloves, murmured recognition
and approval. No march of progress, no utilitarian wave
here. Byron's pugilist friend and master, Jackson of
Bond Street, could he have walked in, would have detected

little change, either in the crowd or the hero, since his own day.

Perhaps the most important event connected with St. Paul's Church, in Covent Garden, which in its original form was built by Inigo Jones to be "the handsomest barn in England," was the marriage in 1773 of William Turner of Maiden Lane to Mary Marshall of the same parish; for from that union sprang Joseph Mallord William Turner, the painter, who was baptised there in 1775. Among those buried here are Samuel Butler, the author of "Hudibras," and Peter Pindar (Dr. Wolcot) the scarifier of Guelphs and Whitbreads, who wished his coffin to touch that of his great and satirical predecessor; William Wycherley, who wrote "The Country Wife"; Sir Peter Lely, who painted Stuart beauties; Grinling Gibbons, who carved wood like an angel; Dr. Arne, the musician; and Charles Macklin, the actor, who lived to be 107.

It was in Maiden Lane, close by, that Turner was born, in 1775, and among famous sojourners there were Andrew Marvell and Voltaire. To-day it is given up to the stage, and it is difficult to pass through it without hearing the chorus of some forthcoming musical piece at practice in an upper room. Rule's oyster shop is here, the modern substitute for the historic Cyder Cellar, where a hundred and more years ago Porson drank incredibly and grew wittier with every potation. And it was in Maiden Lane that poor Terriss, the last of the swaggering romantics of the English stage, was murdered by a madman a few years ago. Close by, in Tavistock Street, at the "Country Life" offices, is one of the best modern doors in London.

Between Covent Garden and Drury Lane certain eighteenth-century traces still remain; but east of Drury Lane is a wilderness of modernity. Everything has gone between that street and Lincoln's Inn Fields—everything. Men are not made London County Councillors for nothing.

Still, it must, I suppose, be conceded that the great business houses of Aldwych and Kingsway have their uses. The

largest of the new structures are the Bush Building on
what is called the island site, with its imposing arch;
Australia House at the corner; the Opera House, built
by an American entrepreneur for the exploitation of the
best singing and now a picture palace; and Africa House,
higher up Kingsway, near Holborn, with its elaborate
symbolic pediment. The Bush Building archway, seen
from Kingsway, is magnificent.

Of Covent Garden's two great theatres I have nothing
to say; but the north-east corner house of Russell Street
and Bow Street, with its red tiles and ancient façade,
has much interest, for it was once, in a previous state,
Will's Coffee House, where John Dryden sat night after
night and delivered judgments on new books and plays.
The associations of Will's are too numerous for me to
dare to touch upon them further: they are a book alone.
Next door, at No. 20 Russell Street, a hundred and more
years later, over what is now a fruiterer's, lodged Charles
and Mary Lamb; but the dispenser of tablets does not
recognise the fact, nor that Lamb was born at 2 Crown
Office Row in the Temple, to which we are steadily drawing
near.   Lamb's Russell Street rooms I fancy extended
to the corner house too, and it was from one of these that,
directly they were established there in 1817, Mary Lamb
had the felicity to see a thief being conveyed to Bow
Street police station.

[Bow Street has now completely lost its antiquity and is
no longer interesting.] Nor would Wellington Street be
interesting were it not for its association with Henry
Irving and the Lyceum. It is true that Henry Irving is
no more, and the Lyceum is now dedicated to melodrama;
but the memory of that actor is too vivid for it to be
possible yet to pass his old theatre without a regret.
Never again will that great and courteous gentleman with
whom its old fame is identified be seen on its stage. It
was in a corner of the pit, leaning against the barrier
between that part of the house and the stalls, that I

saw all Irving's best performances in his later years, most
exquisite of which to recall being always his Benedick in
"Much Ado About Nothing"—or, as the programme
hawkers who hovered about the queue in the dark passage
of the Lyceum Tavern used to call it, "Much to-do about
Nothing." Of all the myriad plays I have seen—good
plays, middling plays, and plays in which one's wandering
eyes return again and again most longingly to the magic
word "exit"—I remember no incident with more serene
pleasure than the entry of Miss Terry as Beatrice with
the words "Against my will I am sent to bid you come
in to dinner," and the humorous gravity, a little perplexed
by the skill of this new and alluring antagonist, of Benedick's face as he pondered his counter stroke and found
none. And with it comes the recollection of that other
scene between these two rare and gentle spirits, when, in
"Olivia," Dr. Primrose, having at last found his weeping
daughter, would take her home again. All reluctance and
shame, she demurs and shrinks until he comes beautifully
down to level ground with her, by saying, with that indescribably sweet smile of his, "You ran away with
one man: won't you run back with me?" and wins the
day. Irving may have lacked many qualities of the great
actor; but when he died there passed away from the
English stage something of charm and distinction and
picturesque power that it is not likely soon to recover;
and the world was the poorer by the loss of a commanding personality.

York Street, which was built early in the seventeenth
century, retains much of its old character. It was at
No. 4 that De Quincey wrote his "Confessions"; and
the superb Elliston, who counted fish at dinner "as
nothing," lived at No. 5. I am exploring and naming
only the old streets where the actual historic houses still
stand, because to walk down a dull street because a great
man lived in it before the rebuilder and modern taste had
made it dull, is not an attractive occupation. And I am

omitting all names but those that seem to me to lend a human note to these pages. Streets such as Arundel Street and Norfolk Street in the Strand, which had many literary and other associations, but have been entirely rebuilt and are now merely business thoroughfares lined with fantastic red brick façades, do not seem to me interesting. But Essex Street, close by, does seem to me interesting, because it retains its old Georgian form, and, being a *cul-de-sac* for carriages, is quiet to boot. The Essex Head, it is true, where Sam's Club met under Dr. Johnson's sway, has been rebuilt; but the lower part of the street is much as it was when Henry Erskine learnt oratory at the Robin Hood Club (as some of the speakers of our day learn it at the Cogers') and when the Young Pretender lodged at Lady Primrose's; and the fine gateway remains.

In no street out of the city are omnibuses so constant as in the Strand, although to see the London 'bus at its best, I think Whitehall is the place. As they come down the hill from Charing Cross into the spaciousness of the road opposite the Horse Guards, like ships in full sail, swaying a little under their terrific onset, and shining gaily in all their hues, they are full of the joy of life and transmit some of it to the spectator. What London would be without its coloured omnibuses one dares not think. After the first flush of Spring, almost all her gaiety comes from them. Whitehall is the best at all times, but in April and May, when the trees (always a fortnight earlier than in the country) are vivid on the edge of the Green Park, and the sun has a nearly level ray, there is nothing to equal the smiling loveliness of Piccadilly filled with omnibuses, as seen from the top of the hill, looking east, about Down Street. It is an indescribable scene of streaming colour and gentle vivacity.

Mention of the slanting sun brings me back to the Strand; for there is nothing more beautiful in its way—certainly a way peculiar to London—than that crowded 'bus-filled street at the same afternoon hour, with the light on the white spire of St. Mary's at the east end. It is a graver, less Continental, beauty than Piccadilly's: but it is equally indelible. Almost it makes me forgive the Strand.

St. Mary's church, like St. Martin's-in-the-Fields, is not, as most people would tell you, one of Wren's, but was built by Gibbs. Everything possible was done, some few years ago, to get permission to demolish it, for what were called the "Strand improvements"; but happily in vain. All honour to the resisters. The famous Maypole in the Strand stood on the site of this church. A cedar trunk, one hundred and thirty-four feet high, it was erected in 1661 in honour either of the Restoration or (and here comes in the sweet of ignorance) because a Strand farrier's daughter, the wife of General Monk, had become the Duchess of Albemarle. It is very unfair to Gibbs to have allowed such giant edifices as Australia House and the Bush Building to be erected so near St. Mary's spire. But the Bush Building is a splendid addition to London's architecture, all the same.

Close to St. Mary's church is Strand Lane, a narrow alley descending to the river, notable for containing one of the most unexpected and interesting survivals in all London: nothing less than a bath constructed by the Romans when they inhabited Britain, and still usable, although not, I believe, used. A modest sixpence (this is one of the few charges that have not been increased since the War) entitles one to enter and examine this curiosity.

St. Clement's Inn, close by St. Clement Danes, a few years ago was still a backwater of peace, but is now obliterated and new houses bear its name—Clement's Inn, where young Master Shallow of Warwickshire, Little John Doit of Staffordshire, Black George Barnes of Staffordshire, and Francis Pickbone and Will Squele, a Cotswold man, were the devil's own swinge-bucklers. How could we pull it down? But we would pull down anything.

And New Inn, close by, of which Sir Thomas More was
a member—that has gone too.   Men, as I remarked
before, are not made County Councillors for nothing.

With St. Clement Danes church, just to the east of St.
Mary's Le Strand, and, like that, most gloriously in the
very middle of the road, we come at last to the true
Wren.   It was in this church, one of London's whitest
where it is white—of a whiteness, under certain conditions
of light, surpassing alabaster—that Dr. Johnson had his
pew, from which, we are told, he made his responses
with tremulous earnestness.   The pew was in the north
gallery, where a tablet marks the spot, styling him (and
who shall demur?) "the philosopher, the poet, the great
lexicographer, the profound moralist and chief writer of
his time."   Among those buried either here or in the cemetery of the church in Portugal Street, now demolished,
are Thomas Otway and Nathaniel Lee, the dramatists;
Joe Miller, who made all the jokes, and in addition to
being a "facetious companion," as his epitaph says, was
a "tender husband" and "sincere friend," as humorists
should be;   Dr. Kitchiner, the author of "The Cook's
Oracle" and himself a "notable fork"; and Ackermann,
the publisher of the "Repository," which everyone who
loves the London of the Regency, its buildings and costumes, in the fairest of all the methods of counterfeiting a
city's life, namely copper-plate and aquatint, should know,
and if possible possess.

And here at the Griffin, opposite the most fantastically
and romantically conceived Law Courts in the world—
the most astounding assemblage of spires, and turrets,
and gables, and cloisters, that ever sprang from one
Englishman's brain,—we leave the Strand and pass into
Fleet Street, or, in other words, into the City of London.

CHAPTER X

FLEET STREET AND THE LAW

WHEN I first knew London—passing through it on the way to a northern terminus and thence to school—Temple Bar was still standing. But in 1878 it was pulled down, and with its disappearance old London's doom may be said to have sounded. Since that day the demolishers have taken so much courage into their hands that now what is old has to be sought out: whereas Temple Bar thrust antiquity and all that was leisurely and obsolete right into one's notice with unavoidable emphasis. The day on which it was decreed that Fleet Street's traffic must be no longer embarrassed by that beautiful sombre gateway, on that day Dr. Johnson's London gave up the ghost and a new utilitarian London came into being.

By the way, it is worth while to give an afternoon to a walk from Enfield to Watham Cross, through Theobald's Park, in order to stand before Temple Bar in its new setting. Enfield is in itself interesting enough, if only for its associations with one who loved London with a love that was almost a passion, and who never tired of running over her charms and looking with wistful eyes from his rural exile across the fields towards the veil of

smoke beneath which she spread her allurements: I
mean, of course, Charles Lamb. It was an odd chance,
which no one could have foreseen, least of all perhaps
himself, to whom it must have stood for all that was most
solid and permanent and essentially urban, that carried
Temple Bar (beneath whose shadow he was born) to this
new home among green fields, very near his own.

The Bar stands now as one of the gateways to Theo-
baldi's Park. It was bought prior to demolition by Sir
Henry Meux, and every brick and stone was numbered,
so that the work of setting it up again in 1888 exactly
as of old was quite simple. I know of no act of civic
piety prettier than this. And there Temple Bar stands,
and will stand, beneath great trees, a type of the prosperous cit who after a life of hard work amid the hum of
the streets retires to a little place not too far from town
and spends the balance of his days in Diocletian repose.
What sights and pageants Temple Bar must recall and
ruminate upon in its green solitude! The transplantation
of the Elgin Marbles from the Parthenon to the British
Museum—from dominating the Acropolis and Athens to
serving as a source of perplexity to British sightseers in
an overheated gallery of Bloomsbury—is hardly more vio-
lent than the transplantation of Temple Bar from Fleet
Street and the city's feet to Hertfordshire and solitude.

A concrete example of English taste in the eighteen-
seventies is offered by the study of the statuary and
ornamentation of the Griffin—the memorial which was
selected to mark the site of Wren's gateway. It is curious to remember that the heads of traitors were displayed publicly on the spikes of Temple Bar as recently
as 1772. Barbarism is always surprising us by its
proximity.

Even less than the Strand's pavements are those of
Fleet Street fitted for loiterers. In fact we are now in
the City, and urgent haste has begun; not quite as in
Cheapside and Broad Street, for no one here goes without

ST. MARY'S LE STRAND

a hat, but bustle is now in the air, and with every step
eastward we shall be more in the fray. From Fleet
Street, however, though it may in itself seethe with activity, the escape is easy into quietude more perfect
than any that the Strand has offered; for here is the
Temple on the south, and on the north Lincoln's Inn
with its gardens; here also are Clifford's Inn and Ser-
jeants' Inn; and here are the oddest alleys, not narrower
than those between the Strand and Maiden Lane, but
more tortuous and surprising, the air of all of them (if
you can call it air) heavy with the thick oiliness of printer's ink.

Printer's ink is indeed the life blood of Fleet Street
and its environs. The chief newspaper offices of London
are all around us. "The Times," it is true, is fixed a
little to the south-east, on the other side of Ludgate Hill
station; but in Fleet Street, and between it and Holborn
on the north and the river on the south, are nearly all
the others.

On an all-night walk in London, which is an enterprise
quite worth adventuring upon, it is well to be in Fleet
Street between three and five, when it springs into intense
activity as the carts are being loaded with the papers for
the early morning trains. From here one would go to
Covent Garden and smell the flowers—the best antidote
to printer's ink that has been discovered.

The Temple, which spreads her cool courts and gardens all unsuspected within a few yards of Fleet Street,
is best gained by the gateway opposite Chancery Lane, by
the old house with a ceiling of Tudor roses which is now
a County Council preserve. Almost immediately we come
to the Temple church, the most beautiful small church
in London and one of the most beautiful in the world—
so grave in character and austere and decisive in all its
lines; and yet so human too and interesting, with its
marble Templars lying there on their circular pavement
in a repose that has already endured for five centuries

and should last for centuries more. Many of Lamb's old Benchers are buried beneath this church; and here also lie the learned John Selden, and James Howell who wrote the " Epistolæ."

To the north of the church is a plain slab recording that Oliver Goldsmith, that eminent Londoner and child of genius, lies beneath it. He died at No. 2 Brick Court, up two pairs of stairs, in a "closet without any light in it," as Thackeray, who later had rooms below, described the poet's bedroom. That was on April 4, 1774, and the next morning, when the news went out, it was to this door that there came all kinds of unfortunate creatures to whom he had been kind—weeping and friendless now.

To name all the illustrious men who have had chambers in the Temple would not only be an undertaking of great magnitude but would smell overmuch of the Law. Rather would I lay stress on the more human names, such as poor Goldsmith's and Charles Lamb's. It was a little less than a year after Goldsmith had died at 2 Brick Court that at the same number in Crown Office Row Charles Lamb was born—on February 10, 1775. The Row is still there, but it has been rebuilt since Lamb's day, or perhaps only refaced. The gateway opposite leading into the garden is the same, as its date testifies. Lamb claimed to be a Londoner of the Londoners; but few Londoners have the opportunity of spending their childhood amid so much air and within sight of so much greenery as he. Perhaps to these early associations we may attribute some of the joy with which in after life, Londoner as he was (having lent his heart in usury to the City's stones and scenes), he would set out on an expedition among green fields. The building near the church called Lamb House has nothing to do with the essayist.

I ventured just now to mock a little at the Law; and yet it is not fair to do so, for it is the Law that has preserved for London this beautiful Temple where all is peace and eighteenth-century gravity. Yet not everything has it retained, since no longer are the Inns of Court revels held here. It was in the Middle Temple Hall, which is a perfect example of Elizabethan architecture, that "Twelfth Night" was first played.

Lincoln's Inn, the Law's domain on the other side of Fleet Street, has its lawns and seclusion and old world quiet too; but it does not compare with the Temple. The Temple's little enclosed courts, with plane trees in their midst, of the tenderest green imaginable in early spring; her sun-dials and her emblems; her large green spaces sloping to the river; her church and her Master's house; her gateways and alleys and the long serene line of King's Bench Walk—these are possessions which Lincoln's Inn can but envy. And yet New Square is one of the most satisfying of London's many grave parallelograms; and the chapel which Inigo Jones built rises nobly from the ground; and the old gateway in Chancery Lane does something to compensate for the loss of Temple Bar. Its date, 1518, disposes of the story that Ben Jonson helped to build it, with a trowel in one hand and a book in the other, but I like to believe that he did a little desultory bricklaying in this way on some extension to it.

Before going through this comely and venerable gateway there is a very attractive little museum to be visited on the opposite side of the road. For the great white building here is the Record Office, where the State papers are kept and where any student of antiquity may read them, in the little circular room for that purpose, so like one of the tiny offspring of the Reading Room of the British Museum. During the war the documents were housed for safety in Bodmin gaol. As it happened no bomb fell on the Record Office but the chapel of Lincoln's Inn, only a few yards distant, was badly damaged.

Until I visited the little museum, the Record Office had been to me a vast and imposing building, with an enchanting residence for a dwarf or gnome, or even a sugar-plum fairy, in Fetter Lane; a stretch of lawn that must be the envy of every suburban gardener who passes; and the abode of no particular human interest. Now I think of it as the shell which possesses, in its museum, one of the most attractive kernels in this great city: a small, deeply interesting and wholly unfatiguing collection of objects of historical value, where all kinds of unexpected treasures meet the eye, not the least of which is Doomsday Book.

The building where so many historical rarities are to be found was once the Chapel of the House of Converts (the converts being Christianised Jews), and later the Chapel of the Rolls. It is now desanctified, and you may keep on your hat, as those Jews would have done before the proselytiser got them; but certain signs of the old holiness remain, such as stained-glass windows and two or three very fine tombs. Chief of these tombs is that of Dr. John Young, Master of the Rolls early in the sixteenth century, whose monument was designed by the Florentine sculptor, Torrigiano.

The museum would be called historical first and foremost, but any one interested in calligraphy might be pardoned if he claimed that the collection of illustrious signatures to be seen there is its chief glory. These signatures naturally comprise a large number of the most famous English rulers and ministers, but other great names are found too, and not a few foreigners. The actual writing of William Shakespeare may be scrutinised. At least, according to the catalogue, the signature is that of the Bard; but the stranger unprepared with information would have to be forgiven if he maintained that the name written is obviously "Willie Asquith." Again, Napoleon, one of whose documents is displayed in another part of the room, has clearly signed himself "Rosebery." Nelson's writing, both before he lost his right arm and afterwards, may be studied. In a letter (left-handed) to Lord Hobart, written on the *Victory*, at sea, January 4, 1804, "My heart," he says, "is warm, my head is firm, but my body is unequal to my wishes. I am visibly shook, but as long as I can hold out I shall never abandon my truly honourable post."

Neither good writing nor good spelling is prominent in this museum. Perhaps the worst spelling of all is that of Mary Queen of Scots, who ends an appeal to Cecil with these sentences: "I pray God to mouve the quin's hert to consider off me or wors com. I pray you let my harti commendations be ten in als good pert to your bedfalou, as I wische her wilingli to doe weil and be me frind." Chaucer, however, as usual, runs the Quin of Scots very close. Spelling remained lax for many years. Even John Milton, wishing to recommend Andrew Marvell to a post, could get no nearer his name than Mr. Marvile. The other Quin, Elizabeth, is well represented. We find the Sultan of Turkey, Amurath III, addressing her as "refulgent with splendour and glory, most sapient princess of the magnanimous followers of Jesus, most serene controller of all the affairs and business of the people and family of the Nazarenes, most grateful rain-cloud, sweetest fount of splendour and honour." In 1577 she signs a warrant for the delivery to Frobisher of some prisoners "condemned or like to be condemned to death" to "make a viage by the seas for the discovery of new countryes." And then we find poor Leicester on his death-bed asking for a kind smile again: "being the chifest thing in this world I doe pray for, for hir to have good health and longe life. . . . I humbly kyss your foote." Essex, another favourite in disgrace, also has his appeal: "Hast, paper, to that happy presence whence only unhappy I am banished. Kiss thatt fayre correcting hand which layes new plasters to my lighter hurtes, butt to my greatest woond applyeth nothing." But the most poignant letter of all is that scribbled by Sir Philip Sidney in hospital at Arnheim, where he died a few days later from a wound received in the battle of Zutphen.

The note, in Latin, is to Jaen Wyer, and runs thus in English: "Come, my Weier, come. I am in danger of my life, and I want you here. Neither living nor dead shall I be ungrateful. I can write no more, but I earnestly pray you to make haste. Farewell. At Arnem. Yours, Ph. Sidney."

Other notable exhibits—and it must be remembered that all these things are curiosities only in a secondary way, their presence in the Record Office being due to their legal or official character—are the actual "Scrap of Paper" of which so much was heard early in the war; various Gunpowder Plot documents; Defoe's Apology; the Warrant for Shakespeare and others to be King's Players; a drawing illustrating the murder of Darnley; a letter from Laud to Charles I with "You ar right" written by Charles in the margin; and a most pregnant document from the archives of the British Legation in Tuscany, dated March 24, 1822, in which three friends do their best to explain away a recent fracas in Pisa. Their names are Byron, Shelley and Trelawny.

There are also a number of very fine seals, particularly that of Francis the First of France, and a little gold Papal *bulla*. Among other items that testify to the catholicity of the collection is the census paper of Buckingham Palace when the people were numbered in 1851. In this her Majesty is described as "Wife," and the Prince Consort as "Head." American visitors should not miss a "mappe of a part of Hudson's or the North River and Rareton River, which have their outlett into the sea of Sandy Hoocke," 1700, which will show them what the city of New York looked like before it was the city of anything. Where baseball is now played the sport, it seems, used to be shooting bears from behind with a bow and arrow. There is also a letter from George Washington, and a very good example of a Round Robin.

But perhaps the exhibit which will give most comfort of all is an assortment of Rolls. The visitor is thus

THE MADONNA AND CHILD, WITH ST. JOHN AND ST. CATHERINE

AFTER THE PICTURE BY TITIAN IN THE NATIONAL GALLERY

enabled to realise, probably for the first time, what it is that the Master of the Rolls is master of.

To Lincoln's Inn Fields, which is now lawyers' offices and a public playing ground, but was once a Berkeley Square, we come by way of the Inn. On the north and south sides the rebuilders have already set their mark; but the west side, although the wave of reform that flung up Kingsway and Aldwych washes its very roots, is still standing, much as it was in the great days of the seventeenth century, except that what were then mansions of the great are now rookeries of the Law. No. 59 and 60, for example, with its two magnificent brick pillars, was built by Inigo Jones for the Earl of Lindsay. Inside are a few traces of its original splendours. The corner house, now No. 67, with the cloisters, was Newcastle House (previously Powis House), the residence of the great Duke of Newcastle. Lincoln's Inn Fields Theatre, where Pepys used to be so vastly amused (going there so often as to make Mrs. Pepys "as mad as the devil") was on a site now covered by the Museum of the Royal College of Surgeons, to which the curious are admitted by order. Not for me are physiological whims and treasures of anatomy preserved in spirits of wine; rather would I stay outside and reflect on the first night of Congreve's "Love for Love" on April 30, 1695, with Mrs. Bracegirdle as Angelica, or of the première of "The Beggar's Opera," thirty and more years later, with Lavinia Fenton so bewitching as Polly Peachum that she carried by storm the heart of the Duke of Bolton and became his Duchess. A little while ago I was reflecting that barbarism, although now, of course, extinct, is yet very recent; but to dip however casually into the history of London is to be continually reminded that for the most part nothing changes. The papers are still rarely without news of the marriages of noblemen to actresses.

On the north side of Lincoln's Inn Fields is the Soane Museum, a curious medley of odds and ends with a few

priceless things among them and a very capricious system
of throwing open its doors.   One must, however, visit it,
for otherwise one would never see Hogarth's delicately
coloured election series or "The Rake's Progress" in the
original, and since in two or three of the subsidiary
figures of "The Humours of an Election Entertainment"
he comes nearer Jan Steen than in any of his work this
would be a pity; and one would never see Canaletto's
fine painting of the Grand Canal—better than any of that
master's work at the Wallace Collection, I think; nor
Giulio Clovio's illuminations to St. Paul's Epistles; nor
a very interesting Watteau; nor several quaint missals,
among them one whence the Bastard of Bourbon got his
religion; nor a MS. of Lamb's Margaret of Newcastle;
nor the MS. of Tasso's "Gerusalemme Liberata"; nor
two of Reynolds' sketch books; nor many exquisite
cameos and intaglios; nor two fine Turners; nor Christopher Wren's watch; nor the silver pistol which Peter
the Great ravished from a Turkish Bey; nor paintings
on silk by Labelle, little delicate trifles as pretty as Baxter
prints; nor enough broken pieces of statuary—gargoyles,
busts, capitals, and so forth—to build a street of grottoes;
nor the famous alabaster sarcophagus of Seti I, King of
Egypt about 1370 B.C.

It is the duty of all who now take a walk down Fleet
Street to visit the scenes associated with the great name
of Johnson.   You may thread Bolt Court: you may
worship, as he did, in St. Clement Danes.   But whether
the wooden seat in the Cheshire Cheese which bears a
brass plate sanctifying it to the Doctor was really his
is another matter.   None the less it has drawn many
English sightseers and all Americans.   The Cheshire
Cheese represents the old guard in English restauration.
How long it will be able to hold out I dare not prophesy.
There are indeed already signs at the Cheshire Cheese
that devotion to old ideas is not what it was.   The
famous pudding (lark and oyster, steak and kidney) was

produced, I seem to recollect, with more ritual, more of an air, many years ago than to-day. I have eaten of it but once, and shall eat of it no more. Not to my charge shall be laid the luring of any sweet-voiced lark into a Fleet Street kitchen, or indeed any kitchen whatsoever; but others have other views, and for them the arrival of the dish has long been one of London's crowded moments. Americans cross the Atlantic to partake of it and write their opinion in the visitors' book, which, not less depressingly facetious than all its kind, is rather more interesting by reason of an occasional name that has some artistic correlation. Old ale, a sanded floor, hot punch, and seats of a discomfort beyond that of the old third-class railway compartments or a travelling circus, complete the illusion of Johnsonian revelry.

But for the pilgrim who thrills at the name of the Great Lexicographer the true Mecca is now his house in Gough Square, piously saved for the nation and filled with relics, by Cecil Harmsworth. I know of no memorial house better arranged or more scrupulously maintained than this, except perhaps George Washington's at Mount Vernon.

More than any other street Fleet Street, in spite of all its new buildings, has kept an old London feeling. I think this is due in a great measure to its irregular façades, each one different and some very odd, and its many clocks and signs. To look down Fleet Street on a sunny afternoon is to get a very vivid sense of almost eighteenth-century animation. Modern as it all is, it always recalls to my mind the Old London street at one of the early South Kensington exhibitions. Every variety of architecture may be seen here—from the putative palace of Cardinal Wolsey to the "Daily Telegraph" office, from Sell's building, with its sun-dial, to St. Dunstan's-in-the-West; while to glance down Middle Temple Lane is to have a genuine peep at the eighteenth century.

St. Dunstan's-in-the-West is Fleet Street's jewel, with

its very curious, very beautiful, open-work tower, as exceptional in its way as St. Dunstan's-in-the-East, although not the artistic equal of that delicate structure. The architect of the western St. Dunstan's was one Shaw, and it is not yet a hundred years of age, having been begun in 1831, all the old associations belonging to that which preceded it—the St. Dunstan's under whose shadow Charles Lamb says he was born; of which Donne was vicar; and which in the seventeenth century was surrounded by booksellers' shops, among them Smethwick's, who published "Romeo and Juliet" and "Hamlet," and Marriot's, who put forth "The Compleat Angler." That sweet singer Thomas Campion was buried there. Over the side door of St. Dunstan's, on the right, is a contemporary statue of Queen Elizabeth which was brought to this position in 1766 from its old place on Lud Gate.

The other Fleet Street church, St. Bride's, which is just off the road on the south, is older and has far more dignity: it is indeed one of Wren's finest efforts. Elsewhere I have said something of the spire under a busy sky. In a house in the churchyard Milton once lived, and beneath the church lies the author of "Pamela" and "Clarissa Harlowe," under the central aisle.

It is at the Barley Mow, close by, in Salisbury Square, that the ancient society of the Cogers hold their parliament every Saturday night and settle questions of state over pipe and glass. One should certainly visit one of these debates, where so many speakers have first raised their voices and demolished the Government. Students of race will not be surprised to hear that there was never a Cogers' palaver without a brogue in it.

THE AVENUE, MIDDELHARNIS

AFTER THE PICTURE BY HOBBEMA IN THE NATIONAL GALLERY

CHAPTER XI

ST. PAUL'S AND THE CHARTERHOUSE

Observing in London—The London gaze—A few questions—St.
Paul's—Sir Christopher Wren—Temples of Prosperity—Spires of
Genius—St. Paul's from a Distance—London from St. Paul's—
The High Roads to the Country—Florid Monuments—The Great
Painters — The Thames Streets — Wren again — Billingsgate —
St. Sepulchre's and Condemned Men—The Great Fire—The Cock
Lane Ghost—Bartholomew's Hospital—St. Bartholomew the Great—
A Wonderful Church—Cloth Fair—Smithfield Martyrs—The Char-
terhouse—The Old Gentlemen—Famous Schoolboys—A Spring Walk
—Highgate and Hampstead Heath—The Friendly Inns—A word
on Hampstead and Kate Greenaway.

THERE are so many arresting movements in
London, as indeed in all hives of men, that to
observe widely is very difficult. Just as one is
said not to be able to see a wood for trees, so one cannot
rightly see a city for its citizens, London for its Londoners.
I believe, to give an example of defective London observation, that one's tendency is to think that all its greater
streets are straight; whereas hardly any are. Here is a
question on that fallacy, suggested to me one day as I
stood at the point which we have now reached: "From
the middle of the road under the railway bridge at the
foot of Ludgate Hill how much of St. Paul's do you see?"
I would wager that the majority of Londoners would
expect to see the whole façade; but they would be very
wrong.

In one of his delightful books Dr. Jessopp remarks that
whereas country people look up, Londoners look down.
It is largely this habit which has limited their observing

powers; but London has itself to blame. I assume that one can observe well only by taking large views, and in London this is impossible, even if one would, partly from the circumscribing effect of bricks and mortar, partly from the dim light of a London distance, and partly from the need of avoiding collisions. One's eyes unconsciously acquire a habit of restricted vision: our observation specialises, like that of the little girl in Mrs. Meynell's book about children, who beguiled the tedium of her walks by collecting shopkeepers named Jones. Perhaps that is the kind of observation for which we in London have become best suited.

I remember how amazed I was, some years ago, when one clear Sunday morning, as I was walking in Fleet Street, I chanced on looking down Bouverie Street to see, framed between its walls, the Crystal Palace gleaming in the far distance. That, however, was an exceptional sight. Far less uncommon yet quite obvious characteristics cause astonishment when they are pointed out. It comes, for example, as a surprise to many people if you refer to the hill in Piccadilly. "What hill?" they ask. Indeed, if there is one thing more remarkable than one's own ignorance of London it is that of other people. Walking one day in Cheapside, from west to east, I was struck by the unfamiliar aspect of the building which blocked the end of that thoroughfare. It turned out to be a new set of offices at the foot of Cornhill, and it caused me to wonder how many people shared my belief that as one walks eastwards down Cheapside one ought to have a full view of the Royal Exchange; which is not, as a matter of fact, visible until one is almost out of the Poultry. And this error led me to examine other similar fancies, and in many cases to find them equally wrong. I amused myself in consequence by drawing up a little paper in London topography, or rather in London observation. Here are a few of the questions which I jotted down:—

1. If the Nelson Column were to fall intact upon its side in a due southerly direction, where would Nelson's head lie?

2. If circumstances should confine your perambulations to an area comprised in a radius of three hundred yards from the Griffin in Fleet Street, what streets and how much of them would be open to you? Could you get to the theatre?

3. Give in detail the route of what is in your opinion the shortest walking-distance from (*a*) St. Pancras to Victoria, (*b*) Paddington to London Bridge, (*c*) the Lyceum to Oxford Circus, (*d*) the Zoological Gardens to the Albert Hall, (*e*) the Bank to the Tower, (*f*) Seat P4 in the British Museum Reading Room to seat C7.

4. Between what points of the compass do the following streets run: the Strand, Northumberland Avenue, Fenchurch Street, Edgware Road, Knightsbridge, Tottenham Court Road, Cockspur Street, Bow Street, Whitehall, Westminster Bridge, Waterloo Bridge and London Bridge?

5. Give the approximate taxi fare between Charing Cross and (*a*) the Elephant and Castle, (*b*) the Spaniards, (*c*) Liverpool Street, (*d*) the Marble Arch, (*e*) the Brompton Oratory, (*f*) the People's Palace, (*g*) the Agricultural Hall.

6. If you followed that diameter of the four-mile radius which starts from the West Hill, Highgate, where would you collide with the opposite circumference?

7. Does it surprise you to learn that Westminster Bridge, if continued in a straight line for two or three miles on the Surrey side, would run into Tower Bridge, or somewhere very near it?

8. Where are Hanging Sword Alley, William and Mary Yard and Whetstone Park?

Of St. Paul's Cathedral I find it very difficult to write. Within, it is to me the least genial of cathedrals, the least kindly. It has neither tenderness nor mystery. I

would not call it exactly hard and churlish, like some of
the white-washed Lutheran temples: it is simply so much
noble masonry without sympathy.

Wren, of course, had no religion: one sees that in
every church he built. He was a wonderful architect;
he heaped stone on stone as no Englishman has ever
done, before or since; one feels that he must have known
by inspired prevision exactly how the smoke and fog of
the future would affect his favourite medium; but he
had no religion, no secret places in his soul, no colour,
His churches are churches for a business man, and a
successful one at that: not for a penitent, not for a
perplexed and troubled soul, not for an emotional sufferer.
Poor people look out of place in them. Wren's churches
are for prosperity.

To make satisfying exteriors—especially to make the
right spires—was Wren's happy destiny. He never, or
almost never, failed here. Within, his churches are for
the most part merely consecrated comfortable rooms:
without, they are London's most precious, most magical
possession. At first they may not please; but—and
especially if one studies the city from a height—one comes
to realise their beauty and their extraordinary fittingness.
On a bright day of scudding clouds, such as I remember
in January of this year, when I was sitting in a room at
the highest point of the Temple, the spire of a Wren
church can have as many expressions, can reflect as many
moods, as a subtle and sympathetic woman. I was watching St. Bride's with absolute fascination as it smiled and
frowned, doubted and understood.

St. Paul's of course can hardly be ranked with Wren's
churches at all: it is so vast, so isolated. It is too vast
in its present Anglican hands for human nature's daily
needs. The Roman Catholics, by their incense, their con-
fessionals, their constant stream of worshippers, their
little side chapels, their many services, and, perhaps most
of all, by their broken-light, bring down even their largest

cathedrals to reasonable dimensions, so that one does not feel lost in them. They might humanise St. Paul's. But as it is, St. Paul's is a desert: nothing is done for you, and its lighting is almost commercial. The dominant impression it conveys is of vastness: one emerges with no hush on one's soul.

St. Paul's should, I think, be loved from a distance; an interview should not be courted. The triumph of St. Paul's is that, vast and serene, it broods protectively over the greatest city in the world, and is worthy of its office. The dome is magnificent: there is nothing finer: and that to me is St. Paul's—a mighty mothering dome; not cold aisles and monstrous groups of statuary, not a whispering gallery and worried mosaics, not tourists with red guide-books and typists eating their lunch. All that I want to forget.

St. Paul's best appeal, true appeal, is external. It has no religious significance to me: it is the artistic culmination of London city, it is the symbol of London. And as such it is always thrilling. One of the best near views is from the footbridge from Charing Cross to Waterloo; one of the best distant views is from Parliament Hill; another is from Greenwich Park where the dome seems to be held up by the Tower Bridge. By no effort of imagination can one think of London without it.

Yet go to St. Paul's one must, if only to reverse this view and see London from its dome. On a clear day, which in London means a windy day, you cannot have a more interesting sight than this great unwieldy city from the ball of its sentinel cathedral—all spread out on every side, with a streak of river in the midst: all grey and busy right away to the green fields.

To trace the great roads from this height is one of the most interesting things. For it is pleasant to think that all the roads even of the crowded congested business centre take one in time into the country, into the world, right to the sea. In time, for example, Ludgate Hill is going

to be Fleet Street, and Fleet Street the Strand, and the
Strand King William Street, and so on to Leicester Square
and Coventry Street and Picadilly; and Piccadilly leads
to Hounslow and Staines and the west of England.
Behind us is Cannon Street, which leads to London
Bridge and the Borough High Street and Tabard Street
to Watling Street and Gravesend and Rochester and the
Kentish coast: or viâ London Bridge and the Borough
High Street, to Newington Causeway, to Clapham, Epsom,
Leatherhead and Dorking to the Sussex coast; or through
Guildford to the Hog's Back and Hampshire. Cheapside
leads to Cornhill and Leadenhall Street and Aldgate, and
Aldgate to the Whitechapel Road and Romford, Brent-
wood, Chelmsford and the east; Bishopsgate leads to
Edmonton, Hoddesden, Cheshunt, Ware and the north-
east; the City Road leads to Islington, Highgate and
the North; and Cheapside to Holborn, Oxford Street,
the Edgware Road, St. Albans and the north-west. From
the ball of St. Paul's one can follow all these roads for a
little way on their great journeys.

A few years ago such eventualities were not considered
as they now are, the Londoner associating liberty only
with the rail. But now that the motor car has come,
the road has returned to its own again, not only in fact
but in our thoughts. No motorist thinks only of the
portion of road that he happens to be on: he looks ahead
and thinks of its course and destination. This is good.
This is one of the best things that the motor has done.
Compared with such an enlargement of vision, such a
quickening of the imagination, its speed is unimpor-
tant. The motor's great achievement is its gift of
England to the English, the home counties to the
Londoner.

It is in St. Paul's that our great soldiers and sailors
and painters are commemorated. The painters are
modest; but the monuments to the warriors are large
and florid (rather like the Dutch), usually personifying

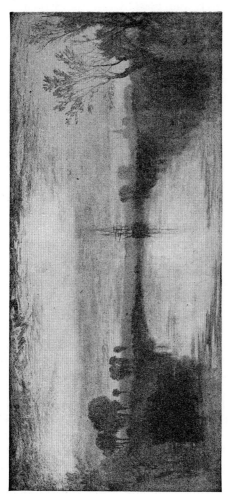

CHICHESTER CANAL

AFTER THE PICTURE BY TURNER IN THE TATE GALLERY

the hero in action. Nothing is so wrong as for sculpture
to perpetuate an arrested movement: great art, and
particularly marmoreal art, treats of repose; but the
sculptors of St. Paul's, the Bacons, and Bailleys, and
Westmacotts, did not think so, and we therefore have
Sir Ralph Abercromby for ever falling from his horse,
and Sir John Moore for ever being just lowered into his
grave, though not at all as the poem describes. Latterly,
however, taste has improved, for the completed Wellington monument has dignity and tranquillity, while Lord
Leighton's sarcophagus is beautiful.

The old rule which seems to have insisted upon every
statue being eight feet high, although doubtless a wise
one in so large a building, leads to some rather quaint
effects: as when one comes suddenly upon a half-naked
Colossus of truculent mien, fit opponent for Hacken-
schmidt, and finds the name of Samuel Johnson beneath it.
Anomalies in marble are so very noticeable.

For other memorials to distinguished men one must
descend, at a cost of sixpence, into the crypt (the soldiers
and sailors above are free), where Sir Christopher Wren
lies, and where many of the greatest painters are buried
—among them Turner and Reynolds, Lawrence and
Millais. Here too lie Nelson and Wellington. Latterly
the crypt has been set apart as the resting-place or
memorial-place of some of our lesser but authentic men
of genius, such as W. E. Henley, that burly fighter and
sweet poet, and Randolph Caldecott, best of illustrators
for the young, and now and then a gifted stranger within
our gates, such as E. A. Abbey.

One of the parts of commercial London that I like best
is the slope of the hill between St. Paul's and the river.
All kinds of old narrow lanes wind down this hill to the
water, crossing Upper Thames Street on the way—all
strongly stamped by the past and all very busy and noisy.
Nowhere in London do the feet of horses make so clat-
tering a disturbance as hereabouts, and the motor vehicle

has hardly yet found its way here. These lanes with the odd names—Godliman Street, Benet Lane, Sermon Lane, Trig Lane, Distaff Lane, Little Divinity Lane, Garlick Hill, College Hill, Stew Lane—are all winding and narrow and obsolete, and without exception, contrary to the best interests of business; yet they persist, and one is glad of it. And all make for the wharves and the river, and ultimately the open sea.

The Great Fire made very short work of Thames Street —as indeed a fire always does of riverside buildings—and everything that one now sees dates from the hither side of that disaster. The churches are all Wren's, whose industry amazes more and more:—St. Benet's (where Inigo Jones is buried); St. James's in Garlickhithe, with a figure of the apostle over its fine assertive clock); St. Michael's, on College Hill, with some carving of Wren's confederate Grinling Gibbons, and a window to Dick Whittington, who was buried here as often as he was Lord Mayor of London. By Cannon Street's arch one passes the very thinnest end that any architectural wedge ever had, and so comes into Lower Thames Street, where we quickly find Wren again—at St. Magnus the Martyr, at the foot of Fish Street Hill, on which the Monument, like a tall bully, lifts its head and lies. St. Magnus's is one of London's larger churches, and in its way is very fine. Miles Coverdale, who gave the English their Bible, is buried here. The glass is not good, nor is it good in any Wren church that I have seen, but it rarely reaches a lower point than in St. Dunstan's-in-the-East (which has the beautiful tower). Before we come to this church we pass Pudding Lane, where the Great Fire began (we shall see directly where it stopped), and to Billingsgate fish market. Both the Thames Streets, Upper and Lower, are very genuine, and very interesting, with their warehouses and their wharves; although I should feel there by night that one must meet rats. The whole walk from Blackfriars Station to the Tower is worth taking, with

IN THE TEMPLE GARDENS (Fountain Court)

plenty of material to the hand of a Méryon or Muirhead Bone on the way; but at Billingsgate I draw the line —Billingsgate, which is always muddy whatever the weather, and always noisy and slimy and fishy beyond words. One comes away indeed vowing never to eat fish again.

From St. Paul's, when I was last there, I walked to the church of St. Bartholomew the Great in Smithfield, feeling that I needed a little Norman and Early English humanising in the genuine atmosphere of antiquity; for St. Paul's, for all its sacred dust, is too much like the mausoleum of a Lord Mayor. I walked through a narrow passage into Paternoster Row, and so to Amen Corner and Warwick Lane. I peeped into Amen Court, that quiet ecclesiastical backwater where St. Paul's canons live, but have at the present moment no Sydney Smith among them; nor among the minor canons is there a Thomas Ingoldsby. I peeped also into Warwick Square, one of whose old residential houses still stands amid the offices, with a top hamper of woodwork and a parliament of pigeons on its coping. And so on into Newgate Street, where all has changed—the site of Christ's Hospital being now covered by Post Office buildings, and Newgate's dark and sinister prison having given way to the gleaming new Central Criminal Court in yellow stone with its gold figure of Justice on top. St. Sepulchre's Church has not yet been pulled down, it is true; but I suppose it has merely been overlooked, so noble is it and worthy of preservation.

St. Sepulchre's, whose four vanes and their inability to swing exactly together have made a city proverb, has a long association with crime which, however kindly meant, lends it a sinister air. Its clock for centuries gave the hours to the hangman at Newgate across the way: at first to warn him that it was time to start for Tyburn, and later that the moment was ripe for the execution in the prison itself. Life must have been very interesting

and full—to the innocent or undetected—in Holborn and
Oxford Street in those old days when condemned men
were hanged at Tyburn Tree: processions so constantly
passing, with every circumstance of publicity and ribaldry.
St. Sepulchre's connection with executions did not end
at merely giving the time: it had refinements of torture
at its fingers' ends. By the zeal of a citizen of London
named Robert Doewe, who left a sum of money for the
purpose, the clerk of the church was forced to take his
bell in hand on the eve of a hanging, and proceed twice,
once at night and once in the morning, to the prison,
where, standing beneath the window of the wretch's cell,
he gave out certain tolls and called upon him in a dreary
rhyme to make his peace with God if he would avoid
eternal flames. And then, on the departure of the cart
for Tyburn, the clerk had to appear again and offer
prayers; and lest any of these searching attentions were
omitted or shirked, the Beadle of the Merchant Taylors'
Hall was provided with a stipend to see that the clerk
duly carried them out with a becoming Christian rigour.
So much for St. Sepulchre's official interest in the condemned; but it played also an amateur part in another
and prettier, although not much humaner, ritual, for
it was from its steps that a nosegay was presented
to every traveller to that Tyburn from which none
returned.

Our church has fifteenth century masonry in it, but
for the most part is seventeenth, having been destroyed
by the Great Fire. St. Sepulchre's was indeed that de-
stroyer's last ecclesiastical victim, for a few yards farther
up Giltspur Street, at Pie Corner, it died away and was
no more, having raged all the way from Pudding Lane
by the Monument. Pie Corner was just by Cock Lane,
the scene, in 1762, of the most ridiculous imposture which
ever laid London by the heels—the Cock Lane ghost.
When last I stood looking down this lane, which now
belongs almost entirely to commerce, a catsmeat man

went by, pushing a barrow and calling his wares, and it seemed he must have walked straight out of one of Hogarth's pictures.

I have said in an earlier chapter that Shepherd Market in Mayfair gives one the best impression at this moment of the busy shopkeeping London of the Augustan essayists. The best idea of a London of an earlier time that still remains, is I think to be found in Cloth Fair and Bartholomew Close, where sixteenth-century houses still stand, and sixteenth-century narrownesses and dirt are everywhere. If there is the true old London anywhere, it is in the passages on the north side of St. Bartholomew the Great.

But before we reach Bartholomew Close we must pass St. Bartholomew's Hospital, or Barts' as it is called, on the south side of Smithfield, one of London's great temples of healing. Its square in summer is quite a little park, with its patients taking the air and the children playing among them, and there is always a bustle of students and nurses and waiting-maids, crossing and re-crossing from one grey building to another.

The late Sir Norman Moore, the physician, who wrote the history of St. Bartholomew's Hospital, offered to take me round the ancient wall of London on any moonlight night I might name. It was a favourite walk of his. Like so many invitations to which no date is affixed, this was neglected by me until too late; and I have often regretted my foolishness, for Sir Norman Moore was an antiquary with a mind richly stored and a great gift of expository conversation. I recommend the excursion to any society of persons interested in London. The route is very easy to trace. In this connection I should like to mention an excellent Society of London walking lovers and London explorers, the Ashburton London Fellowship, with head-quarters at 28 Red Lion Square, whose members constantly meet either to attend lectures or to pay carefully organised visits to historical sites. To look through a few of their programmes is to realise how inexhaustible this city is.

The way to Bartholomew Close is through the hospital to Little Britain, and so into this ramifying old-world region, once a centre of printers (Benjamin Franklin practised his trade there) and now given up to warehouses and offices and in its narrow parts to small shops; but never for an instant belonging to the twentieth century or even the nineteenth.

The church itself—St. Bartholomew the Great—is one of the architectural jewels of the city. Not that it is so perfect or so beautiful; but that it is so curious, so genuine, so un-Wrenlike, so unexpected, so modest. I think its humility and friendliness are its greatest charm. It hides away behind West Smithfield's houses, with its own little crazy graveyard before it, but keeps its door always open. You enter and are in the middle ages.

I am not attempting to describe the church, which is a very attractive jumble of architectural styles, with a triforium that one longs to walk around, and noble doors, and massive Norman pillars, and a devious ambulatory. Indeed there is no need, for no London church is so often depicted. On the morning I was last there it was like students' day at the National Gallery, as many as four young women being hard at work transferring different aspects to paper, while two others were engaged on Prior Bolton's window, which is a kind of private box in the south side of the choir, built into one of the arches of the triforium, where this prior, who flourished early in the sixteenth century, may have sat.

An older relic still is the coloured tomb of the founder —in the sanctuary—the merry and melodious Rahere, who founded the Priory of St. Bartholomew in the reign of Henry I. Seven Henries later it was of course dissolved. Having loitered sufficiently in the church, one should walk round its exterior and make a point of seeing the sexton's house (to which I have already alluded)

CORNELIUS VAN DER GEEST
AFTER THE PICTURE BY VAN DYCK IN THE NATIONAL GALLERY

which clings to the north wall as a child to its mother
—the quaintest old house in London, with its tiny Tudor
bricks and infinitesimal windows.

Cloth Fair begins here, a congeries of narrow streets
and dreadful old women, where once was the centre of
the drapery trade that now flourishes in St. Paul's Churchyard. From Cloth Fair I passed into Smithfield's large
vacancy, where Bartholomew Fair—which was in its
serious side a fair for cloth—used to be held every Bartholomew's Day until 1855, when the law stepped in and
said No. The pleasure portion was the most extraordinary chaos of catchpenny booths, theatricals, *feræ naturæ*,
wild beasts, cheap jacks and charlatans that England has
ever seen; and I like to think that Charles Lamb led
William Wordsworth through it in 1802.

Through the fleshly horrors of Smithfield Market, where
Hebrew middlemen smoke large cigars, I advise no one
to wander; and Charterhouse Square, whither we are now
bound, can be reached easily by Long Lane and Hayne
Street, well outside the domain of the carcase and the
bloodstained porter.

To Charterhouse Square, a region of peace, within
sound of Aldersgate's commercial zeal, we are coming,
not to see the Merchant Taylors' school, or even the
charming Georgian houses that are left, but to explore
the monastery that gives it its name. After a curiously
varied career, the Charterhouse is now fixed (I hope for
many centuries to come, although the gate porter tells
me alarming stories of offers from speculative builders)
as an almshouse for old gentlemen. It was built in the
fourteenth century as a monastery for Carthusians.
Then came the dread Henry VIII with his odd and
implacable conscience, hardly less devastating than the
speculative builder or the modern County Councillor, who
cast out the monks and beheaded the prior, and made
the house a private residence for rich courtiers—Sir
Thomas Audley, Lord North, the Duke of Northumber-

land, the Duke of Norfolk, the Duke of Suffolk in turn
occupying it and entertaining there. But in 1611 Mr.
Thomas Sutton bought it and endowed it with a sum of
£200,000 as a hospital and a school. In the school forty
boys were to be educated free, with sixty others who paid
fees; in the hospital "eighty gentlemen by descent and
in poverty" were to be maintained—above the age of
fifty, if sound, but of forty, if maimed in war. Both
intentions were admirably realised, although changes have
come in. In 1872, for example, the school was moved
to Godalming, and in 1885 the number of pensioners was
reduced by twenty-five owing to loss of revenue. But
the fifty-five that remain could not spend their declining
days more sweetly and serenely than within these grey
walls.

The Charterhouse is very beautiful, very quiet. Its
most famous pensioner, although an imaginary one, will
always be Colonel Newcome—a proper tribute to the
genius of Thackeray, who was educated at the school
here. Among its pensioners in real life have been such
different dramatists as Elkanah Settle and John Maddison
Morton, the author of "Box and Cox." Among famous
schoolboys of the Charterhouse—old Carthusians, as we
call them—some of whom are celebrated in the little
passage that leads to the chapel, are John Leech and
George Grote, Addison and Steele, Crashaw and Black-
stone, John Wesley and Sir Henry Havelock.

The last time I went to the Charterhouse was the first
day of spring last year, and when I came out the sky
was so clear and the air so soft that I gave up all my
other plans, and turning into Aldersgate, walked all the
way to Highgate: up Aldersgate, which is now wholly
commercial but which in Tudor times was fashionable;
up the Goswell Road (where Mr. Pickwick lodged with
Mrs. Bardell); along Upper Street, that fine old-world
highway; past Islington Green, now a municipal enclosure; through Highbury; up the long Holloway Road

(where I weakened and took a tram); up Highgate Hill; and so to that healthy northern suburb where time still tarries. All this I did for old sake's sake, because it was at Highgate, on the very top of the hill, that I used to live—just north of the Grove, where Carlyle heard Coleridge discourse endlessly of the sum-jective and the om-jective.

To me Highgate is still London's most fascinating suburb, for it has a quietness and an unpretentiousness that are foreign to Hampstead. On how many sweet May evenings have I walked along Hampstead Lane to the Spaniard's, past Caen's dark recesses, where it is whispered badgers are still to be found, and sitting in one of the tavern's arbours, have heard the nightingale singing in Bishop's Wood. The Spaniard's then—in the eighteen-nineties—was one of the best of the old London inns still surviving—without the foreign waiters and the coloured wine glasses to bring in the false new note. And I was never tired of leading my friends thither to show them Dick Turpin's knife and fork in a case on the wall. Sometimes we would walk on to Jack Straw's Castle, along that fine high ridgeway across the Heath known as the Spaniard's Road, and watch London twinkling far away beneath us. Or disregarding Jack Straw's Castle we would plunge down from Constable's knoll of Scotch firs, over rough sandy bridle paths, to the Bull and Bush in the hollow at North End, and there find refreshment.

I am speaking of the spring and summer; but Hampstead Heath is not less attractive in winter too, and in winter there used to be at the Bull and Bush a brew of barley wine, as it was called, that was very warming. Such brews are no longer common. What one misses from London windows in winter is any alluring invitation to hot cordial drinks. The publicans announce the commencement of the goose club, but there is no longer any tidings of mulled ale. It is sad but true that the Londoner's—indeed I might say the Englishman's—first and last word in alcoholic cheer is whisky. Even in the coldest weather no stand is made for the genial beverages of the past. To the end Dickens brewed punch and saw that it was good; but with Dickens, or very shortly after, passed away all interest in that enkindling Christianising bowl.

And who now asks for a port wine negus? But when I first came to London in 1892, in the good old days when Furnivall's Inn still stood, and Ridler's Hotel beamed hospitably across Holborn, I used to frequent a little inner sitting-room in that hostelry, where long clay pipes were provided, and where a stately waiter used to bring a negus that was worth drinking, with cinnamon floating on the top like drift wood after a wreck.

In Highgate and Hampstead I should love to linger: but they are outside the radius so far as this book is concerned. Yet of Hampstead I must say a word here, if only to correct the suggestion that it is pretentious. Pretentious only in its modern roads—its Fitzjohn's Avenues, and so forth: there is no pretentiousness about Church Row, which, until the flats were built on the north side, was the most beautiful English street I ever saw, or expect to see, and is still well worth climbing a hill ten times as steep as Hampstead's. With this early simple part of Hampstead, and the little passages and cottages between Church Row and the pond on the summit, the memory of Kate Greenaway is in my mind inseparably bound. To think of one is to think of the other. One feels that she must have lived here; as indeed she did—just below Church Row, in Frognal, but not, I grieve to say, in an old house. Hampstead has had many literary and artistic associations, from Keats (in Well Walk) to George du Maurier and Mr. John Galsworthy (in the Grove) but Kate Greenaway is my Hampstead symbol.

I remember what a shock it was to hear that she was

dead. For one had never thought of death in connection with this serene and joyous artist. Her name had called up for so long only pleasant, sunny associations: memories of green meadows with grave little girls and boys a-maying; quiet, restful rooms (in Church Row!) with tiny fireplaces, daffodils in blue vases on the high mantel-pieces, and grave little girls and boys a-playing; and trim streets, where everything was well-kept and well-swept, and all the roofs were red and all the garden gates and fences green, and more grave little girls carried dolls, and more grave little boys rolled hoops, and very young mothers with high waists gossiped over their grave little babies' infinitesimal heads. Some such scenes as these had for twenty years been rising before one whenever Kate Greenaway's name was heard, bringing with them a gentle breath of ancient repose and simplicity and a faint scent of pot pourri. And to think the hand that devised this innocent communism of quaintness and felicity, this juvenile Arcadia, was still for ever!

That was in 1901, when for some years Miss Greenaway had not been the power that once she was. Her greatest triumphs were in the early eighties, when she illustrated Ann and Jane Taylor's "Original Poems," and wrote and illustrated verses of her own writing, and put forth every Christmas a little almanack, with scenes fitting to every month and delicate and dainty borders of the old-world flowers she loved best. It might almost be said that she invented the daffodil. That was the time when flowers were being newly discovered, and while the æsthetes were worshipping the sunflower and the lily Miss Greenaway was bidding the cheeriest little daisies spring from the grass and the chubbiest little roses burst from the bushes, and teaching thousands of uninitiated eyes how beautiful the daffodil is. Wordsworth had done so before, it is true; but between Wordsworth and Kate Greenaway how wide a gulf of stuffy taste was fixed—the forties, the fifties, the sixties, and the seventies! Kate Greenaway came like a fresh southern breeze after a fog. The æsthetes were useful, but they were artificial: they never attained to her open-air radiances. In the words of a critic whom I was reading somewhere the other evening, Kate Greenaway newly dressed the children of England; and the effects of her influence will probably never be lost. And to a great extent she refurnished England too. There is not an intelligent upholsterer or furniture dealer in the country at this moment whose warehouses do not bear witness to Miss Greenaway's unobtrusive, yet effectual, teaching. She was the arch-priestess of happy simplicity.

As an illustrator of dramatic stories, such as the domestic tragedies set forth by the sisters Taylor, or Bret Harte's "Queen of Pirate Isle," or "The Pied Piper of Hamelin," Miss Greenaway was not quite successful. Her genius bent rather to repose than action; or, at least, to any action more complex than skipping or dancing, picking flowers, crying, or taking tea. (No one in the whole history of art has drawn more attractive tea tables—old Hampstead tea tables, I am sure.) Drama was beyond her capacity, and her want of sympathy with anything unhappy or forceful also unfitted her. Her pictures prove her the soul of gentleness. Had she set out to make a tiger it would have purred like the friendliest tabby; nothing could induce her pencil to abandon its natural bent for soft contours and grave kindlinesses. Hence her crones were merely good-natured young women doing their best —and doing it very badly—to look old; her witches were benevolent grandmothers. To illustrate was not her *métier*. But to create—that she did to perfection. She literally made a new world where sorrow never entered —nothing but the momentary sadness of a little child— where the sun always shone, where ugliness had no place and life was always young. No poet can do much more than this. It seems to me that among the sweet influences of the nineteenth century Kate Greenaway stands very

ST. PAUL'S FROM THE RIVER

high. The debt we owe to her is beyond payment; but I hope that some memorial will be considered. Randolph Caldecott has a memorial in the crypt of St. Paul's; Lewis Carroll in the Great Ormond Street Children's Hospital; Kate Greenaway ought to have a group of statuary (in the manner of the Hans Christian Andersen monument) in Church Row, Hampstead.

And now we must get back to the city again, but before we do so let us, since it is Friday, turn our steps to a very curious place on that day. I wonder how Mr. Wilfred Whitten, that inveterate and glowing Metropolitan, would reply to the question, Where, if anywhere, in London is to be seen in this late day the best approximation to a Hogarthian scene? But let me share with all propounders of riddles (except a few unhappy ones baffled by the cleverness or tactlessness of the company) the triumph of supplying also the answer. The answer is the Caledonia market on a Friday. I was last there on a bitter afternoon, and the thought of Hogarth was continuous in that vast concourse of dealers and bargain-hunters.

It was a killing day: an east wind swept the eminence: Caledonia was at its sternest and wildest. The dealers were blue with cold; their wives huddled over braziers; every hot-chestnut man was hemmed in by a little warmth-seeking crowd as closely as though he was in a fit; on the floor of this vast open space were spread the wares of the day, all of which had been brought thither that morning, and arranged to best advantage, and most of which would have to be packed up and taken away that evening. Horses and carts were anchored here and there for the removal of the more prosperous merchants' goods, the horses shivering in the blast; for the rest there were hand barrows by the hundred. The goods covered, I suppose, several acres; and a hundred pounds would have cleared the market. For the most part it was rubbish—

old iron, old clothes, old household utensils, such curiosities as a pawnbroker lends nothing on, "dud" Sheffield plate, tools, oleographs, and so forth, all huddled together. But there were specialists too. One dealer, for example, had nothing but old corsets, and if there is a less engaging sight than a huddle of old corsets I hope never to see it. Another had fire-irons and nothing else; another, painters' brushes which had seen their best days; another, odd pieces of wainscotting; another, old umbrellas; and so forth. But these specialists were few; the majority of the stocks were miscellaneous.

As to the dealers themselves, their general air was of a willing receptivity rather than aggressive disburdenment. Here and there one proclaimed the merits of his wares; the majority shivered and watched. Perhaps it was the grey chill of the day; perhaps in warmer weather all are vocal. Few of them were properly dressed for such bleakness; all had the cynical expression of the Londoner under Heaven's ban; a Hogarthian plainness, if not ugliness, heightened by the exposure, marked every face.

The bargain-hunters were more prosperous looking, and happier because less cold, for they at any rate had the power of locomotion denied to one who wished either to sell or preserve his wares. Rumour has it that many of the articles which are offered for sale at this market have been acquired by the most primitive means known to acquisitive man; and there is no doubt that among the frequenters of the market are many who hold that hands were made before title-deeds. The merchant therefore, even if he has given up hope of selling, must still be rooted to his pitch.

Many of the crowd were as purely sight-seeing as myself; but there were the intent ones too, with their string bags or other bags, hoping always for a find, whether for their own domestic use or to sell again: keen-eyed men and women with long eager fingers.

For the real bargains, I am told, one must go early;

MERCURY INSTRUCTING CUPID

AFTER THE PICTURE BY CORREGGIO IN THE NATIONAL GALLERY

and it is a reasonable precaution. But to what extent the real bargain is obtainable I have no notion. Most persons, I find, have a remarkable story of Caledonian luck; but it has happened always to others, not to themselves. No doubt there have been *coups*, especially when the dealer had the best reason for wishing that his own temporary ownership of the article should cease at the earliest possible moment and the purchaser hurry away with it; but I not only saw with those eyes on that Friday nothing that a collector of any taste would buy, but nothing that any but a confirmed and undiscriminating kleptomaniac would steal.

More fun was that partially covered portion of the market where the stalls have new articles. This was a downright fair, and the spirit of the fair prevailed. Every household requisite was offered at I suppose a far cheaper rate than a shopkeeper with his rent to pay could possibly manage, and when you had bought your fill you could eat winkles and cockles and mussels and shrimps or drink hot coffee. Nothing lacking but roundabouts and cocoanuts, and everywhere signs that buying and selling and chaffering are still among the deepest of human joys, and that London in the twentieth century, when put to it, can reproduce the eighteenth with amazing fidelity.

CHAPTER XII

CHEAPSIDE AND THE CITY CHURCHES

Crowded pavements—Sunday in the City—A receded tide of worshippers—Temples of Cheery Ease—Two Weekday Congregations—St. Stephen's, Walbrook—Bishopsgate Churches—The Westminster Abbey of the City—Houndsditch toy shops—Postmen's Park—Bunhill Fields—The City Road—Colebrooke Row and Charles Lamb—London Pigeons—The Guildhall—The Lord Mayor in State—The City and Literature.

W E are now in a part of London that really is too busy to wander in. London neither likes you to walk faster than itself nor slower; it likes you to adopt its own pace. In the heart of the city you cannot do this and see anything. To study Cheapside and its narrow tributaries, the very narrowness of which is eloquent of the past and at the same time so much a part of the present that it is used in a thoroughly British manner to imprison carts and carters for five or six hours a day, you must choose a Sunday; but if you can loiter in these parts on a Sunday without becoming so depressed as to want to scream aloud, you are made of sterner stuff than I. For my part, I would rather be actually bruised by the jostlings of Cheapside on Monday than have solitary elbow room there on the day of rest, when the cheerful shops are shut and the dreary bells ring out. For the city on Sunday is to me a wilderness of melancholy. Church bells are tolerable only when one hears a single peal; to hear many in rivalry is to suffer.

The city churches are many and are well cared for; but their day is over. During the week we are too busy

142

making money, or not making it, to spare time for religion; while on Sunday we are elsewhere. I do not wish to suggest that there are not city men who value the opportunity which the open doors of the churches give them for a little escape from Mammon during the day; but for the most part the city church strikes one as obsolete. It belongs to the period when merchants not only made their money in the city but lived there too; before Sydenham Hill and Brighton, Chislehurst and Weybridge were discovered. No one lives in. the city any longer, save the Lord Mayor and a few caretakers; and all the gentlemen who would once have convoyed their wives and families up the aisles into the lethargic pews are now either doing the same thing in the suburbs or evading that duty on the golf links.

Times change: the city church remains, calm and self-possessed, offering sanctuary to any one who needs it; but one cannot believe that were they all pulled down to-morrow any one would really resent it except a few simple-hearted old-fashioned city gentlemen and an æsthetic minority writing to the papers from Kensington, while the competition for the sites on which to erect commodious and convenient business premises would be instant and terrific. My own feelings about what ought to be done with them are mixed, for I believe that as sanctuaries they are precious and desirable but I see also that the revenue possible might be of the more practical use. Perhaps the best solution would be to keep the most beautiful and let the others go. Personally I rarely go into the city without spending a few minutes in one or other of these abodes of peace; but that is a circumstance of no value, because I go to the city only out of curiosity. I am not of it; indeed, I am lost in it, and I can find myself again only by resting a while in one of these very formal havens. Silent they are not; the roar of the city cannot be quite shut out; but one hears it only as one hears in a shell the murmur of the sea.

Comfort—ecclesiastical comfort—is the note of the city church. It reflects the mind of the comfortable citizen for whom it was built, who liked things plain but good, and, though he did not want so far to misbehave as to think of religion as a cheerful topic, was still averse from Calvinistic gloom. (In St. Michael's on College Hill, for instance, is a notice over the door bearing the congenial promise to the congregation: "Plenteousness within His palaces.") St. Mary Woolnoth's, just by the Mansion House, is light, almost gay. The black woodwork and the coloured walls have a pleasant effect. The pulpit is an interesting example of the cabinetmaker's art. There is seating accommodation for very few persons, and that guards against overcrowding. The heating arrangements are good. St. Botolph's, in Aldgate, at the corner of Houndsditch, is another bright and cheery little church. This has a gallery and some elaborate plaster work on the ceiling. Comfort and well-being are strongly in evidence—not to the point of decimating a golf links, of course, but comfort and well-being none the less.

One of the most unexpected of London churches is St. Stephen's, Walbrook (behind the Mansion House), into the side of which a bookshop has been built. Without, it is nothing uncommon and its spire is ordinary Wren; but within it is very imposing and rather fine, having a lofty dome and a number of stately pillars. I do not, however, agree with a London friend whose advice to me was to disregard all the city churches so long as I saw this one. At the opposite pole is St. Ethelburga's in Bishopsgate Street Within, a very modest shrinking little fane. Like All Hallows, Barking, St. Ethelburga's escaped the Fire, and it stands, a relic of Early English architecture, in the midst of the busiest part of the city. But beyond its isolation, age and simplicity, it has little to recommend it. The famous city church of St. Helen's is in Great St. Helen's Place, a little to the south, and it is worth visiting for the tombs alone—for here lie London's greatest merchants, from Sir Thomas Gresham down-wards: it is the Westminster Abbey of the city, the Valhalla of commerce. It has, however, one poet too; for the possibility that a William Shakespeare who lived in the parish in 1598 was the Swan of Avon led an American gentleman to erect a window to the dramatist.

In Leadenhall Street one may see where Lamb's India House stood; and Leadenhall Market, which fills several estuaries here, is interesting for its live-stock shops, where one may buy puppies and bantams, Persian cats and bullfinches, and even, I believe, foxes for the chase—if one sinks so low. Cornhill has two churches almost touching each other—St. Peter's and St. Michael's—but neither is interesting, although St. Michael's tower can catch the sun very pleasantly.

For the most part the city church no longer has its graveyard; or if it has, the graves have been levelled and a little green space for luncheon-hour recreation has been made instead. One of the pleasantest of these is that of St. Botolph Without, Aldersgate, which is known as Postmen's Park. It is here that the late G. F. Watts, the great painter, erected memorials to certain lowly heroes and heroines not in either of the heroic services, who saved Londoners' lives and perished in the effort. If any one has a strong taste for graveyards he should certainly visit Bunhill Fields at Finsbury—if only to lose it. A crazy dirty place is this, with its myriad stones saturated with London soot and all awry, and the hum of factories on the northern side. Defoe's tomb is here, with an obelisk over it, and here also lie Bunyan and Isaac Watts, and William Blake and Thomas Stothard, two gentle old men who were rivals only in their painting of Chaucer's Pilgrims; but one comes out in the depths of depression and had better perhaps not have entered. Opposite is a little museum of relics of John Wesley, whose statue is there too. Another great spiritual man, George Fox, lies close by, in the Friends' burial ground.

From Bunhill Fields one may climb the City Road on a tram—the City Road, once important, once having its place in the most popular comic song of the day, but now a kind of wilderness. The Eagle is now an ordinary public-house, the Grecian's Corinthian period is over; and when I was here last, that most dismal sight, the demolition of a church, was to be seen. But the City Road is worth traversing if only for Colebrooke Row, at the end of which, in the last house on the north side, adjoining Duncan Terrace and next a ginger-beer factory, Charles Lamb once lived, in the days before the New River was covered over; and it was down Lamb's front garden that George Dyer walked when he fell into that stream.

Colebrooke Row is still old-fashioned; hardly anything has been done beyond covering the waterway. I descended to the banks of the canal, which, in its turn, runs at right angles beneath the New River, and talked with the captain of the tug which pulls the barges through the long low tunnel. And then I climbed to Colebrooke Row again and roamed about Upper Street and all that is left of Islington Green, where a statue of Sir Hugh Myddelton stands, and wondered at the success with which Islington has kept itself a self-contained town entirely surrounded by houses, and walked a while in Islington churchyard, and then descended the squalid heights of Pentonville to King's Cross. I cannot call either Pentonville or Clerkenwell interesting, except for preserving so much of the London of a hundred years ago.

But meanwhile we are due in Cheapside again.

The British Museum has the first name for pigeons in London—the pigeon being our sacred bird, our ibis—and truly there are none bigger: they have breasts like cannon balls; but the Guildhall's birds are even tamer. In crossing the courtyard in front of the Guildhall one really has to step carefully to avoid treading on them, so casual are they and so confident that you will behave.

THE CHARTERHOUSE

The Guildhall has in its basement a collection of articles relating to the history of the city, which are sufficiently interesting to be well worth a visit. Relics of Roman occupation; old inn signs, including the Boar's Head in Eastcheap which Falstaff frequented; instruments of punishment from Newgate; old utensils and garments; prints and broadsheets; and so forth. But the chief collection of such articles is now to be seen at the London Museum proper, which we have not yet reached.

While we are here we ought to visit the Guildhall Picture Gallery and see what kind of art the City Fathers patronise. Having written of it at some length in "London Revisited," all that I say here is that it is an interesting and varied collection, with a masterpiece by William Dyce in it. The Royal Exchange, not very distant, has also some attractive mural painting.

The Lord Mayor's departure for or from the Guildhall is a piece of civic pomp that never fails to please the tolerant observer. He drives in a golden chariot, with four horses to draw it and two footmen to stand behind; while an officer in a cocked hat, carrying a sword, rides on in front, and mounted policemen serve as an escort. The Lord Mayor climbs in first, a figure of medieval splendour, in robes and furs and golden chain, more like a Rabbi in a Rembrandt picture than a London magistrate about to send a costermonger to prison; then another elderly and august masquerader is pushed in; and then the mace bearer is added, holding that bauble so that its head is well out of the window. The golden carriage, which is on cee springs and was built to carry Cinderella and none other, swings like a cradle as these medievalists sink into their seats. The powdered footmen leap to their station at the back; the coachman cracks his whip; and the pageant is complete. Then the crowd of cynical Londoners—porters, clerks, errand boys, business men, who have found, as Londoners always will find, time to observe the spectacle (and it is all one to them whether it is a Lord

Mayor, or an Italian laying asphalt—melts, and the twentieth century once more resumes its sway.

I am quite aware that I am treating the city too lightly; but it cannot be helped. One chapter is useless: it wants many books. No sooner does one begin to burrow beneath the surface of it into the past than one realises how fascinating but also how gigantic is the task before one. Reasons of space, apart from other causes, have held my pen. The literary associations of the city alone are endless. It is in Threadneedle Street that Lamb's old South Sea House stood; in Leadenhall Street we have just seen the modern representative of his East India House. It was in a house in Birchin Lane that the infant Macaulay opening the door to his father's friend Hannah More, asked her to step in and wait while he fetched her a glass of "old spirits," such as they drank in "Robinson Crusoe." It was at the corner of Wood Street that Wordsworth's poor Susan imagined herself in the country; and here still stands a famous city tree, but its limbs are sadly lopped.

CHAPTER XIII

THE TOWER AND THE AMPHIBIANS

Tower Hill and its victims—All Hallows, Barking—Ainsworth's romance—The Little Princes—St. John's Chapel—The Praise of Snuff—The Armouries—The Jewels—The Tower Residences—Wellclose Square—The Tower Bridge—Mr. Jacobs' Stories—Roofs and Chimneys—Pessimism in a Train—Reverence for the Law—The Ocean *in Urbe*—The most interesting terminus—Docks—Stepney and Limehouse—China in London—Canal Life—"Thank you, Driver" —An Intruder and the *mot juste*.

ON the way to the Tower from Mark Lane station one crosses Tower Hill—perhaps, if the traffic permits, walking over the very spot on which stood the old scaffold. When I was last there a flock of pigeons was feeding exactly where I judged it to have been—that scaffold on which so many noble heads were struck from their shoulders, from Sir Thomas More and Surrey the poet to Strafford and Algernon Sidney, and a few ignoble ones, not the least of which was Simon Fraser, Lord Lovat's, the last man to be beheaded in England, the block on which he laid his naughty old neck being still to be seen, full of dents, in the Tower itself. That was in 1747. Standing here it is extraordinary to think that, comparatively speaking, so few years have passed since it was possible to behead a man publicly in broad day in the middle of a London street.

Opposite Mark Lane Station, and at the corner of Great Tower Street, which leads into Little Tower Street, and that in its turn into Eastcheap and the city proper, is All Hallows Church, whither many of the victims of

149

the Tower Hill scaffold were carried for burial, among them the Earl of Surrey, Bishop Fisher and Archbishop Laud. All three were, however, afterwards removed elsewhere, Laud, for example, to St. John's College, Oxford. William Penn, who lived to speak contemptuously of churches as steeplehouses, was baptised here in 1644, and the bloody Judge Jeffreys, who harried Penn's sect so mercilessly, was married here to his first wife in the year following the Great Fire, which spared All, Hallows by a kind of miracle—just thrusting out a tongue or two to lick up the porch and then drawing them back. The church, though it has a new spire, is, within, a fine example of medieval architecture, and its brasses are among the best that London contains. Among them is one of William Thynne and his wife, Thynne being worthy of all commendation as the man responsible for the first printed collection of Chaucer's works in 1532.

Another interesting Great Tower Street building, or rather re-building, is the Czar's Head, an inn on the same side as the church, which stands on the site of an older inn of that name to which Peter the Great, when learning at Deptford to build ships, resorted with his friends. Muscovy Court, out of Trinity Square, close by, derives its style from the same monarch. Little Tower Street has in a different way an equally unexpected association, for it was in a house there that James Thomson, the poet of "The Seasons," wrote "Summer." The new Trinity House is a very imposing building.

Harrison Ainsworth's romance "The Tower of London," which I fear I should find a very tawdry work to-day, twenty and more years ago stirred me as few novels now are able to do, and fixed the Tower for all time as a home of dark mystery. Not even the present smugness of its officialdom, the notice boards, the soldiers in its barracks, the dryness of its moat or the formal sixpenny tickets of admission, can utterly obliterate the impression of Ainsworth's pages and Cruikshank's engravings. I still expect

to see Gog and Magog eating a mammoth pasty; I still
look for Xit the dwarf; and in a dark recess fancy I
hear the shuddering sound of the headsman sharpening
his axe. No need, however, for Ainsworth's fictions:—
after reading the barest outline of English history, the
Tower's stones run red enough. Anne Boleyn, Katherine
Howard, Lady Jane Grey, Sir Thomas More, the Earl of
Essex—these are a few who were beheaded in state within
its walls; but what of the others who died secretly by
force, like the little Princes and Sir Thomas Overbury,
and those other thousands of prisoners unknown who ate
their hearts out in the cells within these nine-feet walls?

The ordinary tickets admit only to the jewels and the
armour, but a written application to the Governor pro-
cures an authorisation to see also the dungeons, in the
company of a warder. The room in the Bloody Tower
in which the little Princes were smothered is no longer
shown, as it has become part of a private dwelling; but
the window is pointed out, and with that husk you must
be satisfied. Among the sights to which a special order
entitles you is the cell in which Raleigh wrote the "History
of the World," and that narrow hollow in the wall of the
White Tower, known as Little Ease, in which Guy Fawkes
was immured while waiting for justice and death.

St. John's Chapel, in the White Tower, has a naked
simplicity beyond anything I know, and a massiveness
out of all proportion to its size, which inspires both confidence and reverence. In its long life it has seen many
strange and moving spectacles—from the all-night vigils
of the Knights of the Bath, to Brackenbury's refusal
at the altar side to murder the little Princes and the
renunciation by Richard II of his crown in favour of
Bolingbroke. I had the history of this chapel from a
gentle old Irish beef-eater who sits in a chair and talks
like a book. The names of monarchs and accompanying
dates fell from his tongue in a gentle torrent until I
stopped it with the question "Do *all* the warders in the

Tower take snuff?" He had never been asked this before, and it knocked all the literature and history out of him and re-established his humanity. He became instantly an Irishman and a brother, confessed to his affection for a pinch (as I had detected), and we discussed the merits of the habit as freely as if the royal body of Elizabeth of York had never lain in state within a few yards of us, and no printed notice had warned me that the place being holy I must remove my·hat.

In the Tower armouries every kind of decorative use has been made of old muskets, ramrods and pistols, resulting in ingenious mural patterns which must strike the schoolboy visitor as a most awful waste of desirable material. The armouries contain also some very real weapons indeed: to students of the machinery of death they are invaluable. The evolution of the sword and gun of all nations may be traced here, in glass cases which are so catholic as to contain not only the corkscrew dagger of Java but the harpoon gun of Nantucket. I think nothing impressed me more than a long and sinister catchpole—surely the most unpleasant weapon that ever assailed a man's comfort and dignity. The models of knights in armour cannot but add to the vividness of "Ivanhoe." Among the more recent relics is the uniform which the Duke of Wellington wore as the Constable of the Tower, and the cloak, rolled up far too tightly and squeezed under glass, in which Wolfe died on the Heights of Abraham. It should be spread out. The drums from Blenheim touch the imagination too.

But the best things about the Tower are the Tower itself—its spaces and gateways, and old houses, and odd corners, and grave, hopping ravens—and St. John's Chapel. Interesting as the armour no doubt is, I could easily dispense with it, for there is something very irritating in being filed past policemen in the pursuit of the interesting; and one sees better crown jewels in any pantomime. Of medieval gravity one never tires; but medieval ostentation and gaudiness soon become unendurable. Yet I suppose more people go to the Tower to see the jewels than to see anything else. The odd fact that the infamous but courageous Colonel Blood, by his historic raid on the regalia in 1671, rose instantly from a furtive skulking subterraneous existence to a place at Court and £500 a year might have had the effect of multiplying such attempts; but it does not seem to have done so. No one tries to steal the crown to-day. And yet precedent is rarely so much in the thief's favour.

But the Tower as a whole—that is fine. There is a jumble of wooden walls and windows on one of the ramparts overlooking the river, where I would gladly live, no matter what the duties. What are the qualifications of the Governor of the Tower I know not, but I am an applicant for the post.

London's wild beasts, which now lend excitement to Regent's Park, used to be kept at the Tower, and the old guide-books to it, a hundred and more years ago, are inclined to pay more attention to them than to history. A living lion was more to the authors of these volumes (as to the sightseers also) than many dead kings. One such book which lies before me now, dated 1778, begins with this blameless proposition: "The Desire of seeing the Antiquities and Rareties of our Country is allowed by all to be a laudable Curiosity: to point them out therefore to the Inquisitive, and to direct their Attention to those Things that best deserve Notice, cannot be denied its degree of Merit." The guide then plunges bravely into history, but quickly emerges to describe, with a degree of spirit rare in the remainder of his work, the inhabitants of the menagerie. The chief animals at that time were the lions Dunco, Pompey, Dido, Cæsar, Miss Fanny, Hector, Nero, Cleony and Helen, and the tigers Sir Richard, Jenny, Nancy, and Miss Groggery, who, "though a tigress, discovers no marks of ferocity." The old custom of calling the lions after the living monarchs of the day seems just then to have been in abeyance. In 1834 the menagerie was transferred to Regent's Park; but I think they might have left a cage or two for old sake's sake.

From the Tower I walked down what used to be the Ratcliffe Highway, where De Quincey's favourite murderer Williams (who must, said George Dyer, have been rather an eccentric character) indulged in his famous holocaust a hundred years ago. It is now St. George's Street, and one reaches it by the wall of St. Katherine's Dock, through the scent of pepper and spice, and past the gloomy opening of Nightingale Lane, which has no reference to the beautiful singing bird of May, but takes its name from the Knighten Guild founded by King Edgar in the days when London was Danish.

I returned to Mark Lane station by way of Wellclose Square, which saw the birth of Thomas Day, the author of "Sandford and Merton," and was the site of the Magdalen Chapel of the famous Dr. Dodd, who found Beauties in Shakespeare and was the indefatigable friend of London's unfortunates until he took to luxury and excesses, became a forger, and died, as we saw in an earlier chapter, at Tyburn Tree. The square was once the centre of Denmark in London and is still associated with the sea, a school for seamen's children standing where the old Danish church stood, and seamen's institutes abounding hereabouts. Much of the square's ancient character has been preserved, and on one house are still to be seen some very attractive bas-reliefs of children pursuing the arts.

Of the Mint and its streams of silver and gold I have written in "London Revisited." It is an interesting place to see, but I have not been there since sovereigns and half sovereigns were withdrawn.

The Tower Bridge one should climb often, on clear days and misty. The noblest bridge I know (although its stone work is but veneer, and iron its heart), it is imposing howsoever one sees it, broadside, or obliquely, or looking down from the Bridge Approach: with the roadway intact, or the bascules up to let a vessel through. It is the only gateway that London retains.

A few years ago the district over which the Tower Bridge stands as a kind of sentinel, and of which the docks are the mainstay, had no special significance. It was merely largely populated by those that follow the sea or the seaman. But since then has come Mr. Jacobs to make it real, and now no one who knows his engaging stories can ever walk about Wapping and Shadwell, Limehouse and Rotherhithe, without recalling the humour of this writer. It is a high compliment to a novelist and an indication of his triumph when we can say that he has created a new world, although from the circumstance that we say it only of the comic novelists, it has, I suppose, also a suggestion of limitation. A novelist whose characters for the most part behave like real people escapes the compliment: their world is also ours. We do not talk of Thackeray's world, of George Eliot's world. But we talk often of Dickens' world, which means that Dickens' love of eccentricity so impregnated his characters as to give them all a suspicion of family resemblance, branding them of his world rather more perhaps than of ours. Mr. Jacobs also thus stamps his seafaring men, so that we are coming to talk of the Jacobs' world too. Not that he—or not that Dickens—is false to life, but that both, liking people to be as they like them, tone up life a little to please their own sense of fun. It is one of the differences between the realist and the romancist that the romancist wants to give himself pleasure as well as his reader. The realist is more concerned to do only his duty.

I wish that one might enter the Jacobs' world now and then instead of going to Switzerland or Scotland or the other dull countries where one makes formal holiday. But I fear it is not to be; I fear that the differenec between fact and Mr. Jacobs' presentation of it will never be bridged. I have wandered much and listened much in Wapping and Rotherhithe, but have heard no admirable sarcasms, have met no skippers obviously disguised as women. I have listened to night-watchmen, but they have told me no tales like "The Money Box" or "Bill's Lapse." A lighterman at Rotherhithe (on the green balcony of the Angel) once told me a good story, but it is quite unfit for print and belongs peculiarly and painfully to our own world. I have heard the captains of barges and wherries exchanging repartees, but they were for the most part merely beastly. It is sad but true: the Jacobs' world is not accessible. Even if one followed Mr. Jacobs about, I doubt whether one would come to it: none the less may one live in hope as one wanders among the wharves and streets of this amphibious district.

If one would explore it with any thoroughness one must walk from the Tower to the East India Docks: it is all there. But the quickest way to the East India Docks is to take the train from Fenchurch Street—that almost secret city terminus—to Blackwall.

If one were to ask a hundred people to name London's most interesting railway terminus, some would choose Charing Cross, some Waterloo, some Euston, some Paddington, and so forth. Not one would say Blackwall; and yet in its way Blackwall is more interesting than any of these others. The interest of Blackwall station is its unique and romantic situation hard by the north bank of the Thames. You get into the train at Fenchurch Street, and in the company of shipping agents and mates, ships-chandlers and stewards, emigrants and engineers, you travel through the chimney pots and grime of London at its grimiest to this ugly station. And suddenly, having given up your ticket, you pass through a door and are in the open world and a fresh breeze, with the river at your very feet—a wherry or two beating up against the wind, a tug dragging out a schooner, and a great steamer from Hong Kong looking for her berth! It is the completest change, and on a fine day the most exhilarating.

And of all London termini Blackwall is most emphatically a terminus, for another yard and your train would be at the bottom of the East India Docks.

Docks are docks all the world over, and there is little to say of the East India Docks that could not be said of the docks at Barry in Wales, at Antwerp or Hamburg. One is everywhere confronted by the same miracles of berthing and extrication.   Perhaps at the East India Docks the miracles are more miraculous, for the leviathans which lie here are so huge, the waterways and gates so narrow.

The last time I was there I returned on foot—down the East India Docks Road, through Poplar and Limehouse and Stepney: past hospitals and sailors' homes and Radical Clubs, and here and there a grave white church, and here and there, just off the main thoroughfare, a Board School with the side street full of children; and public-houses uncountable, and foreign men on the pavement.

Just by Jack's Palace, a sailors' home, at the corner of the West India Docks Road, I met a little band of five Chinese sailors in dirty blue linen.   They were making, I suppose, for Limehouse Court,—an odd little street which is given up to lodging houses and grocers' shops kept by silent discreet Chinese who have married English women and settled down in London.   They stand at their doors, these stolid Celestials, beneath their Chinese signs, for any one to see, and are, I am told, among the best citizens of the East End and the kindest husbands.

A little west of Jack's Palace one ought to turn off to the south just to see the barges in Limehouse Basin, because it is here that they enter the river from Regent's Canal, that sluggish muddy waterway upon which one is always coming unexpectedly in the north-west district of London, and by which, if one were so minded, one could get right away into the heart of green England. Very stealthily it finds its slow and silent way about London, sometimes underground for quite long distances, as at Islington, where the barges are pulled through by a steel hawser—almost scraping the sides and the roof as they go. By Regent's Park and at Paddington you may see boys angling from the tow path; but no one ever saw them land a fish. I have long intended one day to strike a bargain with a bargee and become his shipmate for a while and see a little of England in this way; but somehow the opportunity never comes. Yet it should, for outside the city—at Hemel Hempsted or Berkhamsted for example—these craft are gay and smiling as any in Holland, and the banks are never dull.

At the hospital just opposite the entrance to the East India Docks and the Blackwall Tunnel—that curious subterranean and subaqueous roadway beneath the Thames, through which one may ride on the top of an omnibus, as one rides beneath Kingsway in a tram— notice boards are set up asking the drivers, for the sake of those that are ill within, to walk their horses past the building. That is a common enough request, but what gives it a peculiar interest here is that the carter, having complied (or not) with the modest demand, is confronted at the end of the façade by another board saying "Thank you, driver."

The Rotherhithe Tunnel is newer: an endless glazed tube with reverberating echoes, in which traffic is like thunder.

In this and other of the poorer quarters of London, where every one else is engaged in the struggle for life, one feels a little that it is an impertinence to be inquisitively wandering at all: that one has no right here unless one is part of the same machine. A little bold Jewess, aged nine or thereabouts, on her way home from school, seemed to share this view, for she looked at me with impudently scrutinising eyes (not ceasing the while to scratch her leg), and then shouted something which I failed to understand but which her companion enjoyed to the full. It was an epithet of scorn, I am sure, and it seemed to challenge my right to be there, doing nothing but examining the fauna of the district for superior literary purposes. And I quite agreed with her. I left her still scratching her leg, the triumphant heroine of her circle, the satisfied author of the *mot juste.*

CHAPTER XIV

WHITECHAPEL AND THE BORO'

East of Bishopsgate—A new London and a New People—Love and Death—A Little Tragedy—The Female Lightning Extractor— A broad and vivid Road—The Trinity Almshouses—Epping Forest —Victoria Park—The Sandbank and the People's Palace—The Ghetto—Norton Folgate—The Bookstalls of London—The Paris Quais—Over London Bridge—St. Saviour's—Two Epitaphs— Debtors' Prisons—Dickens and Chaucer—Guy's Hospital.

LONDON east of Bishopsgate Street is another city altogether. It leads its own life, quite independent of the west, has its own social grades, its own pleasures, its own customs and code of morality, its own ambitions, its own theatres and music halls, its own smart set. The West End is in the habit of pitying the East: but the young bloods of the Mile End Road, which is at once the Bond Street, Strand and Piccadilly of this city, have as much reason to pity the West End. Life goes quite as merrily here: indeed, more so. There is a Continental bustle in this fine road—a finer, freer road than the rest of London can boast—and an infinitely truer feeling of friendliness. People know each other here. Friends on 'buses whistle to friends on the pavements. Talkative foreigners lend cheerfulness and picturesqueness. In the summer the fruit stalls are almost continuous—in early autumn purple with grapes. Nowhere else in London, in England, is fruit so eaten. Sunday here is no day of gloom: to a large part of the population it is shopping day, to a large part it is the only holiday.

There is no call to pity the Mile End Road or Whitechapel High Street. It is they rather than Bloomsbury
and Bayswater that have solved the problem of how to
live in London. If the art of life is, as I believe, largely
the suppression of self-consciousness, these people are
artists. They are as frank and unconcerned in their
courtships as the West Enders are in their shopping.
They will embrace on the top of a 'bus: anywhere. The
last summer evening I was in the Mile End Road Cupid
was terrifically busy.

But the last winter day I was there, I remember, it
was the other end of life that was more noticeable; for
funeral after funeral went by, all very ostentatious and
all at the trot. Most of them were babies' funerals: one
carriage only, with the poor little coffin under the box
seat, and the driver and bearer in white hat bands; but
one was imposing indeed, with a glass hearse under bushes
of plumes—an ostrich-feather shrubbery, a splendid coffin
snowed under flowers, half a dozen mourning coaches
filled with men and women in the blackest of black, three
four-wheelers, a hansom or so, two crowded wagonettes
of the kind that licensed victuallers own and drive on
Sundays, and a market cart packed with what seemed to
be porters from Spitalfields market. I guessed the
deceased to have been a fruit salesman. He was going
home well, as those that die in the East End always do.
No expense is spared then.

These many babies' funerals reminded me vividly of
my first visit to the East End in the eighteen-nineties.
A girl of sixteen, a hand in an umbrella shop, unmarried,
had become a mother, and her baby had died under suspicious circumstances. The case was in the papers, and
a humanitarian friend of mine who was not well enough
to go herself asked me to try and see the girl or her
people and find out if she needed any help. So I went.
The address was a house in one of the squalid streets off
the Commercial Road, and when I called the landlady

said that the girl was at work again and would not be
in for two hours. These hours I spent roaming the neighbourhood, for some time fascinated by the despatch, the
cleverness and the want of principle of a woman who
sold patent medicines from a wagonette, and pulled out
teeth for nothing by way of advertisement. Tooth after
tooth she snatched from the bleeding jaws of the Commercial Road, beneath a naphtha lamp, talking the while
with that high-pitched assurance which belongs to women
who have a genius for business, and selling pain-killers
and pills by the score between the extractions.

After a while I went back to the house and found the
little wan mother, a wistful but wholly independent child,
who was already perplexed enough by offers of help from
kindly aliens in that other London (to say nothing of
local missionaries), but had determined to resume her
own life as if nothing had happened. And so I came
away, but not before her landlord had pitched a tale of
his own embarrassments that far transcended, to his mind,
any difficulty that the girl might be in. And then I rode
back to London on a 'bus, behind a second engineer who
was taking a Limehouse barmaid to the Tivoli.

I believe that an observant loiterer in the Mile End
Road would bring away a richer harvest than from any
street in London. There seems to me always to be light
there, and it is so wide and open that one's eyes are not
worried and perplexed. Here also, and in its continua-
tions, the Whitechapel High Street and Aldgate, one can
reconstruct the past almost more easily than anywhere
in London. There are fewer changes; the width of the
road has not been tampered with; some of the inns still
retain their sign posts with a swinging sign; and many
old houses remain—such as those in Butchers' Row in
Aldgate, one of the most attractive collections of seventeenth-century façades that have been left. There is
something very primitive and old-English in the shops
too, not only of the butchers, but the ancient wine mer-

chant's in the midst of them, whose old whisky is very warming to the dealers who assemble for the hay market in the middle of the road, just above here, three mornings a week.

The Whitechapel Art Gallery has periodical exhibitions that are always worth visiting, for they are arranged with a taste both catholic and fine.

But the architectural jewel of the Mile End Road is the Trinity Almshouses—a quiet square of snug little residences dating from the seventeenth century, for old men who have been mariners, and old women who are mariners' widows or daughters—sixty and more of them. In the midst is a grass plot, and at the end a chapel, and the Governor's house is by one gate and the Reading Room by the other. Home is the sailor, home from the sea, in this still backwater; and here he smokes and gossips till the end, within sound of the roar not of his ancient element but of humanity.

On a fine Sunday afternoon in summer the Mile End Road is crowded with vehicles—dog-carts, wagonettes, donkey-carts, every kind of democratic and obsolete carriage, in addition to motor 'buses, on their way to Wanstead and Epping and the River Lea, which is east London's Jordan. Epping Forest is out of the scheme of this book, or I could write of it with some fervour: of its fine seclusion and its open air, its thickets of hornbeam and groves of beech, its gorse and rivulets, its protected birds and deer, its determined roads and shy footpaths, and its occasional straggling Georgian towns. The Forest, although motor cars rush through it, is properly the last stronghold of the gig; the bicycle also, which is fast disappearing from patrician roads, may still be counted in its thousands here. Epping Forest knows nothing of progress: with perfect content and self-satisfaction it hugs the past and will hug it. It is still almost of the days of *Pickwick*, certainly not more recent than Leech.

The Sunday gigs and wagonettes, the donkey-carts and

bicycles are, as I say, on their way to Epping and the
open country: the trams and omnibuses are packed with
people bound for one of the cemeteries or Victoria Park.
This park, which lies between Hackney and Bethnal
Green, is a park indeed: an open space that is really used
and vanted, in a way that Hyde Park and Regent's Park
and St. James's Park are not wanted.   London in its
western districts would still have air without them; but
Hackney and Bethnal Green would have nothing were it
not for Victoria Park.   Battersea Park is made to do its
work with some thoroughness; but it is a mere desolate
unpeopled waste compared with Victoria Park.   Whether
the sandbank, which a few years ago was placed there for
children to dig in, still remains, I know not: but when I
was there last in warm weather, a few summers since, it
was more populous than an ant hill and the most successful practical amelioration of a hard lot that had been
known—in a district which had just seen the total failure
of the People's Palace, that huge building in the Mile
End Road that was to civilise and refine this wonderful
East End nation, but which all too soon declined into a
college and a desert.   I sometimes doubt indeed if it is
not the Mile End Road's destiny to civilise the rest of
London.   As I have said, these people lead far more
genuine and sensible lives—and to do that, though it may
not be all civilisation, is a long way towards it.

There is no difficulty in naming the prevailing type in
Aldgate and Whitechapel High Street—olive skin, dark
hair, hook nose.   Here the Jews predominate.   But if you
would see them in their masses, unleavened by Christian,
go to Middlesex Street (which used to be called Petticoat
Lane) on Sunday, or Wentworth Street any day except
Saturday.   Wentworth Street is almost impassable for its
stalls and chafferers.   Save for its grime, it is impossible
to believe it in England and within a few minutes of the
Bank.   The faces are foreign; the clothes are foreign,
nearly all the women being wrapped in dark red shawls;

the language is largely foreign, Yiddish being generally known here; and many of the articles on the stalls are foreign—from pickled fish and gherkins to scarfs of brilliant hue. Most of the Jews one sees hereabouts have some connection with the old clothes trade, the central exchange of which is just off Houndsditch—in Phil's Buildings—for the right to enter which you pay a penny, and once inside would gladly pay five shillings to be let out. Yet I suppose there are people who take season tickets.

Norton Folgate and Shoreditch are very different from Whitechapel High Street and the Mile End Road. They are quieter and much narrower. But they too have their old houses, and a chemist at a corner, I notice, still retains his old sign of a Golden Key. The London streets in the days of the hanging signs and gables must have been very picturesque. One does not see that we have gained anything to compensate for their loss—electric light and roll shutters do not count at all in the balance. Spital Square, off Norton Folgate, has been little impaired by the rebuilder, and some of its Georgian doors might open at any moment, one feels, to allow a silk merchant in knee-breeches to step forth.

Shoreditch, like Aldgate High Street, has its stalls: many for whelks and oysters, which are steadily patronised, quite as a matter of course, all day long, and a few for old books. I bought for threepence when I was there last a very unprincipled satire in verse on poor Caroline of Brunswick, entitled "Messalina"; a work on Female Accomplishment (as much unlike the other as a book could be); and "Little Henry and His Bearer." The Aldgate stalls are famous for the bargains one may find there; but one must look long under unfavourable conditions, and I have had no luck. The Farringdon Street stalls have served me better. London having no quays, as Paris has, it is here and to the Charing Cross Road that one must go for old books—to Aldgate and Farringdon Street in particular. I wonder that the West

End has no street of stalls where one might turn over books and prints.

The Embankment, since it leads nowhere, is utterly neglected. The Londoner hates to be out of the swim, and therefore he would rather be jostled in Parliament Street and Whitehall, the Strand and Fleet Street, on his way to Blackfriars from Westminster, than walk direct but unaccompanied beside the river. Hence a mile of good broad coping on the Embankment wall is unused, where in Paris it would be bright with trays of books and prints and curiosities.

It is at Aldgate that on the east the city proper ends; but although the pump still stands, the gate is no more Chaucer was once the tenant of the dwelling-house over the gate and, being a wine merchant, of the cellars beneath it. Mention of the poet reminds me that we have not yet been to the Borough to see the Tabard; and this is a good opportunity—by 'bus—it will need two 'buses—to London Bridge. Not the London Bridge of the old prints, with its houses and shops massed higher and thicker than any on Firenze's Ponte Vecchio, but the very utilitarian structure that ousted it.

London Bridge is the highest point to which great vessels can come: beyond are only tugs and such minor craft as can lower their funnels or masts and so creep beneath the arches. It has always typified London's business to me, because when I used as a child to come to town on my way to school, we came to London Bridge station, and the first great excitement was to cross the river here: the second, to lunch at Crosby Hall amid Tudor trappings. I still always loiter on London Bridge —looking over at the bustling stevedores and listening to the donkey engines and the cranes. From this point the Tower Bridge is the gate of London indeed, and the Tower indescribably solemn and medieval. St. Dunstan's-in-the-East hangs in the sky, a fairy spire, the only white and radiant thing amid the dun and grey.

St. Saviour's, which is now grandly known as Southwark Cathedral, is architecture of a different type, but it is beautiful too and sits as comfortably as any brooding hen. It is interesting both in its old parts and its new —very new indeed, but harmonious, and carefully reproducing what has been lost. In the vestry you may still see a Norman arch or two from the twelfth century. After a fire in the thirteenth century it was built again; and again and again since has it been enlarged and repaired. But it should now rest a while, secure from masons. Be sure to ask the verger for the story of St. Mary Overy, who founded the priory of which this is the church: he tells it better than I could, and believes it too. He will also give you some interesting views on American glass as you stand before the window presented by Harvard University, and will recite epitaphs to you, with much taste and feeling, including the lines on the World's Nonsuch, a beautiful and holy virgin of fourteen. Among these epitaphs is one upon Lockyer, the Cockle and Holloway, Beecham and Carter of his time—the middle of the seventeenth century:—

> His Virtues and his Pills are so well known
> That Envy can't confine them under Stone.
> But they'll survive his dust and not expire
> Till all things else at th' Universal Fire.

Yet where are the pills of Lockyer? Where are the galleons of Spain? Of another worthy parishioner, Garrard, a grocer, it was written:—

> Weep not for him, since he is gone before
> To Heaven, where Grocers there are many more.

The church has old tombs and new windows, those in the new nave being very happily chosen and designed: one to Shakespeare, for his connection with Bankside and its Theatres; one to Massinger, who is buried here; one to John Fletcher, who is buried here too; one to Alleyn the actor; one to Gower, the Father of English Poetry, who is buried here and founded a chantry; one to Chaucer, who sent forth his pilgrims from the Tabard hard by; and one to Bunyan, erected with pennies subscribed by Southwark children. Although the church is so lenient to literature and the stage, no hero from the neighbouring bear pit and bull-baiting arena is celebrated here.

The Tabard to-day is just a new inn on the site of the old and is not interesting; but there is an inn close to it, a few yards north, on the east side of the High Street, which preserves more of old coaching London than any that is now left, and is, I think, the only one remaining that keeps its galleries. I mean the George. When I came to London the White Hart, a little to the north of this, still retained its yard and galleries—just as in the days when Samuel Weller was the boots here and first met Mr. Pickwick on his way to catch Jingle and Miss Wardle. So did the Bull and the Bell in Holborn. But these have all been renewed or removed, and the George is now alone. It stands in its yard, painted a cheerful colour, and the coffee room has a hot fire and high-backed bays to sit in, and the bar is a paradise of bottles. Surely the spirit of Dickens, who so loved the Borough, broods here. Surely the ghosts of Bob Sawyer and Ben Allen drop in now and then from Lant Street, and it is not too far for Mr. Micawber's genial spook to send for a bottle of something encouraging, from the King's Bench prison.

One generally has the feeling that one is in a London of a many years earlier date than that across London Bridge. Perhaps it is beer that keeps progress in check, for the hop merchants congregate here.

The church of St. George the Martyr—brick and stone (you see the spire in Hogarth's "Southwark Fair")— brings other memories of Dickens, for it was in the vestry here that little Dorrit slept, while the prisoners who died in the Marshalsea and King's Bench prison lie in its burial ground, now partly built over. The King's Bench prison, which existed so largely for debtors, had many illustrious

ST. DUNSTAN'S-IN-THE-EAST

visitors besides Mr. Micawber, sent thither not only by the eternal want of pence but also for some of the more positive offences. Among them was John Wilkes (for libel), Haydon, who painted his "Mock Election" here, William Combe, who wrote Syntax's Tours here, and William Hone, who edited his "Table Book" while in captivity. Hone was not in the prison but in its "rules"— which included several streets round about, but no public-house and no theatre. Alleviations were however found. The Dorrit family were in the Marshalsea, which adjoined the King's Bench and had, like all the debtors' prisons, a skittle alley in which the gentlemen might, in Dickens's phrase, "bowl down their troubles." If you walk into Leyton's Buildings, which is very old and picturesque and has a noble timber yard at the end of it, you will be within this prison area. The Marshalsea not only harboured gentlemen who could not meet their bills, but had a compound for smugglers also. Nearly three hundred years ago some of the sweetest notes that ever struck a bliss upon the air of a prison cell rose from the Marshalsea, for here George Wither wrote his "Shepherd's Hunting."

One should certainly walk up St. Thomas's Street, if only to see the doorway of the house to the east of the Chapter House, and also to peep into Guy's, so venerable and staid and useful, and so populous with students and nurses, all wearing that air of resolute and assertive good health—more, of immortality—that always seems to belong to the officers of a hospital. And yet—and yet— John Keats was once a student at this very institution!

CHAPTER XV

HOLBORN AND BLOOMSBURY

The changing Seasons—London at her best—Signs of Winter—
True Londoners—Staple Inn—Ely Place—Gray's Inn—Lord Bacon
—Dr. Johnson and the Bookseller—Bedford Row—The Foundling
Hospital—Sunday Services—Culture and Advanced Theology—The
Fifth Commandment—Queen Square—Edward Irving—Lord Thur-
low—Red Lion Square and the Painters—St. George's and the
Brewer—St. Giles's—Bloomsbury—Gower Street and the Wall
Fruit—Egypt and Greece in London.

I HAVE so often by a curious chance been in Holborn
on those days in February and October when the
certainty of spring and winter suddenly makes itself
felt that I have come to associate the changing seasons
inseparably with that road. One can be very conscious
there of the approach of spring, very sure that the reign
of winter is at hand. Why, I do not know, unless it is
that being wide and on high ground Holborn gives the
Londoner more than his share of sky, and where else
should we look for portents?

I must confess to becoming very restless in London in
the early spring. As one hurries over the asphalt the
thought of primroses is intolerable. And London has a
way of driving home one's losses by its many flower-sellers
and by the crocuses and daffodils in the parks. But later
—after the first rapture is over and the primroses no
longer have to be sought but thrust themselves upon one
—I can remain in London with more composure and wait
for the hot weather. London to my mind has four periods
when she is more than tolerable, when she is the most

THE ADORATION OF THE KINGS
FROM THE PAINTING BY JAN GOSSART DE MABUSE IN THE NATIONAL GALLERY

desirable abode of all. These are May, when the freshness
of the leaves and the clarity of the atmosphere unite to
lend her an almost Continental brightness and charm;
August at night; November at dusk when the presages
of winter are in the air; and the few days before Christmas,
when a good-natured bustle and an electric excitement and
anticipation fill the streets. Were I my own master (or
what is called one's own master) I would leave London
immediately after Christmas and never set foot in her
precincts again till the first match at Lord's; and soon
after that I would be off again.

But November would see me back; for although London
beneath a May sun is London at her loveliest, it is when
the signs of winter begin to accumulate that to me she
is most friendly, most homely. I admire her in May, but
I am quite ready to leave her: in November I am glad
that I shall not be going away for a long time. She
assumes the winter garb so cheerfully and naturally. With
the first fog of November she begins to be happy. "Now,"
one seems to hear her say, "now I am myself again.
Summer was all very well, but clear air and warmth
are not really in my line. I am a grey city and a dingy:
smoke is the breath of my life: stir your fires and let
us be comfortable and gloomy again." In the old days
one of the surest signs of winter in London was straw
in the 'buses; but there is not much of it now. The
chestnut roasters, however, remain: still as certain har-
bingers of the winter as the swallows are of the summer.
At the street corners you see their merry little furnaces
glowing through the peep-holes, and if you will, and are
not ashamed, you may fill your pockets with two-penny-
worth, and thus, at a ridiculously small expenditure,
provide yourself with food and hand-warmers in one. A
foreign chestnut-vendor whom I saw the other day in
the Strand kept supplies both of roast chestnuts and ice-
cream on the same barrow, so that his patrons by pur-
chasing of each could, alternately eating and licking,

transport themselves to July or December, Spitzbergen
or Sierra Leone.   The hot-potato men are perennials,
although perhaps they ply their business with less assiduity
in summer than winter.   I like best those over whose
furnace is an arch of spikes, each one impaling a Magnum
Bonum—like the heads that used to ornament Temple
Bar.   ("Behold the head of a tater," as a witty lady
once remarked.)   The sparrows now are a thought tamer
than in summer, and the pigeons would be so if that
were possible.   The chairs have all gone from the
parks.

From the fact that I have already confessed to a desire
to leave London for quite long periods, and from the
confession which I now make that few pleasures in life
seem to me to surpass the feeling of repose and anticipation and liberty that comes to one as one leans back in
the carriage of an express train steaming steadily and
noiselessly out of one of the great London stations, the
deduction is easy that I am but an indifferent Londoner.
With the best intentions in the world I cannot have
deceived any reader into thinking me a good one.   I am
too critical: the true Londoner loves his city not only
passionately but indiscriminately.   She is all in all to
him.   He loves every aspect of her, every particular,
because all go to the completion of his ideal, his mistress.
None the less (although I suggest that my travels would
assist in disqualifying me), his love does not prevent him
from leaving her: you meet true Londoners all over the
world; indeed it is abroad that you find them most
articulate, for the London tendency to ridicule emotion
and abbreviate displays of sentiment (except on the melodramatic stage) prevents them at home from showing
their love as freely as they can do abroad.   At home they
are sardonic, suspicious, chary of praise; but in the lonely
places of the earth and in times of depression all the
Londoner comes out.

Every one knows how Private Ortheris, in Mr. Kipling's

story, went mad in the heat of India and babbled not of
green fields but of the Strand and the Adelphi arches,
orange peel, wet pavements and flaring gas jets; and on
the day on which I am writing these words I find in a
paper a quotation from an article in a medical magazine,
by the lady superintendent of a country sanatorium for
consumptives, who says that once having a patient who
was unmistakably dying, and having written to his friends
to receive him again, they replied that his home off the
Euston Road was so wretched that they hoped she could
keep him; which she would have done but for the man
himself, who implored her to send him back "where he
could hear once more the 'buses in the Euston Road."
There, in these two men, one in India and one dying in
East Anglia, speaks the true Londoner. No transitory
visitor to the city can ever acquire this love; I doubt
if any one can who did not spend his childhood in
it.

The Londoner speaking here is the real thing: the
home sickness which he feels is not to be counterfeited.
It is not the least sad part of Charles Lamb's latter days
that he was doomed to Enfield and Edmonton, and that
when he did get to London now and then it was peopled
by ghosts and knew him not. No wonder he shed tears
to find that St. Dunstan's iron figures—the wonders of
his infancy, as those in Cheapside have been the wonders
of ours—had vanished. This is the real love of London,
which I for one cannot pretend to, much as I should
value it. London is neither my mother nor my stepmother; but I love her always a little, and now and then
well on the other side of idolatry.

There is that other type of Londoner, too, that is in
love not with its sights and savours but with its intellectual variety—a type fixed for me in the late Theodore
Watts-Dunton, whom when, almost a boy, I was for the
first time in his company, I heard say that he "dared
not leave London for fear some new and interesting

figure should arrive during his absence and be missed by him."

Meanwhile what of Holborn and Bloomsbury?

Holborn is chiefly remarkable for that row of old houses opposite Gray's Inn Road which gives so false an impression of this city to visitors who enter it at Euston or St. Pancras or King's Cross, and speeding down the Gray's Inn Road in their hansoms, see this wonderful piece of medievalism before them. "Is London like that?" they say; and prepare for pleasures that will not be fulfilled. The houses, which are piously preserved by the Prudential directors, form the north side of Staple Inn, one of the quietest and most charming of the small Inns of Court, with trees full of sparrows, whose clamour towards evening is incredibly assertive, and a beautiful little hall. It is all very old and rather crazy, and it would be well for us now to see it as often as we can, lest its knell suddenly sound and we have not the chance again. Something of the same effect of quietude is to be obtained in the precincts of the Mercers' School, a little to the east, especially in the outer court; but this is a very minute backwater. For quietude with space you must seek Gray's Inn.

But before exploring Gray's Inn one might look into Ely Place on the other side of the road, at the beginning of Charterhouse Street, for it is old and historic, marking the site of the palace where John of Gaunt died. Sir Christopher Hatton, who danced before Elizabeth, secured a part of the building and made himself a spacious home there, a tenancy still commemorated by Hatton Garden, close by, where the diamond merchants have their mart. Ely Place, as it now stands, was built at the end of the eighteenth century, but the chapel of the ancient palace still remains, and has passed to the Roman Catholics, who have made it beautiful. The crypt is one of the quietest sanctuaries in London.

Gray's Inn has let the rebuilder in here and there, but

he has been well watched, and in a very little time, under London's grimy influence, his work will fall into line with the Inn's prevailing style. The large Square is still the serene abode of antiquity—not too remote, but sufficiently so for peace. The most illustrious of Gray's Inn's members is Francis Bacon, Lord Verulam, who acted as its treasurer and kept his rooms here to the end. He identified himself with all the activities of the Inn, grave and gay, and helped in laying out its gardens. To meditate upon the great Chancellor most fittingly one must saunter at evening in Gray's Inn Walk, beneath the trees, the descendants of those which he planted with his own hand. It was here perhaps that his own sage and melodious thoughts on gardens came to him.

Among Gray's Inn's other illustrious residents for long or short periods were Ritson the antiquary and vegetarian, Oliver Goldsmith, Southey and Macaulay. It was behind Gray's Inn that Mr. Justice Shallow fought with Sampson Stockfish, a fruiterer. Tonson, the publisher and book-seller, had his shop by Gray's Inn Gate in Holborn before he moved to the Shakespeare's Head in the Strand. Osborne, the bookseller of "impassive dulness," and "en-tirely destitute of shame," whom Dr. Johnson knocked down, had his shop here too. The story goes that the Great Lexicographer there floored him with a folio and set his learned foot upon his neck; but this, it is sad to relate, was not so. "Sir, he was impertinent to me and I beat him. But it was not in his shop: it was in my own chambers"—that is the true version. Booksellers (perhaps from fear) have rather abandoned this neigh-bourhood now, although there are a few in the little alleys about—in Red Lion Passage for example, and in both Turnstile Streets; but curiosity shops abound.

Through Gray's Inn one may gain Bedford Row, which might almost be a part of the inn itself, so quiet and Georgian is it—the best-preserved and widest Georgian

street in London, occupied in its earliest days by aristocrats and plutocrats, but now wholly in the hands of the
Law. I like to think it was at No. 14 that Abernethy
fired prescriptions and advice at his outraged patients.
Bedford Row is utterly un-modern.

I noted as I passed through it one day recently a
carriage and pair of old-fashioned build drawn up before
one of the houses. It had the amplitude of the last
century's youth. There was no rumble, but had there
been one it would have seemed no excrescence. A coronet
was on the panel, and the coachman was aged and comfortable and serene. The footman by the door had also
the air of security that comes of service in a quiet and
ancient family. Suddenly from the sombre Georgian
house emerged a swift young clerk with a sign to the
waiting servants. The coachman's back lost its curve,
the venerable horses lifted their ears, the footman stood
erect and vigilant, as a little, lively, be-ribboned lady and
her portly and dignified man of law appeared in the
passage and slowly descended the steps. The little lady's
hand was on his arm; she was feeble and very old, and
his handsome white head was bent towards her to catch
her final instructions. They crossed the pavement with
tiny steps, and with old-world gravity and courtesy he
relinquished her to the footman and bowed his farewells.
She nodded to him as the carriage rolled steadily away,
and I had a full glimpse of her face, hitherto hidden by
her bonnet. It wore an expression kindly and relieved,
and I felt assured that her mission had been rather to
add an unexpected and benevolent codicil than to dis-
inherit any one. It all seemed so rightly a part of the
life of Bedford Row.

By Great James Street, which is a northern continua-
tion of Bedford Row on the other side of Theobald's
(pronounced Tibbald's) Road, and, like it, Georgian and
wainscotted with oak and out-moded, one comes to
Mecklenburgh Square and the Foundling Hospital (known

THE MONUMENT

locally as the "Fondling") : the heart of old Bloomsbury. Visitors are shown over the Hospital on certain
days in the week; and I think I advise the visit to be
made. It is a pleasant institution to see, and on the
walls of the long low rooms are some interesting pictures—its founder, the good Captain Coram, painted by
Hogarth, who was closely associated with the charity;
scriptural texts illustrating our duties to the fatherless
translated into paint by the same master and by such
contemporaries as Highmore, Wills and Hayman; portraits of governors by the score; and a portion of a
cartoon by Raphael. Here also may be seen medals
belonging to foundlings who have become warriors; cases
of odd trinkets attached to foundlings in the old days
when these poor little forlorn love-children were deposited
in the permanent cradle at the gates; signatures of kings;
old MSS.; and the keyboard and tuning fork that were
used by the great George Frederick Handel when he was
organist here. All these and other curiosities will be
shown you by a sturdy boy, who will then open the door
suddenly upon foundlings in class, and foundlings at play,
the infant school being packed with stolid and solid
children all exactly alike in their brown clothes and white
pinafores and all profoundly grateful for a visitor to
stare at.

The boys for the most part become soldiers and sailors :
the girls go into service. In the early days the boys
were named after heroes of the battlefield and the
ocean, and the girls after whom I know not, but St. Xita
is their patroness, one and all. To-day there may be a
new system of nomenclature; but if not, one may expect
to find Drakes and Rodneys, Nelsons and Collingwoods,
Beresfords and Fishers, Wellingtons and Havelocks, Gor-
dons and Burnabys, Roberts and Kitcheners, Haigs and
Beattys. The first boy baby admitted was very prettily
named Thomas Coram, and the first girl baby Eunice
Coram, after their kindly stepfather and stepmother.

London, as I have hinted, does little enough for its guests on Sundays; but morning service at the Foundling Hospital must certainly be grouped among its entertainments. We are not as a people given to mingle much taste or charm with our charity: we never quite forgive the pauper or the unfortunate; but there is charm here. Anyone that wishes may attend, provided that he adds a silver coin to the offertory (here emerging the shining usefulness of the threepenny bit!).

Before the Foundling Hospital was built, in 1739, there were fields here, and in 1719 a very early cricket match was played in them between the Men of Kent and the Men of London for £60. I know not which won. At No. 77 Guilford Street, in 1803, lived Sydney Smith. Although in the centre of Queen Square, which leads out of Guilford Street to the west, stands a statue of Queen Charlotte, the enclosure was named after Queen Anne, in whose reign it was built. Many traces of its early state remain. Hospitals now throng here, where once were gentlemen and scholars: among them Antony Askew, physician and Grecian and the friend of all learning; and Dr. Campbell of the "Biographia Britannica," whose house Dr. Johnson frequented until the shivering fear came upon him that the Scotsmen who flocked there might accuse him of borrowing his good things from their countrymen. Another friend of Johnson, Dr. Charles Burney, also lived in Queen Square. In a house on the west side, an architect once told me, is still to be seen a perfect example of an ancient English well. Having no opening into Guilford Street except for foot passengers, Queen Square remains one of the quietest spots in London, and scholars might well live there now. Perhaps they do. Such houses would naturally harbour book-worms and scholiasts. During the War a German bomb fell bang in the middle of the garden.

Few streets have changed less, except in residents, than Gloucester Street, running between Queen Square and

Theobald's Road, which dates from Anne or George I and has all its original architecture, with two centuries of dirt added. It is long and narrow and gives in perfection the old Bloomsbury vista. At No. 19 lodged Edward Irving, the preacher, when he first came to London, little dreaming perhaps that his followers some forty years later were to build the cathedral of the Catholic and Apostolic, or Irvingite, body in Gordon Square. Great Ormond Street, leading out of Queen Square on the east, has much history too, especially at No. 45, lately the Working Men's College, for it was here that Lord Chancellor Thurlow was living when in 1784 the Great Seal was stolen. Here also Thurlow entertained the poet Crabbe and thought him "as like Parson Adams as twelve to a dozen." Macaulay lived at No. 50 from 1823 to 1831, but the house is now no more: part of the Children's Hospital stands on its site. No. 44 Great Ormond Street is one of the most attractive of the old Georgian houses, with some fine ironwork to increase its charm.

From Great Ormond Street we gain Lamb's Conduit Street, which, crossing Theobald's Road, becomes Red Lion Street, an old and narrow street between Bedford Row and Red Lion Square. No. 9 Red Lion Street is famous as being the house in which the firm of William Morris first began its existence and entered upon its career of revolutionising taste in furniture and driving Victorian stuffiness from our houses. At No. 17 Red Lion Square lodged Burne-Jones and Rossetti. Haydon, another painter of individuality, lived on the west side of the square; and Henry Meyer, at his studio at No. 3, in the spring of 1826, gave sittings to a little dark gentleman in knee-breeches with a fine Titian head "full of dumb eloquence," who had just left the India House on a pension—Charles Lamb by name. The picture may be seen at the India Office in Whitehall to-day, commemorating if not the most assiduous of its clerks the

one who covered its official writing paper with the best
and tenderest literature.

Between Red Lion Square and the British Museum,
whither we are now bound, one object of interest alone is
to be seen—St. George's Church in Hart Street, famous
for its pyramidal spire, culminating in a statue not of
George the Saint but of George the First; placed there,
to London's intense amusement, by Hucks the brewer.
Hogarth, who liked to set a London spire in the back-
ground of his satirical scenes, has this in his terrible
"Gin Lane," just as St. Giles, close by, is in his "Beer
Street." Munden the actor, whose grimaces and drol-
leries Lamb has made immortal, was buried in the churchyard of St. George's, now transformed into a recreation
ground. Above the old player with the bouquet of faces
Bloomsbury children now frolic.

St. Giles's-in-the-Fields is so near that we ought perhaps
to glance at it before exploring the Museum and the rest
of Bloomsbury. It is still in the midst of not too savoury
a neighbourhood, although no longer the obvious antipodes
to St. James's that it used to be in literature and
speech. When we want contrasts now we speak of the
West End and the East End. St. Giles's is a dead
letter. The present church is not so old as one might
think: much later than Wren: and it is interesting
rather for its forerunner's name than for itself, and also
for being the last resting-place of such men as George
Chapman, who translated Homer into swinging Elizabethan English, and the sweetest of garden poets, Andrew
Marvell.

Bloomsbury, which is the adopted home of the econ-
omical American visitor and the Hindu student; Bloomsbury, whose myriad boarding-houses give the lie to the
poet's statement that East and West can never meet;
is bounded on the south by Oxford Street and High
Holborn; on the north by the Euston Road; on the
east by Southampton Row; and on the west by Totten-

ham Court Road. It has few shops and many residents, and is a stronghold of middle-class respectability and learning. The British Museum is its heart: its lungs are Bedford Square and Russell Square, Gordon Square and Woburn Square: and its aorta is Gower Street, which goes on for ever. Lawyers and law students live here, to be near the Inns of Court, and bookish men live here, to be near the Museum; Bloomsbury is discreet and handy: it is near everything, and although not fashionable, any one, I understand, may live there without losing caste. It belongs to the Ducal House of Bedford, which has given its names very freely to its streets and squares.

To my mind Gower Street is not quite old enough to be interesting, but it has had some very human inhabitants of eminence, and has one or two still. Millais lived with his father at No. 87; the great Peter de Wint, who painted English cornfields as no one ever did before or since, died at No. 40. In its early days Gower Street was famous for—what? Its rural character and its fruit. Mrs. Siddons lived in a house there, the back of which was "most effectually in the country and delightfully pleasant"; while Lord Eldon's peaches (at the back of No. 42), Col. Sutherland's grapes (at No. 33), and William Bentham's nectarines were the talk of all who ate them.

Every one who cares for the beautiful sensitive art of John Flaxman, the friend of Blake, should penetrate to the dome of University College, where is a fine collection of his drawings and reliefs. In the Rotunda has lately been placed a mural painting by Professor Tonks commemorating the War. The College also possesses the embalmed body of Jeremy Bentham, who sits in a glass case dressed in his Quakerish clothes. On his shoulders is a new head made of wax; at his feet is his real one, mummified. Other objects of interest in this neighbourhood are the allegorical frescoes at University Hall in

Gordon Square, filled with portraits of great Englishmen;
the memorial to Christina Rossetti in Christ Church,
Woburn Square; and two unexpected and imposing
pieces of architecture—St. Pancras Church in the Euston
Road, and Euston station. Euston station, seen at night
or through a mist, is one of the most impressive sights
in London. As Aubrey Beardsley, the marvellous youth
who perished in his decadence, used to say, Euston station
made it unnecessary to visit Egypt. I would not add
that St. Pancras Church makes it unnecessary to visit
Greece; but it is a very interesting summary of Greek
traditions, its main building being an adaptation of the
Ionic temple of the Erechtheion on the Acropolis at Athens,
its tower deriving from the Horologium or Temple of the
Winds, and its dependencies, with their noble caryatides,
being adaptations of the south portico of the Pandroseion,
also at Athens.

Bloomsbury, as I have said, gives harbourage to all
colours, and the Baboo law student is one of the common-
est incidents of its streets. But the oddest alien I ever
saw there was in the area of the house of a medical friend
in Woburn Square. While waiting on the steps for the
bell to be answered I heard the sound of brushing, and
looking down, I saw a small negro boy busily polishing a
boot. He glanced up with a friendly smile, his eyes and
teeth gleaming, and I noticed that on his right wrist was
a broad ivory ring. "So you're no longer an Aboli-
tionist!" I said to the doctor when I at last gained his
room. "No," he answered: "at least, my sister isn't.
That's a boy my brother-in-law has just brought from
West Africa. He didn't exactly want him, but the boy
was wild to see England, and at the last minute jumped
on board." "And what does the ring on his arm mean?"
I asked. "Oh, he's a king's son out there. That's a symbol
of authority. At home he has the power of life and
death over fifty slaves."

When I came away the boy was still busily at work,

but he had changed the boots for knife-cleaning. He cast another merry smile up to me as I descended the steps—the king's son with the power of life and death over fifty slaves.

CHAPTER XVI

THE BRITISH MUSEUM AND SOHO

The Bloomsbury History of the World—Great statuary—Julius Cæsar and Demeter—The Elgin Marbles—Terra-cotta and bronze—MSS.—London's foreign quarter—Soho Square and Golden Square—Soho—Cheap restaurants—The old artists' quarter—Wardour Street and Berners Street—The great Hoax—Madame Tussaud's—Clothes without Illusion—The Chamber of Horrors—Thoughts on the Killing of Men—The Vivifying of "Little Arthur"—Waxworks at Night—An Experience in the Edgware Road.

THE British Museum is the history of the world: in its Bloomsbury galleries the history of civilisation, in its Cromwell Road galleries the history of nature. The lesson of the Museum is the transitoriness of man and the littleness of his greatest deeds. That is the burden of its every Bloomsbury room. The ghosts of dead peoples, once dominant, inhabit it; the dust of empires fills its air. One may turn in from Oxford Street and in half an hour pass all the nations of the earth, commanding and servile, cultured and uncouth, under review. The finest achievements of Greek Sculpture are here, and here are the painted canoes of the South Sea islander; the Egyptian Book of the Dead is here, and here, in the Reading Room, is a copy of the work you are now judiciously skipping; the obelisk of Shalmaneser is here, and here are cinematoscope records of London street scenes, here are phonographic records of great Englishmen's voices.

It is too much for one mind to grasp. Nor do I try. The Roman Emperors, the Græco-Roman sculptures, the

JEAN ARNOLFINI AND JEANNE, HIS WIFE
AFTER THE PICTURE BY JAN VAN EYCK IN THE NATIONAL GALLERY

bronzes, the terra-cottas, the Etruscan vases, the gems, the ceramics and glass, the prints, the manuscripts, the Egyptian rooms—these, with the Reading Room, are my British Museum. Among the other things I am too conscious of the typical museum depression: it is all so bleak and instructive.

In vain for me have the archipelagos of the Pacific been ransacked for weapons and canoes; in vain for me have spades been busy in Assyria and Babylonia. Primitive man does not interest me, and Nineveh was not human enough. Not till the Egyptians baked pottery divinely blue and invented most of civilisation's endearing ways did the world begin for me; but I could spare everything that Egypt has yielded us rather than the Demeter of Cnidos, the serenest thing in England, or the head of Julius Cæsar. For although at the Museum the interesting predominates over the beautiful, the beautiful is here too; more than the beautiful, the sublime. For here are the Elgin Marbles: the Three Fates from the Parthenon, and its bas-reliefs, which are among the greatest works of art that man has achieved. We may not have the Winged Victory of Samothrace, or the Venus of Milo, the Laocoön or the Dying Gladiator; but we have these, and we have the Demeter and the Julius Cæsar and the bronze head of Hypnos, although lately a torso has been attached to this not at all to its advantage. Indeed, I doubt if any of the restorations to broken statuary have been good. The nose given to Demeter fortunately was removed again, in deference to public opinion; but Julia Paula, just inside the Roman Gallery, who used to be so mischievous and charming with her broken *retroussé* is now nothing at all with that organ made long and hooked.

One reaches the sculpture galleries by way of the Roman Gallery, where the Emperors are, culminating in the Julius Cæsar, surely the most fascinating male head ever chiselled from marble. I pause always before the pugi-

listic features of Trajanus, and the Caracalla, so rustic
and determined. In the Second Græco-Roman room is a
superb Diskobolos, and here also is a little beautiful torso
of Aphrodite loosening her sandal—that action in which
the great masters so often placed her, that the exquisite
contour of the curved back might be theirs. My favourites in the Third Græco-Roman room are the head of
Aphrodite from the Towneley Collection—No. 1596; the
boy extracting a thorn from his foot, No. 1755; the head
of Apollo Musagetes, No. 1548, the beauty of which
triumphs over the lack of a nose in the amazing way
that the perfect beauty of a statue will—so much so
indeed that one very soon comes not to miss the broken
portions at all. It is almost as if one acquires a second
vision that subconsciously supplies the missing parts and
enables one to see it whole; or rather prevents one from
noticing that it is incomplete. I love also the head in
Asiatic attire—No. 1769—on the same side, and the
terminal figure opposite—No. 1742—on which the winds
and the rains have laid their softening hand.

But all these give way to the Ceres, or Demeter, in the
Greek ante-room. This is to me the most beautiful piece
of sculpture in the British Museum. It came from the
sanctuary of Demeter at Cnidos—a temple to worship in
indeed! I know of no Madonna in the painting of any
old master more maternal and serene and wise and holy
than this marble goddess from the fourth century B.C., a
photograph of which will be found opposite page 186.

In a case on the right of the Ephesus Room, as you
enter from this ante-room, are two gems—another little
Aphrodite, No. 1417, with a back of liquid softness; and
a draped figure of the same goddess, from her temple
at Cyrene—the lower half only—the folds of the dress
being exquisite beyond words.

And so we enter the room which brings more people to
Bloomsbury than any other treasure here—the room of
the Elgin Marbles, which certain sentimentalists would

THE DEMETER OF CNIDOS

AFTER THE STATUE IN THE BRITISH MUSEUM

restore to Greece but which I for one think better here. The group of Fates is the most wonderful; and it is difficult to imagine how much more impressive they would be if they were unmutilated. As it is, they have more dignity and more beauty than the ordinary observer can witness unmoved. Broken fragments as they are, they are the last word in plastic art; and one wonders how the Athenians dared look at their temple in its perfection. On a lower plane, but great and satisfying and beautiful beyond description, are some of the reliefs from the frieze—the perfection of the treatment of the horse in decorative art. Such horses, such horsemen: life and loveliness in every line.

From marble it is interesting to pass to terra-cotta; from the sublime to the charming: from the tremendous to the pretty. It is, however, charm and prettiness of a very high order, some of the little figures from Tanagra and Eretria being exquisite. Note in particular these numbers for their grace and their quaintness: C. 299, an aged nurse and child; C. 278, mother and child; C. 245, a girl with a fan; C. 214, the writing lesson; C. 250, a woman draped and hooded (this is reproduced in the admirable official catalogue); C. 308, a little girl, and C. 196r, a Cupid. The domesticity of so many of these figures—the women with fans, the girls playing astragali, and so forth—always brings to my mind that idyll of Theocritus in which the two frivolous women chat together.

After the terra-cottas we come to the bronzes, chief among which is the wonderful Hypnos from Perugia. Of the treasures of these rooms I can say nothing: they are endless. And so we pass on to the four Vase rooms, and then come to ancient Egypt, where everything that we do now and deem novel and exciting (short of electricity and motors) seems to have been old game.

Parallel with the Egyptian rooms are a series of smaller rooms illustrating the history of religion, leading to the Ethnographical Gallery, which leads in its turn to netsukés (the variety and perfection of which are alike bewildering), ceramics and prints.

The collection of English and foreign pottery and porcelain and glass is fascinatingly displayed, and one may lose oneself completely here, whether it is before Lowestoft and Chelsea or old Greek prismatic glass, Delft or Nankin, Sèvres or Wedgwood, Persian tiles or Rhodian plates.

One reaches the ground floor again by way of the Medieval Room, which contains many odd treasures but is perhaps rather too much like an old curiosity shop, such as Balzac describes in the "Peau de Chagrin" or Stevenson in "Markheim."

But before descending again, one ought to see the ornaments and gems—marvellous intaglios and cameos beyond price from Egypt and Greece and Rome; precious stones of every variety, and wonderful imitations of precious stones of every variety, which, false as they may be, are still quite precious enough for me; gold work of all periods; the famous Portland Vase of blue glass; and frescoes from Pompeii.

One of the most interesting things in the Hall of Inscriptions on the way to the Reading Room is the slab of marble which used to be hung outside a Roman circus, with the words on it, in Latin: "Circus Full. Great Shouting. Doors Closed." Few things bring the modernity of Romans, or the ancientry of ourselves, so vividly before one.

A continuous exhibition of illuminated books, famous MSS., letters and early printed books is held in the cases in the library galleries to the right of the Entrance Hall. Here one may see Books of Mours, Bibles and missals, with quaint and patient drawings by Flemish and Italian artists; the handwriting of kings and scholars, Boer generals and divines; manuscripts of poems by Keats and Pope, illustrating the laborious stages by which perfection is reached; an early story by Charlotte Brontë in

THE EARTHLY PARADISE

FROM THE CHINESE PAINTING IN THE BRITISH MUSEUM

a hand too small to be legible to the naked eye; a commonplace book of Milton's; and books from the presses of Caxton and Gutenberg. Not the least interesting of recent exhibits is Captain Scott's diary open at the page where his hand was numbed for ever. Here also are manuscript pages of the "Iliad" and the "Odyssey" from old Greek libraries, with comments by old Greek scholars.

The gallery adjoining the print rooms, in the new White Building, should be visited constantly, for always there is something new. At the far end is the exquisite "Earthly Paradise," one of the many Chinese paintings that have been acquired since this book was written. Here also are usually Japanese prints. The rest of the great room is given to a changing exhibition of recent acquisitions: chiefly drawings, etchings and water colours by modern artists. No one interested in art can afford to neglect this remarkable place.

It is not until one has wandered in the British Museum for some weeks that one begins to realise how inexhaustible it is. To know it is impossible; but the task of extracting its secrets is made less difficult by acquiring and studying its excellent catalogues, which are on sale in the Entrance Hall. Apart from their immediate use they are very good reading.

The quickest way to Soho from the Museum is down Shaftesbury Avenue; or one may fight one's way through the blended odours of beer, pickles and jam, all in the making, to Soho Square, and recover one's self-respect in the Roman Catholic church of St. Patrick, which is there. So Italian is its interior that you cannot believe you are in London at all.

Soho proper lies between Oxford Street, Charing Cross Road, Leicester Square, and Warwick Street; but the corresponding parallelogram north of Oxford Street, bounded by the Tottenham Court Road, the Euston Road, and Great Portland Street, is now almost equally foreign, the pavements of Great Portland Street in particular being very cosmopolitan. I have been told that in the Percy Street and Cleveland Street neighbourhood many of the great anarchist plots have been hatched; certain it is that London has offered as many advantages to the political desperado as any city, except perhaps Geneva.

The foreign residents of Soho proper are almost exclusively French; north of Oxford Street we find Italians too. Poorer Italians still, organ grinders from Chiaveri, monkey boys from further south and ice-cream men from Naples, live on Saffron Hill, by Leather Lane; Swiss mechanics live in Clerkenwell; poor Jews live in Whitechapel, as we have seen; middle-class Jews in Maida Vale; rich Jews in Bayswater and Hampstead. American settlers are fond of Hampstead; American visitors like the Embankment hotels or Bloomsbury. Although there are many exceptions, one can generalise quite safely on London's settlements, not only of foreigners, but of professional and artistic groups. Thus the artists live in Chelsea, Kensington, St. John's Wood, and Hampstead; the chief doctors are in and about Harley Street; Music Hall performers like to cross the river on their way home; musicians congregate about Baker Street; Kensington has many literary people.

In addition to Leicester Square, which is however far less French than it used to be, Soho has two squares—Soho Square and Golden Square. It is Soho Square which gives the name to the district—"So ho!" an old cry of the harriers, but why thus applied no one knows. The story that it was previously called Monmouth Square and King's Square, and changed to Soho Square after Sedgmoor, where "So ho!" was Monmouth's battle-call, is, I believe, disproved; the reverse being the fact —the battle-cry coming from the neighbourhood. The Duke of Monmouth was the first resident here—in 1681 —his house being on the south side, between Frith Street

STAPLE INN

and Greek Street. Other residents in the Square were
Sir Cloudesley Shovel, the admiral, "Vathek" Beckford,
and Sir Joseph Banks, the botanist. A statue of Charles
the Second used to stand in the centre, facing the house
of his unlucky natural son. George the Second still
stands in Golden Square, half a mile to the west, which
a few years ago it would have been imperative to visit,
for it had, on the south side, one of the comeliest of
London's Georgian houses; but that too has now gone
and the square is uninteresting. Miss Kilmansegg ought
to have lived here, but did not. Golden Square was,
however, the abode of Ralph Nickleby, and in real life,
among others, of Angelica Kaufmann, the artist (Mrs.
Ritchie's charming "Miss Angel"), and Cardinal Wise-
man, who may or may not have been Bishop Blougram
who apologised.

Soho has never been the same since Shaftesbury Avenue
and the Charing Cross Road ploughed through her midst,
and to eat in her restaurants became a fashion. Before
those days she was a city apart, a Continental city within
a London city, living her own life; but now she is open
to all. In fact you now see more English than French
in her Lisle Street and Gerrard Street and Old Compton
Street restaurants. It is the English who eat there, the
French and Italian proprietors who retire with fortunes.
In the old days Wardour Street may be said to have
been the main artery of Soho, but now her most char-
acteristically French street is Old Compton Street. Here
are comestible shops, exactly as in the Rue St. Honoré,
and the greatest profusion of cheap restaurants, most of
which soon have their day and disappear. Since the
habit of eating away from home has seized London, it
has become quite a pursuit to discover new cheap *tables
d'hôte* in this neighbourhood. We now swap catalogues
of their merits as we used to swap stories.

Many of Soho's streets retain their old character. Gerrard Street, for example, although the headquarters of

telephoning and one of the thoroughfares captured by the cinema industry, is yet full of the past. One of the cheap restaurants here is in Edmund Burke's old house; a little farther east, on the same side, at No. 43, is the house where Dryden died. Both have tablets. At the corner of Gerrard Street and Greek Street, at the Turk's Head, the "Literary Club" which Reynolds founded used to meet. Here also the Artists' Club met; for a hundred and fifty years ago this was the centre of the artists' quarter. Hogarth and Reynolds lived in Leicester Square; Hogarth's painting Academy was in St. Martin's Lane. Reynolds, Wilson, Hayman and Gainsborough met at the Turk's Head with regularity and limited themselves to half a pint of wine apiece. Sir Thomas Lawrence lived in Greek Street, and there Wedgwood had show rooms.

Frith Street was the early home of Edmund Kean, and Macready had lodgings there in 1816. At No. 6 (a tablet marks the house) William Hazlitt died, in 1830. Charles Lamb stood by his bed. "Well, I've had a happy life," said Hazlitt. He was buried at St. Anne's, between Dean Street and Wardour Street.

The artists' quarter extended due north beyond Oxford Street to Newman Street and Berners Street. Dean Street was full of artists—Thornhill, Hayman, Hamilton, Bailey, James Ward, all lived there, and Christie's auction rooms were there too. It was Fanny Kelly, Lamb's friend, who built the Royalty Theatre. In Newman Street lived and died Benjamin West—at No. 14; Stothard at 28. Fanny Kemble was born in this street.

Berners Street is still one of the most sensible streets in London, of a width that modern vestries have not had the wit to imitate. With the Middlesex Hospital at the end it has a very attractive vista. This also was given up to the painters: Fuseli was at No. 13, Opie at No. 8, Henry Bone, whose miniatures we saw at the Wallace Collection, at 15. At No. 7 lived the wretched

Fauntleroy, the banker and forger, whom Bernard Barton, the Quaker poet, was urged by a mischievous friend never to emulate. It was upon the lady at No. 54, a Mrs. Tottingham, that Theodore Hook played his dreary "Berners Street hoax," which consisted in sending hundreds of tradesmen to her door at the same hour with articles she had not ordered and did not want, including a hearse. David Roberts, who painted cathedrals like an angel, did not live here, but it was while walking alone Berners Street that he received the apoplectic stroke from which he died.

If I do not dally longer in this part of London it is because I do not care much for it. It is a little seamy, and after Berners Street no longer quite the real thing —not old enough on the one hand, or clean enough on the other. Let us look at the old curiosity shops of Great Portland Street and so pass through the discreet medical district of Harley Street and Welbeck Street to a British institution which it would never do to miss— Madame Tussaud's.

The imposing red façade of Madame Tussaud's in Marylebone Road must give the foreigner a totally false impression of English taste in amusement; for the exhibition does not really bear the intimate relation to the city that its size might lead one to expect. Who goes to Madame Tussaud's I cannot say. All I know is that whenever I have asked friends and acquaintances of my own (as I have been doing lately) if they have been, they reply in the negative, or date their only visit many years ago. I wonder if men of eminence steal in now and then to see what their effigies are like and what notice they are drawing, as painters are said to lurk in the vicinity of their canvases at the Royal Academy to pick up crumbs of comfort. I wonder if Mr. Kipling has ever seen the demure figure that smirks beneath his name; I wonder if the late Dr. Barnardo really wore, "in the form," as the spiritualists say, a collar such as he wears

in his waxen representation? There is hardly a figure
in this exhibition that conveys any illusion of life.
Their complexions are not right; their hair is not right.
Their clothes are obviously the clothes of the inanimate;
they have no notion what to do with their hands.

Thinking it over, I have come to the conclusion that
not only the unreality, but also the eeriness, almost fear-
someness, of a waxwork, reside principally in its clothes.
A naked waxwork, though unpleasant, would not be so
bad: it is the clothes wanting life to vivify and justify
it that make it so terrible, just as clothes on a corpse
add to the horror of death. One wonders where the
clothes come from. Do they also, like the features and
hair of these figures, approximate to life, or are they
chosen at random? Mr. Burns, it is well known, relinquished one of his blue serge suits in exchange for a new
one; but the others? Lord Balfour, for example? Are
there underclothes too? Does the Tussaud establishment include a tailor and a modiste? To these questions
I could no doubt obtain a satisfactory reply by merely
writing to the exhibition; but there are occasions when
it is more amusing to remain in the domain of conjecture.
This is one.

I wandered into Madame Tussaud's a little while ago
entirely for the purpose of saying something about it in
this book. As it was a foggy day, I had some difficulty
in disentangling the visitors from the effigies; but when
I did so I saw that they wore a provincial air. I felt a
little provincial myself as I passed from figure to figure
and turned to the catalogue to see if I were looking at
the late Daniel Leno or Mr. Asquith.

The Chamber of Horrors at Madame Tussaud's i
London's Cabaret des Néants, London's Wiertz Museum
Horrors are not encouraged in England, and London ha
no other official collection of them, if we except the assem
blage of articles of crime that Scotland Yard cherishes
But jemmies and pistols and knives are not in themselve

horrors, whereas wax decapitated heads dropping blood,
coloured pictures of diseases, models of criminals being
tortured, a hangman and a condemned man on the scaffold
—these exist by virtue of their horrifying power, and you
are asked for an extra sixpence frankly as a payment for
shudders.

It is all ugly and coarse, and in part very silly, as
when you are confronted by a dock crammed with effigies
of the more notorious murderers (the only really interesting murderers, of course, being those who have escaped
detection or even suspicion: but how should Madame
Tussaud's patrons know this?) all blooming with the
ruddy tints of health. But one must not wholly depre-
cate. In the other scale must be put some of the work
of Madame Tussaud herself—her Voltaire, which is to me
one of the most interesting things in London, as his life
mask at the Carnavalet is one of the most interesting
things in Paris; a few of her other heads belonging to
the Reign of Terror, notably the Robespierre; the very
guillotine that shed so much of France's best and bravest
blood; and the relics of Napoleon. We must remember
too that it is very easy and very tempting to be more
considerate for the feelings of children than is necessary.
Children have a beautiful gift of extracting pure gold
from baser material without a stain of the alloy remaining upon them; and we are apt to forget this in our
adult fulminations against vulgarity and ugliness. For
children Madame Tussaud's will always be one of the
ante-rooms to the earthly paradise, whether they go or
not. The name has a magic that nothing can destroy.
And though they should not, if I were taking them, ever
set foot in the subterranean Temple of Turpitude, they
would, I have very good reason to know, come away
from the study of kings and queens of England, and the
historical tableaux—the finding of Harold's body, and the
burning of the cakes by Alfred the Great, the execution
of Mary Queen of Scots and the death of Becket, the sign-

ing of Magna Charta and other scenes in "Little Arthur" —with a far more vivid idea of English history and interest in it than any schoolmaster or governess could give them. And that is a great thing.

None the less, not willingly do these footsteps wander that way again; and I would sooner be the chairman of the Society for Psychical Research's committee for the investigation of haunted houses than spend the night among these silent, stony-eyed mockeries of humanity. Surely they move a little at night. Very slowly, I am sure, very cautiously. . . . You would hear the low grinding sound of two glass eyes being painfully brought into focus. . . .

I could go mad in a waxwork exhibition. Once I nearly did. It was in the Edgware Road, and the admission fee was a penny. A small shop and house had been taken and filled with figures, mostly murderers. The place was badly lit, and by the time I had reached the top floor and had run into a poisoner, Mrs. Hogg and Percy Lefroy Mapleton, I was totally unhinged.

CHAPTER XVII

THE PARKS AND THE ZOO

London's Open Spaces—Slumberers—Park Characteristics—The
Bulbs—The Marble Arch Theologians—Kensington Gardens—"The
Little White Bird"—Regent's Park—The Zoo—The Seals and
Sea Lions—Feeding-time Evolutions—A rival to Man—Lord's—
Fragrant Memories—Dorset Square.

FOR those who have to get there, London's finest
open space—or "lung," as the leader-writers say
—is Hampstead Heath. But Hampstead Heath
is a journey for special occasions: the Parks are at our
doors—Hyde Park and Kensington Gardens, St. James's
Park and Green Park, Regent's Park and Battersea Park.
What London would be like without these tracts of
greenery and such minor oases as the gardens of her
squares one cannot think. In hot weather she is only
just bearable as it is. (Once again I apply the word
London to a very limited central area: for as a matter
of fact there are scores of square miles of houses and
streets in the East End that have no open space near
them, Victoria Park having to suffice for an immense
and over-crowded district, whereas the Westender may
if he likes walk all the way from Kensington to Westminster under trees.)

Each of these parks has its own character; but one
sight is common to all, and that is the supine slumberer.
Even immediately after rain, even on a sunny day in
February (as I have just witnessed), you will see the
London working-man (as we call him) stretched on his

back or on his front asleep in every park. I have seen
them in the Green Park on a hot day in summer so numerous and still that the place looked like a battlefield after
action. Do these men die of rheumatic fever, one wonders, or are the precautions which most of us take against
damp superfluous and rather pitifully self-protective?

To come to characteristics, Battersea Park is for
games; St. James's Park for water fowl; the Green Park
for repose; Hyde Park for fashion and horsemanship;
Kensington Gardens for children and toy boats; and
Regent's Park for botany and wild beasts. You could put
them all into the Bois de Boulogne and lose them, but they
are none the worse for that; and in the early spring
their bulbs are wonderful. One has to be in London
to see how beautifully crocuses can grow among the
grass.

I have said that Hyde Park is for fashion and horsemanship; but it is for other things too—for meets of
the Four-in-Hand club (which still exists in spite of
petrol): for flag-signalling: for oratory. Just within
the park by the Marble Arch is the battle-ground of the
creeds. Here on most afternoons, and certainly on Sundays, you may find husky noisy men of all colours trim-
ming God to their own dimensions or denying Him altogether: each surrounded by a little knot of listless
inquisitive idlers, who pass from one to another quite
impartially. To be articulate being the beginning and end
of all Marble Arch orators, the presence of an audience
matters little or nothing. Now and then an atheist tackles
a neo-Christian speaker, or a Christian tackles an atheist;
but nothing comes of it. Such good or amusing things
as we have been led to suppose are then said are (like
the retorts of 'bus drivers) mostly the invention of the
descriptive humorist in his study.

Unless you want very obvious space, an open sky and
straight paths enclosed by iron railings, or unless you
want to see fashionable people in carriages or in the saddle,

KENSINGTON PALACE FROM THE GARDENS

my advice to the visitor to Hyde Park is to walk along
the north side until he reaches the Serpentine, follow the
east bank of it (among the peacocks) to the bridge, and
then cross the bridge and loiter in Kensington Gardens.
In this way he will see the Serpentine at its best, remote
from the oarsmen and the old gentlemen who sail toy
boats; he will see all the interesting water fowl; and
he will have been among trees and away from crowds all
the time.

Personally I would view with composure a veto pro-
hibiting me from all the parks, so long as I might have
the freedom of Kensington Gardens. Here one sees the
spring come in as surely and sweetly as in any Devonshire lane; here the sheep on a hot day have as unmis-
takable a violet aura as on a Sussex down; here the
thrush sings (how he sings!) and the robin; here the
daffodils fling back the rays of the sun with all the assurance of Kew; here the hawthorns burst into flower as
cheerily as in Kent; here is much shade, and chairs
beneath it, and cool grass to walk on. Here also is a
pleasant little tea-house where I have had breakfast in
June in the open air as if it were France; while in winter
the naked branches of the trees have a perfectly unique
gift of holding the indigo mist: holding it, and enfolding
it, and cherishing it.

And here is the delicious sunk Dutch garden with its
lime tree walls.

Here also are dogs. In all the residential parts of
London dogs are very numerous, but Kensington Gardens
is the place if you would study them. Ordinary families
have one dog only; but the families which use the Gardens have many. And the children. . . . But here I
refer you to "The Little White Bird," where you will
find not only the law of the Gardens by day, but are
let into the secret of Kensington Gardens by night, when
the gates are locked, and all is still, and Peter Pan creeps
into his cockle shell boat. . . . Peter himself, in bronze,

in Sir George Frampton's charming creation, triumphant on a rock with fairies all about him, and little woodland animals such as squirrels and rabbits to play with too, now and for ever dominates the Serpentine.

Regent's Park has the Botanical Gardens and the Zoological Gardens to add to its attractions. The Park itself is green and spacious, yet with too few trees to shade it, and too many wealthy private residents like unto moths fretting its garment. The stockbroker who stealthily encloses strips of a Surrey common must have learned his business in Regent's Park. But to any one who cares for horticulture or wild beasts this is the neighbourhood to live in—in one of the cool white terraces on the park's edge, or thereabouts. When I first came to London I had rooms near by, and every Monday morning I visited the otter and the wombats and the wallabys— Monday being a sixpenny day.

Since this book was written the Zoo has been enormously improved. New buildings have been erected; a new tunnel has been dug, a sudden cloud-burst one day having proved that the old one was a death-trap, for a number of children sheltering there were nearly drowned; and the Mappin Terraces have been set up, chiefly to the glory and honour of His Ursine Majesty.

Some day, I hope, the public generally will be allowed to visit the Zoo on Sundays.

The lions and the elephants will always be the most popular attraction, but I am still faithful to the sea lions and seals who, with the otters, least suggest that captivity is a martyrdom. They frolic while 'tis May, and May is continual with them. But I suppose the best time to see them is half-past three, when they are fed. In their fine home, which is a veritable mermaid's pool, with rocks and caverns and real depths of water, they have room for evolutions of delight: and as their keeper is a particularly sympathetic man with a fine dramatic sense, this makes feeding-time a very enter-

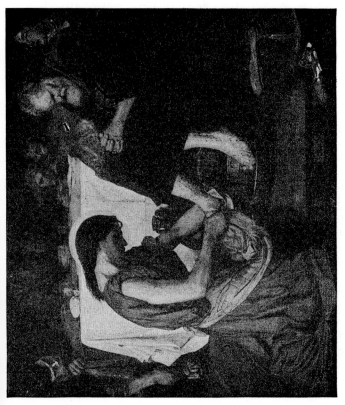

CHRIST WASHING ST. PETER'S FEET

AFTER THE PICTURE BY FORD MADOX BROWN IN THE NATIONAL GALLERY

taining quarter of an hour. It is worth making a special effort to be there then, if only to see how one of these nimble creatures can hurl itself out of the water to a rock all in one movement. It is worth being there then to note the astounding and rapturous celerity with which the sea lions can move in the water—beyond all trains and motor cars—and the grace of them in their properer element.

Seals and sea lions, it is getting to be well known, are the real aristocrats of the brute creation. One had always heard this; but it is only in recent years, since troupes of them have been seen on the variety stage, that one has realised it. When an ordinary wet seal from some chilly northern sea—a thing that we kill to keep warm the shoulders of rich men's wives—can balance a billiard cue on its nose with as much intelligence as the superb Cinquevalli, it is time to wonder if there is not some worthy mental destiny for it more useful in its way than any comforting property of its fur. That most animals can be taught routine, I know; that they can be coached into mechanical feats is a commonplace: but to get one to understand the laws of gravity is a miracle. Not only in a stationary position can this amphibian balance the cue, but move flappingly along with its precarious burden and mount a pedestal. This is very wonderful. And at the Music Halls and Olympia, where these feats are displayed, other things happen too—displays of humour, well-reasoned games of ball between two sea lions in their trainer's absence, and so forth—which show that it is time for us to revise our notions of these gentle creatures. Here is a potential new force. It is undoubtedly time to clothe our wives in other material, and think of the seal less as a skin than a mind. We might try experiments. Suppose the Lord Chancellor really were a Great Seal. . . .

Perhaps the seal is the superman of the future. In any case it should be the subject of a scientific memoir.

When seals and sea lions come nearer our own vaunted abilities than any other member of the brute creation we are entitled to be told why. "Go to the ant" was never a piece of counsel that aroused me; but "Go to the seal" has logic in it.

When the summer comes it is not, however, Hyde Park with its breadth of sky and its peacocks, not Kensington Gardens with its trees and the Round Pond's argosies, not Regent's Park even at sheep-shearing time, not St. James's Park with its water fowl; it is none of these that call me. My open space then is Lord's cricket ground in St. John's Wood (where acacias and lilac flourish). For the Oval, the great south London ground, where Surrey used to beat all comers and may do so again, I have never much cared: it is not comfortable unless one is a member of the Club; and I dislike gasometers. But Lord's I love, although I wish that one could see the game while strolling as once one could. It is now too much of a circus with raised seats. Still, sitting there at ease one may watch minutely the best cricket in the world. It was there that, scarlet with shame, I saw the Australian team of 1896 dismissed on a good wicket for 18, one after another falling to Pougher of Leicestershire, who had rarely terrified batsman before, and terrified none after; it was there that I saw Mr. Webbe bowled by Mordecai Sherwin, who took off the gloves for the purpose, leading to the batsman's famous *mot* that he "felt as if he had been run over by a donkey-cart"; it was there that I saw Mr. Stoddart drive a ball straight from the nursery end along the ground so hard that it rebounded forty measured yards from the Pavilion railings; it was there that I saw three distinct hundreds scored in the University match of 1893; it was there that I saw Sir T. C. O'Brien and Mr. F. G. J. Ford heroically pull the Surrey and Middlesex match out of the fire in, I think, the same year. It was there in 1912 that I saw the great little McCartney miss his 100 by one run.

But when Albert Trott at last realised his ambition of hitting the ball clean over the Pavilion I was not there. Perhaps some one will do it again: cricket is full of thrills, and what man has done man can do.

Those are the moments that I recollected when this book was first written. Many have I experienced at Lord's since, and not least when its most popular latter day hero, Ernest, or "Patsy," Hendren, was batting, but they are too numerous to record.   In 1921 new gates were erected in honour of the memory of W. G. Grace, Mr. Herbert Baker, the designer, calling in the aid of cricket symbolism very happily.

I like to approach Lord's through Dorset Square, which was the site of the original ground, because then I feel I may be passing over the exact spot where Alexander, Duke of Hamilton, was standing when he made his great drive—a hit which sent the ball one hundred and thirty-two yards before it touched earth.   A stone was erected to commemorate this feat.   Where is it now?

CHAPTER XVIII

KENSINGTON AND THE MUSEUMS

Two Burial Grounds—Kensington's Charm—Kensington's Babies
—Victorian Influence—Kensington Palace—The London Museum—
Holland House—Two Painters—The Model Buildings—The Albert
Memorial—Indian Treasures—Machinery for Miles—Heartrending
Bargains—A Palace of Applied Art—Raphael's Cartoons—Water
Colours—John Constable—The Early British Masters—The Jones
Bequest—The Stage and some MSS.—A Perfect One-man Collection
—The Natural History Museum.

KENSINGTON in itself, no less than in its beautiful
name, is the most attractive of the older and
contiguous suburbs. The roads to it are the
pleasantest in London, whether one goes thither through
the greenery of the park and Kensington Gardens, devi-
ously by the Serpentine and among the trees, or by
Kensington Gore, south of the Park, or by the Bayswater
Road, north of it.

The Bayswater route is the least interesting of the
three, save for its two burial grounds—one spreading
behind the beautiful little Chapel of the Ascension, which
is opened all day for rest and meditation and guards the
old cemetery of St. George's, Hanover Square, now no
longer used, where may be seen the grave of Laurence
Sterne: and the other the garden of the keeper's lodge
at Victoria Gate, which is, so far as I know, the only
authorised burial ground for dogs, and is crowded with
little headstones marking the last resting-place of Tiny
and Fido, Max and Prince and Teufel.

Kensington is of course no longer what it was; but

the old Palace still stands on its eastern side, and Holland House still stands on its western side, and Kensington Square is not much injured on the south, and Aubrey House is as beautiful as ever, on the very summit of the hill, and Cam House and Holly Lodge (where Macaulay died) are untouched, below it. Yet active as the builder and rebuilder are they have not been allowed to smirch this reserved and truly aristocratic neighbourhood. Notwithstanding all its flats and new houses it still has its composure and is intellectually contented. Kensington knows: you can teach it nothing.

One new structure at any rate that has been added to Kensington is all to the good: I mean that marvellous little temple of white stone which causes the wayfarer to Iverna Court to rub his eyes—the Armenian chapel erected, at the cost of Mr. Caloust Sarkis, in honour of his parents Mahtesi Sarkis and Dirouki Gulbenkian, in the year 1922 A.D. or 1372 of the Armenian Era. This building is not only beautiful; it is peculiar among most English edifices in having the names of its architects inscribed upon it, as in France: Mewes and Davis. My felicitations!

I said something in an earlier chapter about St. James's Street and Pall Mall and Savile Row being men's streets. Almost equally is the south pavement of Kensington High Street a preserve of women. In fact Kensington is almost wholly populated by women. Why girl babies should so curiously outnumber the boy babies of Kensington is a problem which I cannot attempt to solve. The borough has plenty of scientific men in it to make any hazardous conjectures of mine unnecessary; but I would suggest with all deference that the supply of girl babies may be influenced (1) by the necessity of maintaining the feminine character of the High Street, and (2) by fashion, the most illustrious and powerful woman of the last hundred years having been born at Kensington Palace. I rather lean to the second theory, for Kensington being so much under the dominion of the Victorian idea—with the Palace on the edge of it, the amazing souvenir of the queen (a kind of granite candle) in the High Street, her statue in the gardens, and a sight of the Albert Hall and Memorial inevitably on one's way into London or out of it—it is only natural that some deep impression should be conveyed.

Although Kensington Palace began its royal career with William and Mary, and it was Anne who directed Wren to add the beautiful Orangery, the triumph of the building is its association with Victoria. It was there that on May 24, 1819, she was born; and there that she was sleeping when in the small hours of June 20, 1837, the Archbishop of Canterbury and the Lord Chamberlain awakened her to hail her queen—and "I will be good," she said, very prettily, and kept her word. Both these historic rooms—the room where she was born and the room where she slept—are now incorporated in the London Museum here; and her toys you may see, her dolls' house and her dolls, dear objects to the maternal sightseer, and also her series of amazingly minute official uniforms, together with pictures of herself, her ancestors and children, in great numbers.

The Palace is principally Wren's work and is staid and comely save for a top hamper of stone on the south façade which always troubles my eye. But the little old houses north of the main building on the west are quite charming and may be used as a collyrium. Of the charm of these and many of Kensington's older houses and some of its new I have spoken in the first chapter: although I said nothing there in praise of the Princess Beatrice's stables, which are exquisitely proportioned and always give me a new pleasure.

The leaden statue of William III, the gift to England of the Emperor of Germany, Wilhelm II, when he was a friend of this country, still stands on its inadequate pedestal in front of the south façade.

From the windows of Kensington Palace one has an

unexpectedly verdant prospect. In the foreground is the Round Pond with its busy naval life. One has but to narrow the vision a little, and it is the Solent in Cowes Week. And away beyond the greenery is the City of London smoking above the grimness. Truly Kensington Gardens forms a very delectable oasis. "How thick the tremulous sheep-cries come!" wrote Matthew Arnold, there, half a century ago, and it is still true; one may indeed even see the sheep sheared beneath the elms; and quite one of the most unexpected and charming things to do in London on a June morning is to have breakfast outside the pavilion near the Princes Gate entrance.

Another rare possession of Kensington is Holland House, which stands half-way up the hill, half a mile to the west of the Palace, and may be seen dimly through the trees from the main road and, hiding behind its cedar, more or less intimately through the iron gates in Holland Walk. How long it will remain, who can say? Again and again it has been threatened and a large part of the grounds is now given to a golf school! Holland House is the nearest country mansion to London; while in the country itself are none superior in the picturesque massing of red brick and green copper, and none stored more richly with great memories. It was built in 1607: James the First stayed there in 1612; in 1647 Cromwell and Fairfax walked up and down in the meadow before the house discussing questions of state; William Penn lived there; Addison died there, exhibiting his fortitude *in extremis* to the dissolute Earl of Warwick. At last the house came to Henry Fox, Lord Holland, father of Charles James Fox and grandfather of the famous Lord Holland, the third, who made it a centre of political and literary activity and who now sits in his chair, in bronze, under the trees close to the high road, for all the world to see. A statue of Charles James Fox stands nearer the house.

Of the great days of Holland House less than a hundred years ago let an earlier occupant of the neighbouring Holly Lodge tell—in one of his fine periods:—"The time is coming when perhaps a few old men, the last survivors of our generation, will in vain seek amidst new streets and squares and railway stations for the site of that dwelling which was in their youth the favourite resort of wits and beauties, of painters and poets, of scholars, philosophers and statesmen. They will then remember with strange tenderness many objects once familiar to them, the avenue and the terrace, the busts and the paintings, the carvings, the grotesque gilding, and the enigmatical mottoes. With peculiar fondness they will recall that venerable chamber in which all the antique gravity of a college library was so singularly blended with all that female grace and wit could devise to embellish a drawing-room. They will recollect, not unmoved, those shelves loaded with the varied learning of many lands and many ages, and those portraits in which were preserved the features of the best and wisest Englishmen of two generations. They will recollect how many men who have guided the politics of Europe, who have moved great assemblies by reason and eloquence, who have put life into bronze and canvas, or who have left to posterity things so written as it shall not willingly let them die, were then mixed with all that was loveliest and gayest in the society of the most splendid of capitals. They will remember the peculiar character which belonged to that circle, in which every talent and accomplishment, every art and science, had its place. They will remember how the last debate was discussed in one corner, and the last comedy of Scribe in another: while Wilkie gazed with modest admiration on Sir Joshua's Baretti, while Mackintosh turned over Thomas Aquinas to verify a quotation: while Talleyrand related his conversations with Barras at the Luxembourg, or his ride with Lannes over the field of Austerlitz. They will remember, above

HAMPSTEAD HEATH

AFTER THE PICTURE BY JOHN CONSTABLE IN THE SOUTH KENSINGTON MUSEUM

all, the grace, and the kindness far more admirable than grace, with which the princely hospitality of that ancient mansion was dispensed."—Thus wrote Macaulay.

Within Holland House I have never set foot, but I know its gardens—English and Dutch and Japanese—and I know how beautiful they are, and when one is in them how incredible it seems that London is only just across the way, so to speak.

A little west of Holland Park, in Holland Park Road, is Leighton House, the stately home of the late Lord Leighton, which has been made over to the people as a permanent memorial of the artist. Here one may see his Moorish hall and certain personal relics, and some of his very beautiful drawings and water colour sketches of Greece and the southern seas. Exhibitions of pictures are from time to time held here. In Lisgar Terrace, a few minutes farther west, is the Garden Studio of the late Sir Edward Burne-Jones, the friend and contemporary of these artists, where a number of his drawings and paintings are permanently preserved, to be seen on certain days by any one who presents a visiting-card. Here are the studies for many famous pictures, here are pencil sketches, and a few unfinished works. No modern had a more sensitive pencil than this master, and the Garden Studio should be sought for its drawings alone, apart from its other treasures.

I mentioned, when we were in Park Lane, that the Dorchester House pictures might similarly be viewed. Among London's picture galleries which are not picture galleries, but to which visitors are admitted personally as guests, or by introduction, I ought to mention the College of Surgeons in Lincoln's Inn Field, where magnificent portraits by Hogarth, Reynolds, Opie, Romney and Lawrence may be seen. Also a very remarkable portrait of Sir Anthony Carlisle by Sir Martin Archer Shee. In the College of Physicians—opposite the West end of the National Gallery—other fine medical portraits

are to be found, together with Zoffany's famous painting
of the Life School at the Royal Academy; while the Garrick Club is famous for its theatrical portraits, chiefly by
Zoffany and De Wilde, and it is possible, through a
member, to see these.

To pass from the true Kensington to South Kensington
is to leave gold for silver. South Kensington is all wealth
and masonry. Here are houses at a thousand a year
and buildings that assault the heavens. The Albert
Memorial is the first of a long chain of ambitious edifices
so closely packed together as to suggest that they are
models in a show yard, and if you have the courage you
may order others like them. The Albert Memorial, the
Albert Hall, the Imperial Institute, the Royal College of
Music, the Natural History Museum, the School of Science
and Art, the Victoria and Albert Museum, Brompton
Oratory—these, together with enormous blocks of flats,
almost touch each other: a model memorial, a model con-
cert hall, model museums, model flats, model institutes,
and so forth.

By the way, the groups of statuary at the four corners
of the base of the Albert Memorial, symbolising Europe,
Asia, Africa and America, always seem to me very felici-
tous and attractive. The bison and the cow, the elephant
and the camel, are among the kindliest animals that
stone ever shaped. I have an artist friend who wishes
to treat the Round Pond in a similar spirit, and set up
groups to celebrate Grimm and Andersen and Kate
Greenaway and Lewis Carroll—since the Round Pond is
the children's Mediterranean. A very pretty project it
seems to me; too pretty ever to be carried out.

One thinks of the Victoria and Albert Museum as the
Museum at the corner of Exhibition Road and the Cromwell Road only: but that is only part of it. The Museum
extends into the Imperial Institute, where one may walk
for miles, as it seems, among the wonders of the East.
I cannot describe these riches: all I can say is that

India, China, Japan, Persia, Egypt and Turkey have given of their best—in pottery and carving, glass and porcelain, embroidery and tapestry, bronze and jade. But nothing is to my imagination more interesting and quickening than the first thing that one sees on entering the east door in Imperial Institute Road—the façades of two houses in teak from Ahmadabad in Gujarat. This is old domestic India at a blow. They are wonderful: nothing else in the exhibition is so unexpected.

Before crossing the road for the Victoria and Albert Museum I recommend a visit to the Royal School of Needlework, at the corner, where there are always specimens of beautiful embroidery on view and in the furniture room there is often a bargain.

The Victoria and Albert is one of the most fascinating museums in the world—filled with beauty and humanity. Not a mummy in it, not a South Sea trophy, not a fossil. All is friendly and all interesting. It is South Kensington's mission to instruct England in domestic beauty. Everything that is most beautiful and wonderful in architecture and furniture, sculpture and metal work, jewellery and embroidery, pottery and glass, may here be studied either in the original or in facsimile. The best goldsmith's work in the world is here in electrotype, the best sculpture in casts. The Venus of Milo is here, and the Laocoön, the Elgin Fates, the Marble Faun, Michelangelo's giant David, Donatello's little David, Verrocchio's still smaller David, Michelangelo's two tondos, at the Bargello and in the Royal Academy Diploma Gallery, John of Bologna's Mercury, Verrocchio's cherub and fish fountain, and all the other favourites from the galleries of the world.

It is of course impossible to write of any museum adequately, even in a whole volume, and I have but a few pages. Moreover something new is added every day. Since I wrote this book gifts of a number of very fine Rodins have been made to the Museum and a temporary

exhibition of Mestrović left behind it permanently one
or two very beautiful works of that master. Among
recent acquisitions is the large and remarkable collection
of Japanese lacquer formed by the late William Cleverly
Alexander.

Every day something is added to this wonderful treasure-house. On my last visit I examined for the first
time a glass case wholly devoted to tea-caddies. Every
kind of caddy is there—in wood, in tortoiseshell and in
ivory: a proof of catholicity. Inexhaustible is the only
word for the pleasure and profit which one finds at the
Victoria and Albert Museum; and one thought that is
always present, no matter in what department one may
be wandering—among the exquisite wrought iron, among
the carpets, among the old costumes and embroideries
and chintzes, among the furniture—is this: "Why do
we ever invent new shapes or patterns at all?" This,
I know, is revolutionary or, rather, reactionary; there
should be constant new effort; each age should do its
own creating: and so forth. But O what lovely designs
we are foregoing!

The Museum furthermore is made the despair of every
collector by the custom—a very interesting one and a
very valuable one—but often devastating in its triumph
—of appending to many of its treasures the price that
was paid for it. Some are high; but the bargains! The
bargains are heart-breaking. It is perhaps fortunate that
this custom no longer prevails.

It is to the galleries on the right of the main entrance,
given to Renaissance sculpture, that I always go first
and where I remain longest. For here are certain great
works the possession of which will always make us envied,
even by Berlin, where Herr Bode has brought together
so magnificent an assemblage of kindred masterpieces.
At South Kensington Donatello may be studied in all
his periods and in all his media: light relief, deep relief,
marble, terra-cotta and bronze. Here is the Madonna

and laughing Child of Antonio Rossellino, which I have reproduced for this edition. (Herr Bode, I may say, attributes it to Desiderio da Settignano.) Some beautiful examples of Mino da Fiesole are also here; several Verrocchios, among them a youthful John the Baptist, illustrating the Leonardo type, as we call it, perfectly—Leonardo having studied in Verrocchio's workshop. The great and rare master himself has a relief here entitled an "Allegory of Discord."

The next room is given to the Della Robbias—look particularly at the Child in No. 5633 by Andrea, and also at his little bagpiper in a corner—and to Michelangelo's Cupid or Apollo; and in the next are wax sketches that might be from Michelangelo's hand and might have been done for his giant "David" at Florence. John of Bologna, his pupil, is also here, and at the far end are two interesting heads by a modeller of genius—Bastianini. But the head of a woman attributed to the school of Michelangelo (No. 8538) is the most fascinating thing here, with its air of mischievous disdain. Below is more sculpture—French, ecclesiastical and so forth, with one distinguished case given to our own superb Alfred Gilbert, containing his exquisite "Perseus Arming," in bronze, and his silver "Victory."

Above these galleries are those in which the Salting Bequest is now displayed. We have seen the pictures which this most generous of testators left to the National Gallery; at the British Museum are his drawings; here are his porcelain, his carvings, his miniatures. They fill five rooms and álone form a monument of one man's taste and catholic acquisitiveness. All that I can say here is that everything is worth study, and that for those visitors who do not care so much for beauty as for human interest the miniatures offer a feast of delight, for not only are they very exceptional specimens but several are portraits of exceedingly pretty women. In a side case is an early painting by Nicholas Hilliard of a courtly gentleman leaning against a tree, which has great charm, and here too are a couple of very entertaining leaves from a book of hours by Simon Benninck. The bronze medal portraits in other cases of the same room are also profoundly interesting, and it is worth mentioning here that elsewhere in the Museum are many hundreds of the best of these reproduced faithfully in electrotype as well as original.

Other neighbouring galleries are devoted to carpets, including a prayer carpet from the mosque at Ardabil, dated 1540. That would be the date of completion; for these carpets take many families many years to weave. Here too is much lovely tapestry. Close by are fine specimens of architecture, including wonderful slate door-ways from Genoa, re-erected here; the pretty brick door-way of Keats's school at Enfield; the façade of Paul Pindar's house in Bishopsgate Without; a chimney piece from North Italy by Tullio Lombardi, with the chase in full swing carved upon it; and many other exciting and suggestive examples for the young architect of the day.

Other ground-floor galleries contain examples of the best furniture of all times, with a few reconstructed rooms —one in white pine from Great George Street, Westminster; one from a farm-house near Alençon, with painted panelling; one in old oak from Sizergh Castle, Westmoreland, with a lovely plaster ceiling; and one from the old palace at Bromley-by-Bow. And everything makes one wonder what happened to English taste before English taste was sporadically born again.

In the great galleries of casts, as I have said, work of the finest Renaissance sculpture of the world is repro-duced, including not only statues but tombs, monuments, altars and ciboria. Elsewhere are the reproductions of classical statuary. Ghiberti's Baptistery gates are repro-duced in painted plaster, but the wonderful earlier gates from Hildesheim Cathedral, done early in the eleventh

MRS. COLLMANN
AFTER THE PICTURE BY ALFRED STEVENS IN THE NATIONAL GALLERY

century, are reproduced in electrotype precisely like bronze.

I say no more here, for at the catalogue desk a whole library can be obtained, including one book which gives a complete bird's-eye view of all the collections, and one has but to study this for a little while before beginning the tour to understand one's way about and rightly appreciate the extent of the riches gathered here.

Lastly let me say that I know of no Museum better arranged or less tiring than South Kensington, which has free lifts to every floor.

South Kensington, in addition to its own water colour collection and its Raphael cartoons, has had many valuable bequests, chief among them being the Dyce and Forster books, MSS. and pictures, the Sheepshanks collection of British paintings, the Jones bequest, the Ionides bequest, and the Constable sketches given by Miss Isabel Constable. These, with its wonderful Art Library (which is open to the public), its representative water colours, and its collections of etchings and Japanese prints, make it a Mecca of the art student and connoisseur of painting.

When it comes to value I suppose that the Raphael cartoons are worth all the rest of the Museum put together. To me, as I have said, they are finer than anything of his at the National Gallery, and by the possession of them London, for all its dirt, can defy Rome and Florence and Paris. Those have the Laocoön and the David and the Venus of Milo: we have the Elgin Marbles, the Leonardo's "Holy Family," and the Raphael cartoons.

The picture rooms have recently been reorganised and will probably remain as they are to-day for a long while. The Dyce and Forster collections are now in LXXXIII and LXXXIV: a very miscellaneous set of pictures with here and there something very good or interesting, such as a London river scene by Samuel Scott, Romney's "Serena Reading," a Wilson sketch, portraits of Garrick and Dicky Suett, Henderson and John Philip Kemble, and

Cornelis Jannsen's head of Dr. John Donne. All these are
in Room LXXXIV, together with cases containing a first
folio Shakespeare and other valuable books. In Room
LXXXIII is G. F. Watts' portrait of Carlyle, Dickens by
W. P. Frith, a Bonington, a Greuze and a Terburg, and
in a case the MSS. of "Oliver Twist," "David Cooper-
field" and "Edwin Drood" open at the last unfinished
pages.

In Rooms LXXXII, LXXXI, LXXXVII, LXXVIII
and XC the complete progress of English water-colour
painting, from Paul Sandby to D. Y. Cameron and Muirhead Bone, can be followed. It is a most fascinating
survey and one is continually struck by the excellence of
the second best as well as the best. The heroes of the
first room—LXXXII—are Paul Sandby, Thomas Hearne,
Thomas Malton, John Collet, George Barret, Francis
Towne and that sublime painter, J. R. Cozens, the first
to lift water-colour art from topography to romance.
In the next room—LXXXI—we find Old Crome, Turner,
Girtin, J. B. Knight, Heriot, Callcott and John Varley.
In the third room—LXXXVII—are the De Wints and
the Cotmans and the Copley Fieldings. In the fourth—
LXXXVIII—are Fred Walker, H. G. Hine, J. F. Lewis,
Charles Green, Kate Greenaway and Phil May. And then
in Room XC are the recent and living masters, with, to
my mind, a black river scene by T. L. Shoosmith as the
most remarkable exhibit: "Odel Castle on the Ouse."

The Constable room is another of South Kensington's
unique treasures. I would not say that his best work is
here: but he never painted anything, however hurriedly,
that had not greatness in it, and some of these sketches
are Titanic. It is necessary to visit South Kensington
if one would know this painter thoroughly—his power
over weather, his mileage, his trees and valleys, his clouds
and light. There is a little sketch here called "Spring"
which I associate in my mind with the "Printemps" of
Rosseau at the Thomy-Thierry Collection in the Louvre:

they are wholly different, yet each is final. There is a fishing boat here on Brighton Beach which could not be finer. And the many sketches of Dedham Vale (Constable's Fontainebleau) are all wonderful. You may see here his gift of finding beauty where he was. He did not need to travel over land and sea: while other painters were seeking Spain and Italy, Constable was extracting divinity from Hampstead Heath, compelling the Vale of Health to tell him its secret.

The Sheepshanks Collection of works by late Georgian and Victorian painters is interesting for its fine examples of less known masters as well as its famous works. In addition to Turner's "Royal Yacht Squadron at Cowes," a scene of golden splendour, five lovely Wilsons, two spacious and glorious landscapes by Peter de Wint, among the finest landscapes ever painted in England, three excellent Morlands, another divine view of Mousehold Heath by Old Crome, Gainsborough's beautiful "Queen Charlotte," and representative examples of the anecdotal school, Leslie and Webster and Landseer, the collection has an exquisite view of the Thames from Somerset House by Paul Sandby, three very interesting Ibbetsons, a good David Roberts, a Henry Dawson, very Wilsonic, a George Smith of Chichester, two William Collins and a Joshua Shaw.

The Jones Bequest, which fills a long gallery, is a kind of minor Wallace Collection—pictures, miniatures and furniture, with a florid French tendency. Among the pictures are water colours by Turner and Copley Fielding, two beautiful Guardis opposite a rather similar Wilson, who in his turn is brought to one's mind by a George Smith of Chichester, a rich autumnal John Linnell, a Reynolds, a Gainsborough, a charming Vanloo—children playing musical instruments—and some interesting Tudor portraits, including Henry VIII, probably by Holbein, and Mary Queen of Scots. There is also a charming Madonna and Child by Carlo Crivelli.

The very interesting collection of oil paintings, draw-ings and etchings formed by the late Constantine Alex-ander Ionides, one of England's wealthy Greek residents, is to be seen at South Kensington. A small collection representing the good taste of one humane connoisseur offers perhaps the perfect conditions to the lover of art: and these we have in the Ionides Bequest. A visitor to London bent upon the study of Rembrandt's etchings would go naturally to the Print Room of the British Museum; but they have there no better impressions than some that Mr. Ionides brought together. Mr. Ionides' interest in etching extended to modern masters too—here are Whistler and Legros, Strang and Rodin. Particularly here is Millet, with his "Gleaners," his "Shepherdess Knitting," and other examples of simplicity and sincerity and power. And though the *locus classicus* for Flaxman is University College in Gower Street, the Ionides' Flax-mans should be asked for particularly, and also his col-lection of drawings by Alphonse Legros, one of the most illustrious of our French adopted sons, whose home was in England for many years. Here also are drawings by that great master Henri Daumier, too little of whose work is accessible to the English picture lover: thirteen in all, of which the "Wayside Railway Station" is perhaps the greatest, and "The Print Collector," which it is amusing to compare with Meissonier's at the Wallace Collection, the most finished. Another fascinating drawing is a sketch of Antwerp by Hervier, a French artist of much accom-plishment and charm who is also too little known in England.

The best paintings in the Ionides Collections are in Room XCI, where many beautiful Barbizon pictures are to be seen. Among the others is a fine Bonington, with a glimpse of a boat sailing on the Lake of Geneva seen through a doorway. Guardi, whom we saw to such advan-tage at the Wallace Collection, has here a decorative treatment of a fair in the Piazza of St. Mark at Venice,

with a sky above it of profound blue. One of the most
charming of the old Dutch pictures is a landscape by
Philip de Koninck; while of the new Dutch examples there
is a beautiful little hay wagon by Matthew Maris. The
brothers Antoine and Louis Le Nain, of whom very few
examples are to be found in England, have two pictures
here, very curious and modern. Corot is not quite at
his best in either of his two pictures, although both are
beautiful, but Courbet's "Immensité" (No. 59)—sea and
sand at sunset—is fine. Diaz's "Baigneuse" (No. 60) is
as he alone could have painted it, and Georges Michel,
another French painter whose appearance on English
walls is too infrequent, has a beautiful "Mill" (No. 67)
that might have been derived direct from Constable and
Linnell, yet is individual too. Millet's great picture here,
"The Wood Sawyers" (No. 47), I do not much like: it
has the air of being painted to be sold; but the other
three are very interesting, especially perhaps the "Landscape" (No. 172) in the manner of Corot. Rousseau's
spreading Fontainebleau tree (No. 54) is perhaps the
flower of the Barbizon contribution.

The Natural History Museum, the great building to
the west, in the Cromwell Road, is a museum in the
fullest sense of the word: almost everything in it is
stuffed. But its interest cannot be exaggerated. Life
was never so tactfully, prettily and successfully counterfeited as it is in the galleries on the ground floor, just to
the left of the entrance, which contain the cases of British
birds with their nests. It needs no learning in ornithol-
ogy, no scientific taste, to appreciate these beautiful
cases, where everything that can be done has been done
to ensure realism—even to the sawing down of a tree to
obtain a titmouse's nest in one of its branches. Here
you may see how sand martins arrange their colonies,
and here peep into the nest of the swallows beneath the
eaves; but as to whether Sir James Barrie is right in
thinking that they build there in order to hear fairy

stories, or Hans Andersen is right in holding that their intention is to tell them, the catalogue says nothing. The Museum takes all nature for its province—from whales to humming birds, a case of which occurs charmingly at every turn: from extinct mammoths to gnats, which it enlarges in wax twenty-eight times—to the size of a creature in one of Mr. Wells' terrible books—in order that the student may make no mistake.

Perhaps the most interesting gallery in the whole building is that on the third floor devoted to men and apes, which illustrates not only the Darwinian theory (there is a statue of Darwin on the stairs) but also the indecency of science, for surely it is something worse than bad manners thus to expose the skulls of gentlemen and monkeys. The gentlemen it is true are for the most part foreigners and heathen; but none the less I came away with a disagreeable feeling that the godhead had been tarnished. The most interesting single case in the Museum is perhaps that in the great hall illustrating "Mimicry," where you may see butterflies so like leaves that you do not see them: caterpillars like twigs: and moths like lichen. Between these and the extinct monster, the Diplodocus-Carnegii—which is almost as long as the Cromwell Road itself and seems to have been equally compounded of giraffe, elephant and crocodile, all stretched to breaking point—one can acquire, in the Natural History Museum, some faint idea of the resource, ingenuity and insoluble purposes of life.

CANNON STREET STATION FROM THE RIVER

CHAPTER XIX

Beautiful Chelsea—Turner's Last Days—St. Luke's—Church Street—Cheyne Row's Philosopher—The Carlyles and an Intrusion —Don Saltero's—The Publican and the Museum—Rossetti's break-fast—The Physick Garden—The Royal Hospital—The Pensioners' coats—London's disregard of its river—The Gulls—Speed—Whistler and the Thames again—The National Gallery of British Art—"Every picture tells a Story"—Old Favourites—Great English Painters— The New Turners—Watts and Millais—The Chantrey Bequest—A Sea-piece—Lambeth Palace.

OLD riverside Chelsea has not allowed progress to injure it essentially. Although huge blocks of flats have arisen, and Rossetti's house at No. 16 Cheyne Walk has been rebuilt and refaced, and some very strange architectural freaks may be observed in the neighbourhood of No. 73 (fantastic challenges to the good taste of the older houses in the Walk), the Embankment still retains much of its old character and charm. London has no more attractive sight than Cheyne Walk in Spring, when the leaves are a tender green and through them you see the grave red bricks and white window frames of these Anne and Georgian houses, as satisfactory and restful as those of the Keizersgracht in Amsterdam.

The Walk has had famous inhabitants. To the far western end (at No. 119) Turner retreated in his old age; and here he lived alone as Mr. Booth—or, as the neighbours called him, Admiral Booth, deeming him a retired sailor— hoping never to be found by his friends again, and it is here that, huddled in a dressing-gown, he would climb to the roof at day-break to watch the sun rise. And here he died in 1851, aged nearly eighty. Sir Thomas More, whose house stood where Beaufort Row now is—to the west of Battersea Bridge—still lends his name to the neighbourhood; while his body rests in Chelsea Old Church, as St. Luke's is called—a grave solid building of red brick and stone, with a noble square tower on which a sun-dial and a clock dwell side by side, not perhaps in perfect agreement but certainly in amity. More's wife Joan is also buried here; and here lie the mother of Fletcher the dramatist, and the mother of George Herbert the divine poet, whose funeral sermon was preached in the church by Dr. Donne, and listened to by the biographer both of her son and of her celebrant—Izaak Walton.

Lindsey House, to the west, was Whistler's home for many years; and you find another of his homes—that built for him by Godwin—in Tite Street, a little way up on the right, the White House with a very charming window on the river end. Opposite is Chelsea Lodge, where his compatriot, E. A. Abbey, worked and died. Higher up on the same side is a very nest of artistic activity, Tower House, where John Sargent has wielded his mighty brush.

At the corner of Danvers Street and Cheyne Walk the eye is startled by finding a medieval façade. This is Crosby Hall, which once stood in Bishopsgate Street, but was taken down and re-erected here with great piety. It was built in 1475 and transferred here in 1908.

Church Street, Chelsea, should be explored by any one who is interested in quaint small houses, beginning with a fine piece of square Anne work in the shape of a free school that appears now to be deserted and decaying. Swift, Steele, Arbuthnot, Atterbury and, many years later, both Charles and Henry Kingsley, all lived in Church Street for a while.

Cheyne Row, close by on the east, is made famous by the house—No. 5—in which Carlyle lived from 1834 until 1881, there writing his "French Revolution" and "Frederick the Great," and there smoking with Tennyson and FitzGerald. Private piety has preserved this house as a place of pilgrimage. It is certainly very interesting to see the double-walled study where the philosopher wrote, and to realise that it was by this kitchen fire that he sat with Tennyson; to look over his books and peer at his pipes and letters and portraits; and yet I had a feeling of indiscretion the while. If there is any man's wash-handstand and bath, any woman's bed and chair, that I feel there is no need for me or the public generally to see, they are Mr. and Mrs. Carlyle's. I seemed to hear both of them distilling suitable epithets. It is not as if one could read the books or examine the letters: everything is under lock and key. There the house is, however, exactly as it was left, and better a thousand times that it should be a show for the curious than that it should be pulled down. And, at any rate, it contains Carlyle's death mask and a cast of his hands, after death—very characteristic hands; and his walking stick is on the wall.

The famous Don Saltero's Museum was at 18, Cheyne Walk. It is now no more; and where are its curiosities? Where? Saltero was one Salter, a barber, who opened a coffee house here in 1695 and relied on his collection of oddities to draw custom. It was a sound device and should be followed. (All innkeepers should display a few curiosities, and indeed a few do. I know of one at Feltham in Sussex, and another in Camden Town; while it was in an East Grinstead hostel that I saw Dr. Johnson's chair from the Essex Head. Henekey's, by Gray's Inn, has an old lantern or so. But the innkeeper is not as a rule alive to his opportunities.) At the end of the eighteenth century Don Saltero's collection was dispersed. Chelsea in those days was famous also for its buns and its china. It makes neither now. Why is it that these industries decay? Why is it that one seems to be always too late?

It was at No. 16 Cheyne Walk that Rossetti lived, and it was here that Mr. Meredith was to have joined him, and would have done so but for that dreadful vision, on a bright May morning at noon, of the poet's breakfast —rashers cold and stiff, and two poached eggs "slowly bleeding to death" on them. In the garden at the back Rossetti kept his wild beasts. At No. 4 died Daniel Maclise, and, later, George Eliot. Passing the row of wealthy houses of which old Swan House and Clock House are the most desirable, we come to the Botanic Garden of the Royal Society of Apothecaries, with its trim walks and bewigged statue of Sir Hans Sloane in the midst. Here Linnæus himself once strolled; but we cannot do the same, for the Physick Garden, as it used to be called, is private: yet one may peep through its gate in Swan Walk for another view of it—Swan Walk, whose square houses of an earlier day are among the most attractive in London.

Close by, however, are the Royal Hospital's gardens, which are free to all and constitute Chelsea and Pimlico's public park, filled, whenever the sun is out, with children at play. The Hospital itself, which a pleasant tradition ascribes to Nell Gwynn's kindly impulse but history credits to Charles the Second (his one wise deed, perhaps), is Wren's most considerable non-ecclesiastical building in London. One would not ask it to be altered in any respect, such dignity and good sense has it; while the subsidiary buildings—officers' quarters and so forth—have charm too, with their satisfying proportions and pretty dormer windows. To be taken round the great hall by an old Irish sergeant is a very interesting experience: past the rows of tables where little groups of veterans, nearly all of them bearded, and all, without exception, smoking, are playing cards or bagatelle or reading, one of them now and then rising to hobble to the fire for a light for his pipe, over their heads hanging the flags won from a hundred battlefields, and all around the walls portraits of great commanders. It is a noble hall. On the raised platform at the end is a collection of medals belonging to old Hospitallers who left no kin to claim these trophies, and portraits, among them one of the Iron Duke, who lay here in state after his death, on a table which is still held sacred. In the chapel are more flags. The old soldiers are a more picturesque sight in summer than winter, for in winter their coats are dark blue, but in summer bright scarlet, and these very cheerfully light up the neighbouring streets and the grave precincts of their home.

The Chelsea which people have in mind when they speak of the Chelsea school of painting is more inland and is gathered about the King's Road. It is from this quarter rather than from riverside Chelsea that the soft-hatted men with bull-fighters' whiskers and the bobbed-haired girls set forth on their nightly invasion of the Café Royal.

In an earlier chapter I have said something of Whistler's discovery of the river at Chelsea. Certainly it is here that the urban Thames has most character. By London Bridge it is busier and more important and pretentious; by the Embankment it is more formal and well behaved; but at Chelsea it is at its best: without the fuss and the many bridges of its city course; without the prettiness and flannels of its country course: open, mysterious, and always beautiful with the beauty of gravity.

The Thames never seems to me to belong to London as it should. It is in London, but it is not part of London's life. We walk beside it as little as possible; we cross it hurriedly without throwing it more than a glance; we rarely venture on it. London in fact takes the Thames for granted, just as it takes its great men. If it led anywhere it might be more popular; but it does not. It can carry but few people home, and those are in too much of a hurry to use it; nor can it take us to the theatre or the music hall. That is why a service of Thames steamers will never pay. No one fishes in it from the sides, as Parisian idlers fish in the Seine; no one rows on it for pleasure; no one, as I have already said, haunts its banks in the search for old books and prints. Our river is not interesting to us: its Strand, one of our most crowded streets, has to be a hundred yards inland to become popular. We do not even with any frequency jump into the Thames to end our woes. Living and dying we avoid it.

The only non-utilitarian purpose to which we put the river is to feed the gulls from its bridges. During the past few years the feeding of these strange visitants has become quite a cult, so much so that on Sundays the boys do a roaring trade with penny bags of sprats. There is a fascination in watching these strong wilful birds with the cruel predatory eye and the divinely pure plumage as they swoop and soar, dart and leap, after a crumb or a fish. Every moment more gulls come and more, material-ised out of nowhere, until the air just seethes with beating wings and snapping beaks. In summer they find food enough on the sea shore: it is only in winter that they come up the Thames in any numbers for London's refuse and charity.

When walking from Chelsea towards Westminster one day in the early spring of this year I saw these gulls at rest. They were on the shore of the Battersea side (somewhere near the spot where Colonel Blood hid in the rushes to shoot Charles II as he bathed)—hundreds strong, beautiful white things against the grey mud. It was a fine afternoon and the sun made their whiteness still more radiant.

While I was standing watching them, and realising how beautiful the Chelsea river is, I was once again struck by the impression of great speed which one can get from river traffic moving at really quite a slow rate. A tug came by drawing three or four empty barges. Until this invasion of unrest set in the river had been a perfect calm —not a movement on the surface, nothing but green water and blue sky, and the gulls, and Battersea Park's silent and naked trees. Suddenly this irruption. The tug was making perhaps twelve knots (I have no means of judging), but the effect was of terrific swiftness. She seemed with her attendant barges to flash past. I imagine the narrowness of the river to have something to do with this illusion, because at sea, where a much higher rate is attained, there is no sense of speed at all. (It is true that steamers which were as far apart as the eye could reach a few minutes ago will meet and leave each other in an incredibly short space of time; but the impression then filling the mind is not so much of the speed of the boats as of the mysterious defeat of distance.) And the quality of the speed of this tug boat had nothing of brutality or insolence in it, as a motor car has: it had gaiety, mirth, a kind of cheery impudence. It soothed as well as astonished.

On the same afternoon I was minded to enter the Tate Gallery just to look at Whistler's exquisite nocturne of old Battersea Bridge, which is the perfect adaptation to an English subject of the methods of the Japanese print and conveys the blue mystery of a London night on the river as no other painter has ever done. I have seen all Whistler's work: I have seen his portrait of his mother, and his portrait of Carlyle, and his portrait of Miss Alexander. I have seen his wonderful waves and his decorations for the Peacock Room. I have seen his Princesse du Pays de la Porcelaine and his Connie Gilchrist; his etchings (the Black Lion Wharf stands before me as I write) and his Songs on Stone; and masterly as it all is, I believe that his London river pictures are his finest work—are the work he was born to do above all other men. In his portraits artifice is visible as well as art; in his best river scenes art conquers artifice.

CHAPTER XX

THE TATE GALLERY

BUILT as the home of modern British art, and nobly fulfilling that destiny, the Tate has become in particular a monument to the genius of Turner, Sir Henry Tate's generosity having been supplemented by that of the late Sir Joseph Duveen, the art dealer, to which we owe the new and superb Turner wing. How art dealers normally dispose of their wealth I know not; but undoubtedly Sir Joseph set them an example in symmetrical public benefaction.

The entrance hall, under the dome, is given to sculpture, and here may be seen the late Havard Thomas' "Lycidas" and "Thyrsis" and Mr. Reynolds-Stephens' very lively group, "A Royal Game," in which Queen Elizabeth plays chess with Philip of Spain, with the most fascinating chessmen to represent the galleons and other vessels that then ruled the waves.

In a little room leading out of the large one are some charming small bronzes, including Onslow Ford's "Folly," a mask by W. Reid Dick, and a little portrait figure by Alfred Gilbert.

In Room I we find the great masters of the British School in the eighteenth century; Hogarth, with his *Marriage à la Mode* sequence, and a scene from "The Beggar's Opera" (in a wonderful frame); Reynolds; Wilson, now and then exquisitely lovely as in No. 2647; Romney, Gainsborough, Morland (father and son), Gilbert Stuart and George Stubbs.

229

Then in the octagonal No. II, are a number of Blake's illustrations to Dante and a selection of early water colours, many on loan. And here I might mention that the Tate is worth visiting on the strength solely of its borrowing, so many owners of fine pictures being ready to respond to the call of its Director. I have never yet succeeded in going to the Tate without finding something new.

In Room III are the painters of the British School of the early nineteenth century: Constable, in particular. It is indeed Constable's room, for not only are some of his most famous large pictures on the wall, but on a screen in the centre are many of his vivid oil sketches, where he caught the passing moods of the sky for all time. Here also are Old Crome, David Cox, Wilkie (the famous "John Knox"), Copley, Patrick Nasmyth, James Ward (with the huge cliff landscape), Thomas Stothard ("The Canterbury Pilgrims"), and Landseer. The most modern painter represented is Alfred Stevens, with a very beautiful, although unfinished, mother and child.

We now enter the Pre-Raphaelite Room, which is dominated by Millais, whose statue is on the lawn outside the gallery. Here are several of his best, because earliest, works, chief being the very beautiful "Carpenter's Shop," which is reproduced in this volume. After studying this very remarkable work the visitor should examine the drawing for it, on one of the screens, and see how wise was the artist in his second thoughts. Pictures by all the Pre-Raphaelites are here, including several which may come as a surprise. How many readers of this book, for example, know anything of R. B. Martineau? But his patient and accurate, if uninspired, work may be seen here, and the melodramatic secrets of "The Last Day in the Old Home" (that formidable compilation) laid bare. Ford Madox Brown's "Chaucer" is better worth study. To my mind, after "The Carpenter's Shop," the best work in the room is to be found in the portraits by Alfred Stevens.

THE CARPENTER'S SHOP

FROM THE PAINTING BY SIR JOHN EVERETT MILLAIS IN THE TATE GALLERY

We find Alfred Stevens, that very great artist, again in the little room adjoining, No. V, which belongs more properly to Burne-Jones and Rossetti. In Burne-Jones the gallery is rich, for not only is the "Cophetua" here, but also many drawings for other works, and you may see the beautiful hand at work.

We now come to the special glory of the Tate—the Turner rooms. Turner's bequest to the nation consisted of 100 finished pictures, 182 unfinished, and 19,049 sketches in colours and pencil; and these are now divided between the National Gallery and the Tate, the Tate having the bulk of the paintings. In Room VI are the finished pictures, and it would be a sufficient achievement for one man; but there are hundreds and hundreds of other examples in galleries and private hands all over the world. A most interesting occupation for the student of art in this room is to detect Turner in his little jealous moods, when the praise given to a contemporary would prompt him to attempt something in a manner similar to that of the rival, although no real rivalry existed. Thus, in 491, 496, 462 and particularly in 467, it is possible to see a desire to show how easy it was to be Old Cromey. In 465 and in 475 Wilson was to be surpassed; in 473, the Holy Trinity, with a roguish Child, we may find a hint of Sir Joshua, and in 562 more than a hint of Wilkie, who was, however, one of the artists that Turner admired and whose funeral at sea is the subject of one of the great man's most daring works in this room. The portrait of himself as a young man is of interest—in 1798, when he was twenty-three; and the rough sketch of him at work in old age, by J. T. Smith, should not be missed. For all its titanic strength and amazing variety, this room is somewhat gloomy; but the next room, No. VII, where the unfinished pictures hang, is sheer radiance and joy. Here the magician waves his mahl-stick wand, and we are transported to a land of faery and romance. Some of the pictures here, finished or not, are among the most

beautiful things in the world: I would name in particular
Nos. 1991 ("The Evening Star"), 1998, 560, 2065 and
2064. This room is always enchanted, but never so much
so as when the sun shines.

We now, for a little while, leave British art and come
to some of the great Continental moderns, who have
to themselves a small room, which some day is to be
exchanged for really worthy quarters. Here, in Room
VIII, keeping to the right, we find examples of the genius
of Fantin Latour, Boudin, Renoir, Ingres, Monet, Degas
(strongly represented), Manet (also strongly represented), Daumier, Corot, Daubigny, Bosboom, Mauve, De
Bock, Matthew and James Maris, Forain, Rousseau and
the Belgian *petit maître*, Alfred Stevens. Here also we
find two decorations, rich in his favourite vermilion, by
that strange haunted creature, Gauguin, and a head by
Mestrović.

The next two rooms, IX and X, are given to a selection
of Turner's water colours, including the very amusing
Petworth series, and then we come to the basement
where temporary exhibitions are held, always of interest,
and where, in the passages and on the stairs, more and
more Turner pictures hang. At the head of the stairs
is a portrait of the Sir Joseph Duveen to whose generosity
and enthusiasm the Tate owes so much.

In Room XV we enter upon the long series of pictures
bought from Royal Academy exhibitions under the
bequest of Chantrey the sculptor. The earliest pictures
come later, but as I am following the numerical order
of the rooms we will take those in Room XV now. Here
are some of the later works of Millais, showing alas! how
he declined from the early days that gave the world "The
Carpenter's Shop." Here is a version of one of Leighton's
St. Paul's Dome decorations, "And The Sea Gave up the
Dead," and his "Bath of Psyche." Luke Fildes' "Doctor"
and Frank Dicksee's "Harmony," two other famous
Academy pictures, are in this room, together with good

NOON

FROM THE PAINTING BY COROT IN THE TATE GALLERY

examples by Henry Moore, Alma Tadema, Albert Moore, Alfred Parsons and George Mason. All the Chantrey rooms, I may remark here, give one the impression that one's ghost is revisiting old Academies.

From XV we pass into the big hall, which is called Room XVI, with all its statuary and mural paintings, most noticeable of which is the vast Irish decoration by Augustus John, in which that master displays more than his usual disdain for beauty in detail, however much he may be concerned with it in the mass. Among the sculpture may be found some sensitive work by Jacob Epstein.

In Room XVII are the works left to the nation by the English Titian, George Frederick Watts. The two favourites will, I imagine, always be the "Love and Life" and "Love and Death." The richness and tenderness of the landscape of Loch Leven make one wish that the master had painted more from nature.

Room XVIII is dedicated to the genius of Alfred Stevens, the English Michelangelo, who was both painter and sculptor, carver and superb draughtsman; and who may be studied also at South Kensington.

Room XIX is a Chantrey room with a few other pictures added, such as Fred Walker's "Old Gate" and "The Harbour of Refuge," Cecil Lawson's vast moonlit landscape, and the Legros paintings, which range from the severity of "The Retreat from Moscow" to the Giorgionesque richness of the "Cupid and Psyche." Notable among the Chantrey pictures are the Orchardsons, particularly, to my mind, No. 1519, "Her First Dance." Among the more recent purchases, W. W. Russell's vivid portrait of "Mr. Minney" stands out. The "Fantaisie en Folie" of Robert Brough tells what an artist was lost when he was killed in a railway accident in 1905.

Room XX is given to water colours of mixed periods, ranging from W. J. Müller, in whose work the gallery is so rich (note in particular Nos. 2323 and 2338), to the late John M. Swan, who is represented by some very fine studies of animals. In between come Tom Collier, Fred Walker and Pinwell.

Room XXI, to those persons who prefer novelty to tradition, is the most fascinating room in the Gallery, for here are assembled the new influences in British art, notably Augustus John, whose "Smiling Woman" may be said to rule the walls. I give a reproduction of this masterpiece. The same artist's unfinished "Rachel" strikes me as one of the masterpieces of our era. Here may be found also Henry Lamb's dingy but arresting portrait of Lytton Strachey; a superb still-life by Nicholson, "Lowestoft Bowl," and his portrait of Miss Jekyll, who transformed the face of England by her advocacy of wild gardens and herbaceous borders; two or three perfect little pictures by Henry Tonks; two or three masterly landscapes by Wilson Steer; a very exceptional McEvoy, No. 3176; an Orpen in the direct line from Holland of the seventeenth century, No. 2940; Alfred Stevens, by himself; John's portrait of Col. Lawrence; a dreamy Conder, and Whistler's enchanted "Old Battersea Bridge," or "Nocturne—Blue and Silver."

Room XXII is peculiarly interesting to me, because it is given up to modern water colours, and loans are frequent here. Representative work by such living masters as Orpen, Tonks, Wilson Steer, Muirhead Bone, D. S. MacColl, Augustus John, McEvoy and Sargent are always on view, together with those of artists no longer with us, such as Brabazon, A. W. Rich (who is the painter represented in Orpen's brilliant drawing, "The Model," (No. 3530), and J. D. Innes.

In Room XXIII, an octagon, we find Chantrey sculpture, the most attractive thing there being the ivory box which Pandora holds, in Harry Bates' work.

In Room XXIV are more Chantrey pictures, some of them as recent as the Munnings' "Epsom Downs," No. 3554, while such remote purchases as Frank Bramley's

THE SMILING WOMAN
FROM THE PAINTING BY AUGUSTUS E. JOHN IN THE TATE GALLERY

"Hopeless Dawn," and the sparkling Dutch group by F. D. Millet, the American, are also here. The great Herkomer, in which we see R.A.'s at the delicate task of selecting and rejecting, dominates the room. This was painted in 1908, and too few of the artists depicted are now with us. I would mention also, as adorning this room, two pictures by Glyn Philpot, Charles Sims' "Wood Beyond the World," and the sad and sombre Peppercorn.

In Room XXV, still given to the Chantrey Bequest, nothing gives me so much pleasure as Arnesby Brown's "Line of the Plough." His "Silver Morning," that great cattle piece, is also one of the Tate's treasures. Other notable pictures are the Orpen portraits, H. S. Tuke's "August Blue," Charles Sims' "Fountain," the little glowing shore scene by Bertram Nicholls, D. Y. Cameron's desolate lovely "Stirling Castle," and the two Sargents: Ellen Terry as Lady Macbeth, and the portrait of Ingram Bywater.

There remain the gallery, upstairs, round the Dome, and a dark room, No. XXVI, given to negligible Chantrey works. From its windows, however, one has a fine view of the Thames, which is very much Whistler's river just here. In the gallery are drawings and etchings, including some studies from Stothard's "Canterbury Pilgrims," a number of Charles Keene's *Punch* drawings, and some of the patient and remarkable work of Muirhead Bone.

So much for London's principal picture galleries, of which we have now seen all. But I ought to say that for the art epicure there are still others not quite so conveniently placed, chief of them being Hampton Court and the Dulwich Gallery, while the Bethnal Green Museum ought not to be neglected. At Dulwich is one of the most beautiful Rembrandts in the world, a noble Velazquez, some charming Gainsboroughs and two mellow and spacious Cuyps. The London Museum also has a vast collection of topographical pictures, some very good.

And then, for the real glutton, there are the picture

galleries that are open at intervals, such as the Royal Academy, the gallery over Prince's Restaurant, the Old Water Colour Gallery in Pall Mall East, the Suffolk Street Gallery, the Grosvenor Gallery, and all the smaller galleries connected with picture dealers, such as Messrs. Agnew's, the Fine Art Society, the Leicester Galleries and so forth. For the lover of pictures London spreads a continual feast.

A word should also be said about certain commercial buildings with elaborate schemes of decoration well worth a visit. I mention two only: the office of the Canadian National Railways, which has a sumptuous frieze by that wonderful colourist, Mr. Frank Brangwyn, and the offices of the P. & O. almost next door—they are both in Cockspur Street—with its cool and reserved but very effective ceiling and mural designs by Mr. Frederick Beaumont.

WESTMINSTER AND WHITEHALL

Lambeth Palace—The Archbishops—Queen Anne's Gate and Mansions—The new Cathedral—The Inverted Footstool—Origins of street names—The Abbey—Writing on the Tombs—The Guides —Henry VII's Chapel—Cromwell's body—Waxworks—A window's vicissitudes—The Houses of Parliament—London's Police— Extinct Humour—London's street wit—Whitehall—Relics of Napoleon and Nelson—The Deadily Maxims—The End.

AFTER leaving the Tate, and following the river along Grosvenor Road, we come to Westminster; but I would like first to cross over and look at Lambeth Palace, secure in its serene antiquity, where the Archbishop of Canterbury lives. This one may do by inquiring for permission by letter to the Primate's chaplain. There is a little early English chapel here, dating from the thirteenth century, which is one of the most beautiful things in London; and the cicerone is full of kindly interest in his visitors, and of a very attractive naïve pleasure, ever being renewed, in his work as the exhibitor. The great names here are Boniface, who built the chapel, Chicheley, who built the tower, Howley, who built the residential portion and did much restoring, and such moderns as Tait and Benson, who beautified where they could. It was Archbishop Tait, for example, who set up the present windows, which follow in design those which Laud erected or amended, and which the Puritans broke on seeing, as they thought, popery in them. Laud also gave the screen, and from this Palace he went by barge—in the

old stately manner of the primates—to his death.   It
seems to be a point of honour with the ,Archbishops to
leave some impress of their own personality on the Palace.
Archbishop Benson's window in the little ante-room, or
vestry, to the chapel could hardly be more charming;
and the inlaid marble floor to the altar with which the
present Archbishop's name is associated is a very magnificent addition.

Long rows of Archbishops painted by the best portrait
painters of their day—Holbein, Van Dyck, Lely, Hogarth,
Reynolds, Romney, Gainsborough—hang on the walls of
the dining-hall; but the German tourist who was making
the tour of the rooms at the time that I was would not
look at them.   All his eyes were for the Archbishop's
silver, and in particular a crumb-scoop in the form of a
trowel.

Despite the rebuilder Westminster is still very good
to wander in, for it has the Abbey and the little old streets
behind the Abbey, and St. James's Park, and Queen
Anne's Gate, that most beautiful stronghold of eighteenth century antiquity—while close by it, to empha-
sise its beauty and good taste, are Queen Anne's Mansions.   I always think that one gets a sufficiently raw
idea of the human rabbit-warren from the squares of
paper and marks of stairs and floors and partitions that
are revealed on the walls when a house is in course
of demolition: a sight very common in London;
but I doubt if the impression of man's minuteness
and gregariousress is so vivid as that conveyed by the
spectacle of Queen Anne's Mansions by St. James's Park
station—surely the ugliest block of buildings out of
America, and beyond doubt the most aggressively populous.

Westminster's architectural variety is by no means
exhausted in the buildings I have named, for between
the Army and Navy Stores and Victoria station (which I
fancy is Pimlico) is the wonderful Byzantine Roman

WESTMINSTER ABBEY

Catholic Cathedral. It is characteristic of London
methods that a building so ambitious and remarkable
as this should have been packed into an enclosed space
from which a sight of it as a whole from any point of
view is impossible. Its presence here, in the very heart
of flat-land, would be hardly less amazing to the simple
intelligence of George III than was that of the apple
within the dumpling. One is conscious that it is vast
and domineering and intensely un-English, but of its total
effect and of its proportions, whether good or bad, one
knows nothing. The lofty tower is of course visible
from all points. Sometimes it has mystery and sometimes not, the effect depending upon the amount of it
that is disclosed. From Victoria station I have seen it
through a slight haze wearing an unearthly magical
beauty; and again from another point it has been merely
a factory chimney with a desire for sublimity.

Whatever opinion one may hold as to the architectural
scheme of the new cathedral, there can be no doubt as to
its nobility as sheer building, and no question of the splendid courage behind its dimensions. It appears to me to
conquer by vastness alone, and I seem to discern a certain
grim humour in these people setting as near their old
time Westminster cathedral as might be this new and
flauntingly foreign temple, in which the Abbey and
St. Margaret's could both be packed, still leaving inter-
stices to be filled by a padding of city churches.

For one of London's oddest freaks of ecclesiastical
architecture you have only to seek Smith Square, just
behind the Abbey, and study the church of St. John the
Evangelist, the peculiar oddity of which is its four belfries,
one at each corner. I used to be told when I lived within
sound of its voice that the shape of this church was due
to a passionate kick on the part of the wealthy lady who
endowed it, and who, in disgust at the plans submitted
by her architect, projected the footstool across the room.
"There," said she, pointing to it as it lay upside down,

"build it like that"; and the architect did. That is the Westminster legend, and it is probably false—a derivative from the church's shape rather than the cause of it. St. John's, however, has something more interesting to offer than its design, for it was here that the scathing author of "The Rosciad" and other satires—Charles Churchill, who was born close by in Vine Street (now Romney Street) and educated close by at Westminster School —held for a while the position of curate and lecturer, in succession to his gentle old father. Churchill's name is forgotten now, but during the four years in which he blazed it was a menace and a power.

Smith Square still contains two or three of Westminster's true Georgian houses, of which there were so many when I lived in Cowley Street many years ago. New roads and new buildings, including the towering pile of offices and flats which the Ecclesiastical Commissioners erected, as reckless of the proportions of this neighbourhood as of its traditions, have ruined Westminster. Meanwhile, concurrently with the big schemes, a number of individuals with Georgian tastes have been renovating all the little houses here without impairing their character.

Barton Street took its name from Barton Booth, the actor, who invested his savings in property at Westminster. Cowley Street is named after Barton's native village in Middlesex, and has no association with Cowley the poet, although when I lived there I used to be told that it was from him that it took its style. Such is oral tradition! There is indeed no need to invent any origin for London's street names: their real origin is interesting enough. Why Mount Street? Because Oliver's Mount, a point in the fortification lines round London made by the Parliamentarians in 1643, stood here. Why Golden Square? Because in the neighbourhood was an inn called "The Gelding," which gave its name to the square and was then modified by the inhabitants because they

GIRL AT A WINDOW
FROM THE PAINTING BY REMBRANDT AT DULWICH

did not like it. Why Hay Hill? Because the Aye or
Eye brook once ran there: hence also the two Brook
Streets. But the local tradition probably involves a load
of dried grass. Why Westbourne Grove? Because of
the West Bourne, another stream, now flowing underground into the Serpentine.

Why Covent Garden? Because it was the garden, not
for the sale but for the culture of vegetables, belonging
to the Convent: that is, the Abbey of Westminster.
Why Chelsea? Because the river used to cast up a
"chesel" of sand and pebbles. Selsey in Sussex is the
same word. Why Cheapside? Because at the east end
of it was a market place called Cheaping. Why the
Hummums? Merely a Londonisation of Hammam, or
Turkish Bath, which it was before it became an hotel.
Why the Isle of Dogs? Because when Greenwich was a
royal resort the kennels were here. Why the Strand?
Because it was on the shore of the Thames. Why Bays-
water? Because one of William the Conqueror's officers,
Bainardus of Normandy, became possessed of the land
hereabout (as of Baynard's Castle in Sussex) and one of
his fields at Paddington was called Baynard's Water or
Watering. Why Pall Mall? Because the old game of
Pall Mall was played there. Why Birdcage Walk?
Because Charles II had an aviary there. Why Storey's
Gate? Because Edward Storey, keeper of the aviary,
lived hard by. Why Millbank? Because a water mill
stood where St. Peter's wharf now is turned by the stream
that ran through the Abbey orchard (the Abbey orchard!)
down Great College Street. This was one of the streams
that made Thorney Island, on which Westminster Abbey
and the Houses of Parliament stand. It is an island no
longer, because the streams which divided it from the
main land have been dammed and built over; but an
island it was, its enisling waters being the Mill Bank
stream, the Thames, a brook which ran down Gardiner's
Lane, and, on the east, the Long Ditch in Prince's Street.

Why was Westminster so called? Because St. Paul's was the parent and the Abbey was its western dependency —the west minster.

And here, by way of Dean's Yard, we enter the Abbey, which really needs a volume to itself. Indeed the more I think about it the more reluctant my pen is to behave at all. An old children's book which I happen to have been glancing at this morning, called "Instructive Rambles in London and the adjacent Villages, 1800," puts the case in a nutshell. "On entering the Abbey the grandeur and solemnity of the whole struck them forcibly; and Charles, addressing his father, said, 'By the little I already see, sir, I should think that instead of a single morning it would take many days, nay even weeks, to explore and examine into all the curious antiquities of this building.'" His father agreed with him, and so do I. Equally true is it that it would take many weeks to record one's impressions. To say nothing would perhaps be better: merely to remark "And here we enter the Abbey" and pass on. But I must, I think, say a little.

So much has it been restored, and so crowded is it (to the exclusion of long views), that one may say that the interest of the more public part of the Abbey resides rather in its associations with the dead than in its architecture. To see it as a thing of beauty one must go east of the altar—to the exquisite chapel of Henry VII. The Abbey proper has nothing to show so beautiful as this, grave and vast and impressive as it is; but even with this its real wonderfulness comes from its dead. For if we except the great soldiers and sailors and painters who lie at St. Paul's, and the great poet at Stratford-on-Avon, almost all that is most august and illustrious in English history and literature reposes here.

Entering by the north transept you come instantly upon the great statesmen, the monument to Chatham, at first only a white blur in the dim religious light, being so close to the door. Palmerston, Canning and Gladstone are near by. The younger Pitt and Fox lie here too, but their monuments are elsewhere. We have seen so many of Fox's London residences: this is the last. Beneath the north aisle of the nave lie also men of science—Newton and Darwin and Herschel. In the south aisle of the nave are the graves or monuments of various generals and governors, Kneller,[1] the painter, Isaac Watts, who wrote the hymns, John and Charles Wesley and Major André.

Poets' Corner, which is a portion of the south transept, loses something of its impressiveness by being such a huddle and also by reason of certain trespassers there: a fault due to lax standards of taste in the past. Had it been realised that the space of Westminster Abbey was limited, the right of burial there would long ago have been recognised as too high an honour to be given indiscriminately to all to whom the label of poet was applied. We now use the word with more care. The Rev. William Mason and Nicholas Rowe, John Phillips and St. Evremond, even Gay and Prior, strike one in the light of interlopers. Only by dying when they did could they have found their way hither. And certain of the monuments are far too large, particularly that to John, Duke of Argyll and Greenwich, by the exuberant Roubilliac,— no matter how Canova may have admired it. The plain slabs that cover Johnson and Dickens, Browning and Tennyson, are more to one's liking; or such simple medallions as that to Jenny Lind. Shakespeare and Milton are only commemorated here; but Chaucer and Spenser, Jonson ("O rare Ben Jonson" runs his epitaph) and Dryden, Gray and Cowley—all these and many others lie at Westminster. Ben Jonson was buried standing, near the north wall of the nave, in eighteen inches of ground square. His inscription cost eighteen-pence. But the

---

[1] Kneller refused to be buried in the Abbey: "They do bury such fools there," he said.

grave of the Unknown Soldier has relegated, in the interest and pathos, all these tombs to a second place.

So far all has been free; but the choir is not free (except on Mondays), and you must be conducted there officially. The Abbey guides are good and not impatient men, with quite enough history for ordinary purposes and an amusing pride in their powers of elocution. They lead their little flock from chapel to chapel, like shepherds in the East, treading as familiarly among the dust of kings as if it were the open street.

The first chapel, St. Benedict's, has only one queen, and she a poor unhappy slighted creature—Anne of Cleves; the second chapel, St. Edmund's, has none, the Jane Seymour that lies here being the daughter of the Protector Somerset. Yet here are many noble bodies, notably the Earl and Countess of Shrewsbury; and Eleanor de Bohun beneath a fine brass; and the little sister and brother of the Black Prince, with tiny alabaster figures of themselves atop, who died as long ago as 1340. Here also, a modern among these medievalists, lies the author of "Zanoni" and "My Novel." A Crusader by the doorway testifies to the old laxity of rules regarding visitors, for he is cut all over with names and initials and dates—just as the backs of the figures in the Laocoön group beneath the Vatican are scribbled by Italian sight-seers. How many persons know who it was that first scratched his initials on an Abbey tomb? Of all men, Izaak Walton, who cut his monogram on Casaubon's stone in the south transept in 1658.

The next chapel, St. Nicholas's, is the burial place of the Percys, a family which still has the right to lie here. Here also are the parents of the great Duke of Buckingham, in marble on the lid of their tomb, and in dust below it; and here lies the great Burleigh. Both this chapel and that of St. Edmund call for coloured glass.

We come now to the south aisle of Henry VII's chapel and get a foretaste of the glories of that shrine. A very piteous queen lies here, Mary Queen of Scots, brought hither from Peterboro' by her son James I, and placed within this tomb. Charles the Second lies here also, and William and Mary and Anne and General Monk, and here is a beautiful bronze of the mother of Henry VII. In the north aisle is dust still more august, for here is the tomb of Elizabeth, erected by James I with splendid impartiality. Her sister, Queen Mary, lies here too, but the guide is himself more interested, and takes care that you are more interested, in the marble cradle containing the marble figure of the little Sophia, the three-day-old daughter of James I; in the tomb of the little Lady Mary; and in the casket containing the remains of the murdered princes, brought hither from the Tower. A slab in the floor marks the grave of Joseph Addison, the creator of Sir Roger de Coverley, who wrote in the "Spectator" a passage on the Abbey and its mighty dead which should be in every one's mind as they pass from chapel to chapel of this wonderful choir.

And so we come to the Abbey's most beautiful part— Henry VII's chapel, which is London's Sainte Chapelle. It is perhaps the most beautiful chapel in England, and beyond question the most wonderful, since not only is it an architectural jewel but it holds the dust of some of our greatest monarchs. If Henry VII had done nothing else he would live by this. Woodwork and stonework are alike marvellous, but the ceiling is the extraordinary thing —as light almost as lace, and as delicate. Not the least beautiful things here are the two stone pillars supporting the altar above the grave of Edward VI. Henry VII's tomb is in the chantry at the back of the altar, and in the same vault lies James I. George II and the Guelphs who are buried here have no monuments, but the black-guard Duke of Buckingham whom Fenton stabbed is celebrated by one of the most ambitious tombs in the Abbey, with every circumstance of artificial glory and a row of children to pray for him and women to weep.

The Duke of Richmond, another friend of James I, is hardly less floridly commemorated—close to the tomb of Dean Stanley.

A slab in the next chapel or bay marks the grave where Cromwell lay. After the Restoration, however, when the country entered upon a new age of gold under Charles II, one of the first duties of the Londoner was to remove the Protector's body and treat it as of course it so richly deserved. It was therefore decapitated: the trunk was thrown into a pit at Tyburn and the head was set up on Westminster Hall so firmly that it was more than twenty years before it fell during a high wind. Charles the Second having reigned quite long enough, it was perhaps felt that justice had been done; so the skull was not returned to its pinnacle but allowed to pass into reverent keeping. Cromwell's statue may now be seen, with a lion at his feet, in the shadow of Westminster Hall. The wheel has come full circle: he is there.

Compared with the chapel of Edward the Confessor behind the high altar, to which we now come, that of Henry VII is in age a mere child. Here we pass at once to the thirteenth century, Edward I being the ruling spirit. His tomb is here—the largest and plainest in the Abbey—and here lies his wife Eleanor, for whom the Crosses were built—one of the prettiest thoughts that a King ever had—a cross at every place where her body rested on its way from the North to London, Charing's Cross being the last. Edward the Confessor lies in the shrine in the midst: Henry V in that to the north of it, and preserved above are the saddle, the sword and helmet that he used at Agincourt. But popular interest in this chapel centres in the coronation chair that is kept here, in which every king and queen has sat since Edward I.

We come lastly to the chapel of St. John the Evangelist, crowded with tombs, of which by far the most beautiful, and in some ways the most beautiful in the Abbey, is that of Sir Francis Vere, copied from Michelangelo: four

warriors holding a slab on which are the dead knight's
accoutrements. A cast of this tomb is in South Kensington. The guide, however, draws attention rather to
Roubilliac's masterpiece—in which Death, emerging from
a vault, thrusts a dart at Mrs. Nightingale, while Mr.
Nightingale interposes to prevent the catastrophe. At
Père la Chaise this would seem exceedingly happy and
appropriate; but it suits not our austere Valhalla.
Hidden away behind the great tomb of Lord Norris are
statues of John Philip Kemble and his illustrious sister
Mrs. Siddons.

With the possible exception of Voltaire and one or
two of the heads from the Reign of Terror, there is nothing
at Madame Tussaud's so interesting as the waxworks
belonging to the Dean and Chapter of Westminster,
hidden away up a winding stair over the next chapel—
Abbot Islip's. These one should certainly make an effort
to see, for they are very quaint and they probably approximate very closely to life. The Charles the Second
one can believe in absolutely, and Elizabeth too. Nelson
ought not to be there at all, since he was buried at St.
Paul's and these figures were originally made to rest upon
the Abbey graves until the permanent memorial was ready;
but all the sightseers being diverted from Westminster to
St. Paul's, after Nelson's funeral, the wise Minor Canons
and lay vicars (who took the waxwork profits) set up
a rival Nelson of their own. It is a beautiful figure
anyway.

In the cloisters, which to my mind are more alluring to
wander in than the Abbey itself, are other tombs, for
never were the dead so packed as they are here. Among
those that lie here, chiefly clerical, are a few Thespians:
Foote and Betterton and Mrs. Bracegirdle and Aphra
Behn, and here lies Milton's friend who wrote a sweet
book of airs, Mr. Henry Lawes, and the prettiest of short
epitaphs is here too: "Jane Lister, dear childe, 1688."
The cloisters lead to the ancient Chapter House, an

octagonal room dating from the thirteenth century, which once was all the Parliament house England had, and to the Chamber of the Pyx, where the royal jewels were kept before they went to the Tower; and from the cloisters you gain the residences of the Canons of the Abbey, where all live in the odour and harmony of sanctity. The Deanery hides round the corner to the left as you enter from Dean's Yard, from which you also gain Westminster School, where Ben Jonson and George Herbert, Dryden and Prior, Sir Christopher Wren and Gibbon, Warren Hastings and Cowper, were educated.

St. Margaret's, the little church under the shadow of the Abbey, like its infant child, must be visited for one of the finest windows in England, so rich and grave—a window with a very curious history. It was given by the magistrates of Dordrecht to Henry VII for his Chapel in the Abbey, but as he died before it could be erected, Henry VIII presented it to Waltham Abbey, little thinking how soon he was going to dissolve that establishment. The last Abbot transferred it to New Hall in Essex, which passed through many hands—Sir Thomas Boleyn's, Queen Elizabeth's, the Earl of Sussex's, the great Duke of Buckingham's, Oliver Cromwell's and General Monk's. It was during General Monk's ownership of New Hall that the window was taken from its place and buried in the ground for fear it should be broken by Roundheads, who had a special grudge against glass and the noses of stone saints. It was disinterred when all was safe, but did not reach St. Margaret's until 1758. In this church Sir Walter Raleigh is buried, and here was married Samuel Pepys and (for the second time) John Milton. Latimer preached Lenten sermons here before Edward VI; and it was in the churchyard that Cowper, a boy at Westminster School, was standing when a sexton digging a grave threw out a skull which hit him on the leg and began that alarm of his conscience which the sinister eloquence of John Newton was to maintain with such dire results.

THE VICTORIA TOWER, HOUSE OF LORDS

Of the Houses of Parliament I find myself with nothing to say. They are, I often think, beautiful; and then I wonder if they are, or are merely clever. Certainly if the Victoria Tower is the right size the Clock Tower is too slender. The best view is from the embankment walk by St. Thomas's hospital: seen across the water the long low line of delicate stone is very happy and the central spire could not be more charming. And yet should there be so much ornament, so much daintiness? Should not our senate, should not our law courts, be plain honest buildings innocent of fantastic masonry and architectural whimsies? Somerset House, Hampton Court, Chelsea Hospital, St. James's Palace, the old Admiralty—should we not adhere to their simplicity, their directness? Yet the Houses of Parliament lighted up make a fascinating picture postcard for the young.

Years ago, when I lived in Cowley Street and still reverenced lords and senators, I used on my way home at night to loiter a little in Parliament Square in the hope of seeing the demigods whom our caricaturists had made it so easy to recognise: Sir William Harcourt with a thousand chins; Mr. Gladstone submerged in his collar; Mr. Bowles with his wooden legs and iron hooks. Those were great days, when legislators, hereditary or elected, were exalted and awful. But now all is changed. I am older and the House is transformed. Peers are three a penny, and I loiter in Parliament Square no more.

The whole British Empire, it may be said roughly, is administered between Parliament Square and Trafalgar Square. All the Government offices are here; and whatever Parliament may be doing, their work goes on just the same.

New Scotland Yard is here too: on the right, a huge square red building which was planned for an opera house, abandoned when its foundations were all built, and then was bought by the Government for a central police station. (The two other new opera houses which have

been erected in London in recent times are now given
to more trivial entertainment—music hall or cinema.
Having need for larger premises, the authorities built
a second block, which is joined to the parent edifice by
one of the most massive bridges in London—a very fine
arch indeed, as impressive as the little Venetian flying
passage between the Grand Hotel and its annexe at
Charing Cross is delicate and fanciful. Another good
flying passage joins the two sides of King Charles Street
out of Whitehall.

Without its police London could not be London. They
are as much landmarks as its public buildings, and are
almost as permanent and venerable. The Londoner has
a deep respect for his police, and not a little fear too ;
it is only on the Music Hall stage that they are ridiculed.
A policeman on duty is often assaulted in a rage, but he
is never made fun of. Probably no public servant so
quickly assumes dignity and importance. I suppose that
before they are policemen they are ordinary, impulsive,
even foolish, country youths of large stature (the only
London policeman I ever knew in the chrysalis stage was
a high-spirited fast bowler) ; but instantly the uniform
and the boots are donned they become wise and staid,
deliberate and solid, breathing law and order. It is one
of the best examples of the triumph of clothes. I am not
sure that a policeman's helmet is not a better symbol of
London than the dome of St. Paul : they are indeed rather
similar.

The policeman as a preserver of order is less noticeable
in London than as a friend, a counsellor, a preserver of
the amenities. He regulates the traffic, and from his
glove there is no appeal. He takes old ladies and nurse-
maids across the road, he writes in his book the particu-
lars of collisions, he conveys the victims of motor cars to
the hospital, he tells strangers the way to the Abbey. The
London policeman is indeed the best friend of the foreigner and the provincial. They need never be at a loss

if a policeman is in sight, and they will not do amiss if
they address him as "Inspector."

London, as I have said, fears its policemen.   Drink
now and then brings a man into open defiance, and on
Boat Race night the young barbarians of Oxford and
Cambridge import into the West End a certain exuberance
foreign to this grey city; but for the most part the
policeman's life is uneventful, and his authority is un-
challenged.   The practical joker who used to overturn
the Charleys in their boxes (that thin and tedious jest)
is extinct.   We have no high spirits any more: they
have gone out, they are not good form.   Theodore Hook,
who stands for the highest of all, would die of ennui
could he visit again glimpses of a London moon: Theodore
Hook, some of whose "ordinary habits," I read in a
work on the London of his day, "were to hang pieces of
meat on the bell-handles of suburban villas, in the evening, so that during the night every stray dog that happened to pass would give a tug; by this means the bell
would be set ringing five times an hour to the consternation
of the family, who, with candles in hand, might in vain
search the garden, or peep into the road for the cause.
He would cut signboards in half, and affix the odd pieces
to each other, so that the signboard owners next day
would have the pleasure of witnessing their various occu-
pations interpreted by the most ridiculous announcements
in the world.   He would stitch his friend's clothes up in
such a fashion that when, on the following morning, the
friend got into them, the conclusion that he would at
once jump to was that he had from some extraordinary
and unaccountable cause become fearfully swelled during
the night—a conclusion which Hook would take care to
confirm by expressing his great concern at his friend's
appearance, and entreating him to be allowed to call a
doctor."

These were some of his "ordinary habits."   What a
man!   He would also "carry a Highlander from a tobac-

conist's shop, after dark, and stagger with it towards a
cab, in which he would deposit the painted figure, giving
the cabman the address perhaps of some influential person, and bidding him drive carefully as the gentleman
inside was a nobleman slightly intoxicated." But this
kind of ebullient Londoner is quite extinct, as I have
said, or is found only in the mass at King's and University
Colleges, and I suppose that it is that kill-joy the policeman who has made him so. The police have come in since
Hook's time: perhaps he made them imperative.
Nothing can so dispirit a practical joker as the large firm
hand of the law. The law may to some extent have
become a respecter of persons, but it still has no nose for
a joke. The law refers all jokers to the scrutiny of the
police station, which brings to bear upon them a want
of sympathy more than Caledonian.

London can still produce the wag in great numbers,
but his efforts are entirely verbal and are too little his
own. It is the habit to extol the street wit of London;
but with the best wish in the world, I for one have heard
very little of it. For the most part it consists in repeat-
ing with or without timeliness some catchword or phrase
of the Music Halls. It was customary to credit the old
'bus drivers with an apt and ready tongue; but my experience was that their retorts were either old or pointless.
Show me a 'bus driver, I used to say, and I will show you
a man who is not witty. If he were he would not be a
'bus driver. Chauffeurs are too busy for any form of
speech, witty or otherwise.

The drivers of London all dip into the same long-filled
reservoir of sarcasm, from which no new draught has
emerged these fifty years. But tradition made the 'bus
driver witty, just as it made Herbert Campbell funny;
and it will persist.

As noticeable as the London driver's want of real wit
is his want of freemasonry. Every driver's hand is turned
against every other. No policy of vexatiousness is too

petty for one to put in practice against another: they "bore," they impede, they mock, they abuse each other; while owing to the laxity of police supervision, the narrowness of every London street is emphasised by the selfishness with which the middle of the road is kept. It ought to be compulsory for all slow moving vehicles—all that do not want to pass others—to hug the near kerb. As it is, they keep far too near the middle and reduce the width of the roadway by nearly half. Better still would be to divide busy London into one-way streets as they do in New York and have begun to do in Paris.

To return for a moment to the police, if you would know them at their most charming you must leave an umbrella in a cab and then go to Scotland Yard to recover it; for the men who have charge of this department (which is the nearest thing to the Paris Morgue that London possesses) are models of humorous urbanity. Surrounded for ever by dead umbrellas, harassed day by day by the questions of a thousand urgent incoherent ladies, they are still composed and grave and polite. A visit to the adjoining office for lost miscellaneous property will convince one in a moment that there is nothing that human beings are unable to leave behind them in a London cab.

The old Palace of Whitehall consists now only of the great banqueting hall from which Charles I walked to the scaffold on the tragic morning of January 30, 1649. It was through the second window from the north end, and the scaffold was built out into the street: old prints commemorate the event—the shameful event, may I never cease to think it. There is one such print in the hall itself, in the same case with the king's beautiful silk vest that he wore on the fatal day.

Whitehall now contains some of the most interesting relics in the world; but it is a Museum whose interest is now and then almost too poignant. I, for one, simply cannot look with composure at the Napoleon relics from

Longwood, least of all at the chair in which he always sat. The mere thought of that caged eagle at St. Helena is almost more than one can bear: and these little intimate tokens of his captivity are too much. Yet for stronger eyes there they are at Whitehall, including the skeleton of his favourite horse Marengo.

Here also are relics of Nelson—the last letter he wrote to his dearest Emma, in his nervous modern hand, just before Trafalgar, expressing the wish soon to be happy with her again; the clothes he used to wear; his purse; a portion of the Union Jack that covered him on the *Victory*, for pieces of which his sailors fought among each other; the telescope he put to his blind eye; the sword he was using when his arm was wounded; the mast of the *Victory*, with a cannon ball through it; and a hundred other souvenirs of England's most fascinating hero, the contemplation of which is lifted by the magic of his personality, the sweetness and frailty of it, above vulgar curiosity.

To pass from Nelson to Wellington is like exchanging summer for winter: poetry for prose; romance for science; yet it must be done. Here among other things is Wellington's umbrella, the venerable Paul Pry gamp which he carried in his political days in London, even as Premier, and which is as full of character as anything of his that I ever saw, and wears no incongruous air amid such tokens of his military life as the flags around the gallery which he captured from the French. No one really knows the Iron Duke until he has seen this umbrella. Such an umbrella! If one were confronted with it as a stranger and asked to name its owner, Wellington would be the last man one would think of; yet directly one is told it was Wellington's, one says, "Whose else could it be? Wellington's. Of course."

Among other treasures in this Museum are the jaws of famous or infamous sharks, one of which was thirty-seven feet long; wonderful models of boats made under diffi-

culties by French prisoners out of mutton bones and such
unlikely material—the French prisoners vying always
with the patient Chinese carver of cherry stones for the
championship of the world in ingenuity; Cromwell's
sword; Drake's snuff box and walking stick; relics of
Sir John Moore; relics of Sir John Franklin; relics of
Collingwood; a model of the first battleship to carry
guns, the prettiest, gayest, most ingratiating junk of a
boat, which put to sea to guard our shores in 1846; two
bottles of port from the "Royal George," no doubt
intended for the refreshment of the brave Kempenfeldt;
and very interesting plans of the battles of Trafalgar
and Waterloo. All these and many other objects are
displayed with much pride and not a little simple eloquence
by an old soldier. Certainly there is in London no more
interesting room than this: not only for its history but
its present possessions.

And so, through the obvious and comparatively unper-
plexing traffic of Whitehall, we come to Charing Cross
again and to the end of these rambles, not because there
is no more to say (for I have hardly begun yet) but
because one must not go on too long. As a Londoner
of Londoners, whose knowledge of the town, it has been
put on record, was extensive and peculiar—far more so
than mine will ever be—once remarked, the art of writing
a letter is to leave off at such a point as will "make
them wish there was more." And when one is writing
a book one would like to do the same.

INDEX

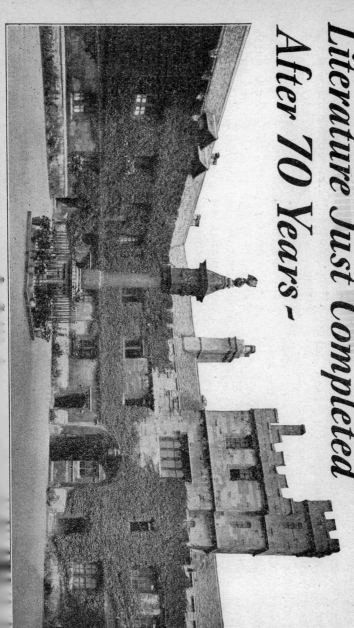

*The Vastest Undertaking In Our
Literature Just Completed
After 70 Years—*

The Supreme Moment in a Language

HENCE, the present publication of the great Oxford Dictionary, after seventy years of work from devoted scholars in England and America (France, Germany and Scandinavia, too), and the expenditure of $2,000,000, may be fairly said to mark the supreme moment in the history of the English language.

This monumental work is the gift of English scholarship to the English speaking peoples. Thirty sub-editors have worked on it for years without any remuneration except the achievement of producing the incomparably best and most comprehensive dictionary in their tongue.

This year marks the completion of the final result of English and American scholarship—an ideal labor of love. More than 2,000 readers were employed. Scholars worked over the great OXFORD in the trenches, in the World War.

Down to the 15th century the language existed in dialects—mostly pure English.

volumes. The Oxford Press requires every year the skins of over 100,000 animals for its leather bindings. Over 400,000 sheets of gold are used annually for its gilt letterings alone. The paper is made at the famous Wolvercote Mill, near Oxford. The great storage warehouses have in stock 5,000,000 volumes.

As to pronunciation, the Oxford, which will be the final authority for at least the next century, has applied directly to the creators of new words and studied each in turn. Sometimes more than thirty letters have been written to scholars and specialists about a single word, consuming weeks of time. The editor notes that at a meeting of a learned society he heard six different eminent physicists pronounce the word GASEOUS six different ways. In dealing with words in which two different pronunciations are current, both are given in the Oxford.

In the great father dictionary, incredible labor and time was often consumed over an item of five or six lines, to produce

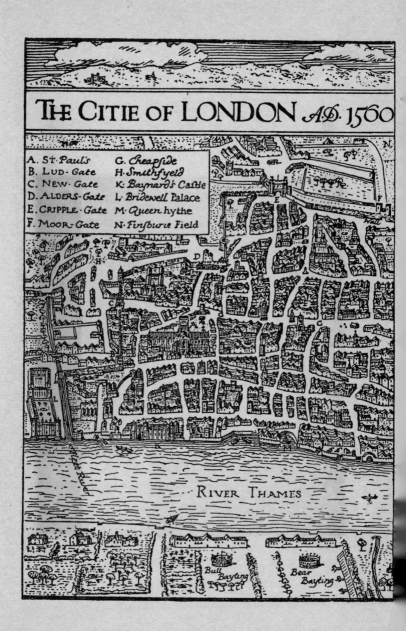

THE CITIE OF LONDON A.D. 1560

A. St. Paul's
B. Lud-Gate
C. New-Gate
D. Alders-Gate
E. Cripple-Gate
F. Moor-Gate

G. Cheapside
H. Smithfyeld
K. Baynard's Castle
L. Bridewell Palace
M. Queen hythe
N. Finsburie Field

RIVER THAMES

Bull Bayting

Bear Bayting